TERRA INCOGNITA

AMERICAN GOVERNANCE AND PUBLIC POLICY SERIES
Series Editor: Barry Rabe, University of Michigan

TERRA INCOGNITA

Vacant Land and Urban Strategies

Ann O'M. Bowman and Michael A. Pagano

GEORGETOWN UNIVERSITY PRESS / WASHINGTON, D.C.

Georgetown University Press, Washington, D.C.
© 2004 by Georgetown University Press. All rights reserved.

Printed in the United States of America

10 9 8 7 6 5 4 3 2 1 2004

Library of Congress Cataloging-in-Publication Data

Bowman, Ann O'M., 1948–
    Terra incognita : vacant land and urban strategies / Ann O'M. Bowman and Michael A. Pagano.
    p. cm. — (American governance and public policy series)
Includes bibliographical references and index.
    ISBN 1-58901-007-8 (pbk. : alk. paper)
  1. Vacant lands—Government policy—United States. 2. Vacant lands—Government policy—United States—Case studies. I. Pagano, Michael A. II. Title. III. American governance and public policy.
HD257.B69 2004
333.77—dc22
                                            2003019870

To Bert E. Swanson
for his contagious zest for urban research, tak.

A. O'M. B.

To Jean Nixon Pagano and Anthony V. Pagano, who
in retirement as much as in their professional and
parenting days continue to teach the art of learning
and discovery as a lifelong journey, a heartfelt grazie.

M. A. P.

Contents

List of Figures

List of Tables

Preface

In an earlier book, *Cityscapes and Capital: The Politics of Urban Development*, we argued that cities use a number of resources to promote development. In conducting the research for that book, we found that significant among those resources was land—and not just any land: vacant land. In the ten cities where we conducted fieldwork, conversations with city officials often came back to the subject of vacant land: how a trash-filled vacant lot could be cleaned up and rezoned for commercial use, how a vacant parcel could be linked to an adjacent tract of land to become a city park, whether the city should purchase a vacant parcel in anticipation of future building needs, how a cluster of abandoned structures could be razed to accommodate an affordable housing complex. Occasionally, these conversations took a different direction: how rapidly disappearing vacant land on the outskirts of the city could be preserved.

Our curiosity was piqued. How much vacant land is there in U.S. cities? What should cities do with it? What kinds of policies do cities have in place that affect vacant land? Our inability to find answers to these questions began a process that led to *Terra Incognita*. At that point, vacant land had not been a subject of much research. In the stacks of our respective universities' libraries, we found dusty copies of two 1960s-era studies that the federal government funded. Those reports provided some baseline, historical figures on the amount of vacant land. Initially, our research sought to update that work. How much vacant land and how many abandoned structures exist in U.S. cities? From those basic questions, the research blossomed into a fascinating and multifaceted project on people, places, and, yes, land.

Although many people have been instrumental, supportive, critical, and generally helpful in the evolution of the project, none played a more crucial role than Rosalind Greenstein of the Lincoln Institute of Land Policy. For her support of this project, we owe a debt of gratitude. The research could not have been undertaken without the financial support of the Lincoln Institute of Land Policy, and we are very appreciative. We hope that the findings, frameworks, and presentation of this book reflect the importance of vacant land to the health, vitality, and prospect of cities and to their residents and visitors.

Many others have offered guidance and insight at various stages of the project. The city officials who allowed us to interview them and monopolize much of their time, especially during the site visit phase of the project, are listed in the appendix A. They provided us with not only data and information but also with an appreciation for the vital, and often overlooked, work of city government. Survey construction was aided by those who were willing "test pilots" and others, including Tom Black, Larry Bohannon, Jane Howington, David Jones, and Cathy Schaeffer. Our research assistants, Audrey Harris and Jennifer Hoffman, compiled massive volumes of data and research during the survey phase of the project and were our links to the survey respondents. At a later stage, Erica Carter and Gregory Plagens, both of the University of South Carolina, provided research assistance. The Lincoln Institute of Land Policy convened a roundtable in the summer of 2000, which proved to be instrumental in our rethinking the project, data, and findings. The participants included Robert Faherty, Lois Geiss, Gary Jastrzab, Nancey Green Leigh, Ray Quay, Ann LeRoyer, and Thomas Wright. The Brookings Institution hosted a roundtable on vacant land issues, giving us an opportunity to discuss our research and get reactions to it. We benefited from the insights offered by Scott Barkin, Paul Brophy, Bruce Katz, John Kromer, Amy Liu, Benjamin Margolis, and Margaret Murphy. The Brookings Institution also supported Michael Pagano in 2001 on a project examining city fiscal incentives and land development. Jennifer Vey of Brookings was most helpful with that project, as were Michael Anderson, Jaime Holland, and Karl Nollenberger. The authors are also indebted to their respective academic institutions and colleagues; Ann to the University of South Carolina and to W. Lynn Shirley, Tom Durkin, and Michael to Philip A. Russo Jr. and Jon Patton of Miami University and to the University of Illinois at Chicago.

Reports, papers, and articles on the research that is published here in final form have been presented in several forums, including ones sponsored by the American Political Science Association and the Urban Affairs Association, and the Who Owns America II conference. We benefited especially from the commentary of Anthony Downs, Robert Lowry, Patrick Shawn Martin, Rachel N. Weber, and anonymous reviewers of the manuscript. In 1999, the Lincoln Institute released a working paper on our findings, "Urban Vacant Land in the United States." In March 2000, *Urban Affairs Review* published an article drawn from our survey work, "Transforming America's Cities: Policies and Conditions of Vacant

Land." In December 2000, the Brookings Institution published *Vacant Land in Cities: An Urban Resource* in the Center on Urban and Metropolitan Policy's Survey Series. And finally, in April 2003, Brookings released Michael Pagano's *City Fiscal Structures and Land Development*, a discussion paper prepared for the Brookings Institution Center on Urban and Metropolitan Policy and CEOs for Cities (www.brookings.edu/es /urban/publications/paganovacant .htm). The photographs that appear in the book were taken by the authors; unless noted otherwise, the maps were created by the authors.

The authors appreciate the encouragement and assistance of Gail Grella, acquisitions editor, and Barry Rabe, series editor, in the development of the final manuscript. The experience of working with the entire Georgetown University Press team was an enjoyable one.

The authors acknowledge the above individuals and institutions. We, however, are solely responsible for errors of omission and commission.

Finally, no project requiring extensive travel and late dinners can ever adequately acknowledge the family members who in their own ways supported their spouses and parents. That a collaborative project of this magnitude has now occurred twice in a decade requires an exceptional debt of gratitude. To Blease and Carson, and to Deborah, Gina, and Andrea, we raise our glasses! *Salute!*

1

The Different Contexts of Vacant Urban Land

Perhaps it is a field that neighborhood children have turned into a playground or an old, abandoned factory that is secured by chain-link fencing and "Keep Out" signs. It might be a surface parking lot wedged between two office towers, or a wetland where a variety of plant life flourishes. It could be an overgrown lot littered with garbage or a crumbling row house where cars without tires are permanently parked. It might be the future site of a gated community or a retail mall. Vacant land is both ubiquitous and diverse and both a problem *and* a resource for city governments.

City governments formulate plans and regulations intended to use or reuse these vacant land parcels. These plans are purposive and strategic, designed to accomplish some greater good. How cities think strategically about their vacant land is the principal focus of this book. Before we turn to the analysis, we explore the various meanings and conceptualizations of vacant land as "good" or "bad." Although the term "vacant land" conjures up vivid mental images, our knowledge of its extensiveness and of policies designed to convert vacant land is limited because there is little comprehensive information and even fewer studies. We begin this assessment of a city's strategic behavior in vacant land conversion, then, by clarifying what is meant by vacant land and the extent to which vacant land is a problem or an opportunity.

VACANT LAND: NEGATIVE AND POSITIVE

The phrase "vacant land" tends to evoke negative images: abandonment, decay, emptiness, and, in some instances, even danger. The

symbolism is compelling. When the former secretary of the U.S. Department of Housing and Urban Development, Henry Cisneros,
sought to portray inner-city decline, he spoke of "boarded-up buildings and trashed vacant lots."[1] Evocative labels such as "dead space"
and "disturbed space" have been levied at bare derelict land, roughly
vegetated wasteland, abandoned buildings, and an assortment of various temporary uses such as materials dumps and construction sites.[2]
As "urban wastelands" and "derelict zones," vacant land is linked to
a host of undesirable conditions and outcomes:

> [A] place may be considered derelict to the extent that the symbols
> of disinvestment, vacancy, and degradation dominate. Where dis-
> repair, litter, emptiness, violation, and other signs of diminished
> habitat prevail, a derelict zone exists in mind if not in reality. . . . It
> symbolizes failure.[3]

Powerful signals are sent to those who pass by decaying structures:

> Abandoned buildings in our inner-city neighborhoods continue to
> erode the local social fabric. They signify the ills of neglect, com-
> municating to people the futility of inner-city living. . . . To invest
> here is to risk losing money . . . abandoned buildings are a sign of
> irreversible deterioration—a process that has attained a critical in-
> ternal momentum.[4]

Abandonment often spreads by contagion. Consider the case of a
once-vibrant shopping district. Store closings, whether induced by the
market or by idiosyncratic factors, reduce retail traffic in the area, thus
jeopardizing remaining merchants. If the economic viability of the lo-
cale weakens, more vacancies occur. Maintenance of the structures
may be curtailed, eventually creating an unsafe situation. Some of the
unoccupied structures may get boarded up, their isolation reinforced by
stark chain-link fencing. Other buildings may provide "homes" to the
homeless.[5] Particularly dangerous structures may be demolished, leaving gaping holes in the area. The newly vacant lots accumulate litter
and trash. At some point, there may be more vacant lots than occupied
buildings; the label "dead space" begins to seem an especially apt
descriptor. As John Accordino and Gary Johnson put it, "Vacant and
abandoned property is a symptom of central city decline that has now
become a problem in its own right."[6] Conventional efforts by a city government to induce investment at the now-distressed site are not likely
to be sufficient.[7] In fact, unsuccessful efforts by a city government to
transform the area add another negative layer to the mix: policy
failure.[8]

Vacant land is often conceived of as a problem, a negative situation that requires correction. Yet beyond this bleak landscape, alternative conceptions of vacant land are possible. Far from being an unrelentingly negative condition, vacant land may come to symbolize opportunity; it may represent a resource that localities want to maximize. During their formative years, cities such as Boston and San Francisco aggressively filled wetlands to create more vacant land. Without it, the cities' development potential would have been limited. The newly created supply of vacant land allowed the cities to flourish.

More than a century later, in West Palm Beach, Florida, creative use of vacant land through infilling and land banking transformed a moribund downtown of empty storefronts into a lively, cafe-lined European-style boulevard, complete with a plaza fountain. Vacant land provided the space and the opportunity for the city government to invest in design-conscious streetscaping and public improvements, and the commercial and housing markets responded favorably. The success of the initiative spawned a second effort, this one led by private developers, to convert 75 acres of vacant land in the downtown area into a $400 million mixed-use development.[9] West Palm Beach is illustrative of the process that one observer has labeled "Dirt into Dollars: Converting Vacant Land into Valuable Development."[10]

These alternative images of vacant land convey availability, space, opportunity, and informality. To at least some members of the public, vacant land is not solely an unalloyed "bad." The Civic Trust's survey of attitudes toward vacant land in the United Kingdom captured the ambivalence: "Not all wasteland sites blight their environment, and even those that do sometimes have positive aspects, redeeming features which make them valued by at least some sections of the community."[11] For some, vacant land's value rests in its nonproductivity, at least as conventionally measured. The indigenous flora and fauna found in these unmanicured settings are natural assets. Vacant lots, along with city parks and rights of way, served as "nature's classrooms" in an urban ecology educational effort sponsored by the National Science Foundation in the late 1980s. Portland, Oregon's, Metropolitan Greenspaces Program operates with a similar logic.[12] It aims to shift land use designations from real estate–generated labels such as "vacant" or "undeveloped" to biologically defined designations, such as "green space" or "greenbelts."

Thus, rather than serving as symbols of urban blight, vacant lots, along with other types of open space in a city, are actually "fortuitous landscapes."[13] Neal Peirce's commentary, "Vacant Urban Land: Hidden Treasure?" underscores this more optimistic orientation toward vacant land.[14] Instead of seeing a vacant lot as a problem to be managed, one can see it as an opportunity to be realized. The vacant lot littered with broken glass and discarded mattresses can be reborn as a community garden yielding a harvest of blossoms and vegetables.[15] The vacant parcel may still be in temporary usage, but its value, tangible and otherwise, is quite different. It comes down to interpretation: "You can treat an abandoned industrial site as an environmental problem. Or you can treat it as an opportunity."[16]

The notion of vacant land as a fortuitous landscape is gaining ground among local policymakers. The deputy mayor of Washington, D.C., put it this way: "If we're going to create some substantial development, we need to get rid of these abandoned and vacant properties."[17] In essence, this is an exercise in "visioning": Look beyond the blight to see what the parcel could become. Abandonment and vacancy are simply stages on the road, perhaps a long road, to renewal. By effectively utilizing its vacant lots and abandoned properties, a city can reinvent itself. Barry Wood, who has studied European vacant land, quotes an Italian planner on Turin: "The existence of vacant land offers Turin a unique opportunity to re-figure the city to meet the needs of the twenty-first century."[18] The same is true in many U.S. cities. The land conversion process may not be simple, however. In some U.S. cities, "industrial brownfields represent the most obvious source of urban land ripe for redevelopment."[19]

DEFINING VACANT LAND

The term "vacant land" is both broad and imprecise, covering various types of nonutilized or underutilized land. A vacant parcel's lack of utilization may result from its physical properties, perhaps a steep slope or small size. Or land may be vacant because of an economic decision to shut down an inefficient industrial facility. In some instances, market considerations fuel vacancy, such as holding land for speculative purposes. Or vacancy may stem from a governmental action, such as the designation of parcels as parkland or a habitat preserve. Thus, vacant land can include "raw dirt," property with abandoned structures, land with recently razed buildings, perimeter agricultural land, contaminated land, and greenfields.

An urban economist, Ray Northam, classified vacant land in U.S. cities into five somewhat mutually exclusive types:[20]

(1) remnant parcels—small in size (ranging from a few hundred square feet to a few thousand), often irregular in shape, haven't been developed in the past; (2) parcels with physical limitations—

unbuildable due to major physical constraints such as steep slope or flood hazard, can be large tracts of land; (3) corporate reserve parcels—land held by corporations for future expansion or relocation, typically local firms such as utility companies; (4) parcels held for speculation—land owned by corporations, estates, or single parties in anticipation of a profitable, market-rate sale at a later time, frequently found in transitional areas; [and] (5) institutional reserve parcels—tracts of land set aside by public or quasi-public entities for future development, given need and funding.

Land with physical limitations and some of the remnant parcels are likely to remain unbuilt into the future, thus constituting a supply of permanently vacant land. For the other types, vacancy is intended to be a temporary condition, although the "temporary" nonuse may continue for decades.

When city governments conduct land inventories, officials wrestle with creating an operational definition of vacant land. Most generally, the label is applied to idle or unused land; however, the definition may be extended to cover underutilized land. For example, a land inventory conducted in one medium-sized Southern city classified a parcel as vacant if one of the following characteristics was met: the parcel had a zero-dollar building value in the local tax assessor's records, it was a tax parcel that did not have a structure on it, or it was a city-owned property considered vacant and developable (e.g., a surface parking lot located in the downtown area).[21] This operational definition of vacant land is strongly influenced by the city's tax structure and its development plan, a not uncommon characteristic in efforts to manage vacant land.

Northam's five-part typology does not explicitly include one large category of vacant land: derelict land. The concept of derelict land evolved from efforts to clean up and restore mineral extraction sites in the United Kingdom. Derelict land is "so damaged by industrial or other development that it cannot be used beneficially without treatment."[22] Land qualifying for the designation "derelict" is eligible for improvement grants from the British government. Somewhat equivalent in the United States are "brownfields," which the U.S. Environmental Protection Agency describes as sites in which real or perceived environmental contamination impedes redevelopment.[23] A closed-down industrial facility where years of environmental abuses have poisoned the soil is an example of a brownfield.

However, as the definition indicates, at some brownfield sites contamination is only "perceived," not "actual." Still, even the perception of contamination is sufficient to dampen enthusiasm for redevelopment,

FIGURE 1.1. Dangerous Vacant Land: A Superfund Site in Camden, New Jersey

and the sites frequently remain vacant. The extent of the brownfield problem has led to federal funding to assist localities in the cleanup and restoration of these sites. The most dangerous brownfields qualify for remediation under the Comprehensive Environmental Response, Compensation, and Liability Act of 1980, more commonly known as the Superfund program. These sites present significant challenges to local governments intent upon the redevelopment and reuse of the properties. The Superfund site pictured in figure 1.1 is located in a dense area of Camden, New Jersey, where its presence hinders efforts at revitalization of other vacant properties nearby.

Another descriptive label for vacant land is the acronym TOADS, which refers to "temporarily obsolete, abandoned, or derelict sites."[24] TOADS are of three varieties:

- formerly productive and valued sites, such as automobile factories, furniture plants, warehouses, or textile mills that have since been abandoned by their owners;
- formerly productive but unwanted sites that housed less desirable activities, such as slaughterhouses, leather tanneries, and paper mills; and
- unused parcels of overgrown land that for various reasons have not been developed.

The third kind of TOADS listed above underscores an important point made earlier: Vacant land is not necessarily damaged or derelict. It can simply be neglected land, that is, unused but capable of some beneficial use.[25] Land that is being held for speculation may take on these characteristics, or it might be "operational land," an unsightly or underutilized section of a current development. For example, an industrial plant might use a portion of its land for storage, and it might lease part of it for a pasture. Operational land may in fact be corporate reserve land. These categorizations are inherently instrumental; the value of land is linked to its productivity, its utility.

The preceding discussion provides the basis for an initial working definition of vacant land: It is unused or abandoned land. Thus, vacant land ranges from never developed parcels to land that once had structures on it. In addition, the definition includes land that supports structures that have been abandoned or become derelict, whether boarded up, partially destroyed, or razed.

This definition allows for two fundamental distinctions in studying vacant land. One basic distinction is the ownership of the land—that is, whether it is publicly or privately held. Ownership affects management and outcomes. The other distinction is whether the land is "developable," regardless of ownership. A host of factors influences developability, including the physical features of the land, the presence (or absence) of legal or financial complications, the local real estate market, and the city or county government's land use plan. These two distinctions have much to do with negative and positive images of vacant land.

DESCRIBING VACANT LAND IN U.S. CITIES

Although vacant land is present in every city, the phenomenon has not been studied comprehensively. Therefore, basic information about the amount of vacant land and its characteristics is not available. More complex questions about the role of city government in regulating and managing vacant land have never been asked in any systematic way.

To address this situation, we undertook a survey of planning directors in U.S. cities with populations of 50,000 or more that was designed to provide basic information on vacant land and to answer some of the more complex questions about public policy toward it. The questionnaire included items on vacant land conditions, supply, policies, and trends. The overall response rate was 35 percent; however, among larger cities (those with populations of 100,000 or more), the response rate reached 50.25 percent. Most of the findings reported in this and subsequent chapters are drawn from the large city database. In an effort to enrich the survey results, fieldwork was conducted in three metropolitan areas, Philadelphia, Phoenix, and Seattle. Data drawn from these site visits shed light on goals, policy choices, and effects. (The survey and fieldwork methodology is described in detail in appendix A.)

The Condition of Vacant Land

Definitions and images of vacant land vary, as the discussion above demonstrates. But what about vacant land conditions? Do cities throughout the nation have the same kind of vacant land, or are the conditions highly variable? The data presented in table 1.1 provide some answers.[26]

In most cities, parcels of vacant land are relatively small in size. Two other conditions are prevalent as well: Vacant land tends to occur in odd-shaped parcels and, in the view of city officials, to be found in the wrong location. These three characteristics individually, and especially in concert, limit the redevelopment potential of vacant land. Small, odd-shaped parcels in the wrong part of the city present serious challenges to the development ambitions of city officials.

Not surprisingly, the supply of vacant land is an issue in most cities. However, in a departure from what might be expected, more cities are concerned about an *undersupply* of vacant land than an oversupply. That is, the lack of an adequate stock of vacant land to accommodate future growth and development characterizes many cities. Vacant land is a shrinking resource in these places. The opposite condition, too much vacant land, is of concern in a large subset of cities, however. An oversupply of vacant land may reflect a long cycle of population out-

TABLE 1.1.   Vacant Land Conditions in U.S. Cities

Condition	No. of Cities
Vacant parcels not large enough	97
Odd-shaped parcels of vacant land	75
Vacant land in "wrong" location	72
Other conditions[a]	60
Vacant land is in undersupply	58
Parcels have been vacant too long	45
Vacant land is in oversupply	43

[a]Other conditions include land that is vacant due to real estate speculation, perceived (or real) contamination, steep slopes, infrastructure problems, or wetlands.

Source: Data are from the authors' vacant land survey, 1997–98; see appendix A.

flow and economic decline and, for these cities, the issue is how to transform vacant land into a valued commodity.

The question of how long land remains vacant is an interesting one. In only about one-quarter of the cities responding to the survey is land considered vacant too long. For most cities, the temporal condition of vacant land is not a serious issue. This suggests that, as a general rule, vacant land is recycled at an acceptable pace in most cities. In sixty of the cities in the study, "other" conditions are relevant. The most common of these other conditions include the holding of vacant land for speculative purposes (in twelve cities), the presence of brownfields (ten), undevelopable slopes of vacant land (eight), the existence of infrastructure problems (six), and classification of vacant land as wetlands (six). The survey data confirm that the label "vacant land" covers myriad characteristics.

Among the subset of larger cities (those with populations of 100,000 or more) responding to the survey, some distinct patterns can be discerned. Vacant land conditions vary, sometimes dramatically, by region and growth rate.[27] In the Northeast, more than half of responding cities have land that remains vacant "too long," compared with only 10 percent of cities in the West. More than 80 percent of the responding Midwestern cities have vacant land parcels that are "not large enough" for development purposes, compared with 50 percent in the South and 42 percent in the West. If we divide the cities into three equal groups based on population growth rates between 1980 and 1995 (slow growth of less than 11 percent, average growth of 11 to 41 percent, or high growth of more than 41 percent), there is notable variation in vacant land conditions. Nearly half of the slow-growth cities report the problem of too-small parcels or land that stays vacant too long. Less than one-fifth of cities with average or high growth rates indicate the existence of those conditions.

That more than half of all cities cited the problem that vacant land parcels were "not large enough" for development, and that one in four noted that vacant land had been in that status "too long," are important issues in urban land reuse. Too-small parcels that stay vacant too long characterize cities in the Northeast and Midwest more than cities in the West or South. In fact, 45 percent of Northeastern cities and 38 percent of Midwestern cities list both factors as major impediments to development, compared with fewer than 10 percent of cities in the West and South. Slow-growth cities, many of which are located in the Northeast and Midwest, are more likely to exhibit both conditions. One-third (34 percent) of the slow-growth cities identified both vacant land factors, whereas 13 percent of the average-growth group and 7 percent of the high-growth cities selected both factors.

The vacant land conditions displayed in table 1.1 present challenges for city governments. How can small parcels, especially when they are not clustered in one area, be assembled into larger ones? What are the development possibilities for odd-shaped vacant lots? How can a "wrong" location be transformed into a "right" one? What can be done to accelerate the movement of long-vacant parcels into productive use? Cities continue to search for answers to these "what works?" questions.

Changes in the Supply of Vacant Land

An insufficient supply of vacant land may limit a city's economic potential.[28] An oversupply of vacant land may depress land prices and, more important, may be part of a larger downward spiral in a community. More than half of all of the cities in this study indicated that they face problems with the supply of vacant land: Either there was too little vacant land (fifty-eight cities) or too much (forty-three). In each instance, city governments are likely to take actions designed to improve the condition. An essential first step in taking action is to learn the causes of the condition. In the survey, city officials speculated about the reasons that their city had increased or decreased its supply of vacant land from the late 1980s to the late 1990s.[29] Figure 1.2 depicts data for larger cities in which the amount of vacant land had increased.[30]

In cities in which the supply of vacant land had increased, several interrelated causal factors exist. Disinvestment from the city and the flight of population to the suburbs are the leading causes, according to city officials. It is a straightforward relationship: If there is not a proportionate replacement of the firms and households leaving the city, density decreases and the amount of vacant land will increase. Seemingly related to these causes are deindustrialization and out-migration, important factors in a large subset of cities. Deindustrialization may have had specific site effects that exacerbate the problem, that is, the closing of old manufacturing facilities may lead to the discovery of contaminated soil at the abandoned sites.

Other site-related problems, such as accessing capital (twelve cities) or assembling land (ten), are less important explanations for increases in the supply of vacant land. In only ten of the responding large cities was annexation said to be responsible for increased vacant land. Somewhat surprisingly, in very few cities are governmental actions such as land use policies and real estate tax policies linked to growth in the amount of vacant land.

Figure 1.3 focuses on cities that experienced a decline in the amount of vacant land from the late 1980s to the late 1990s. Three causes pre-

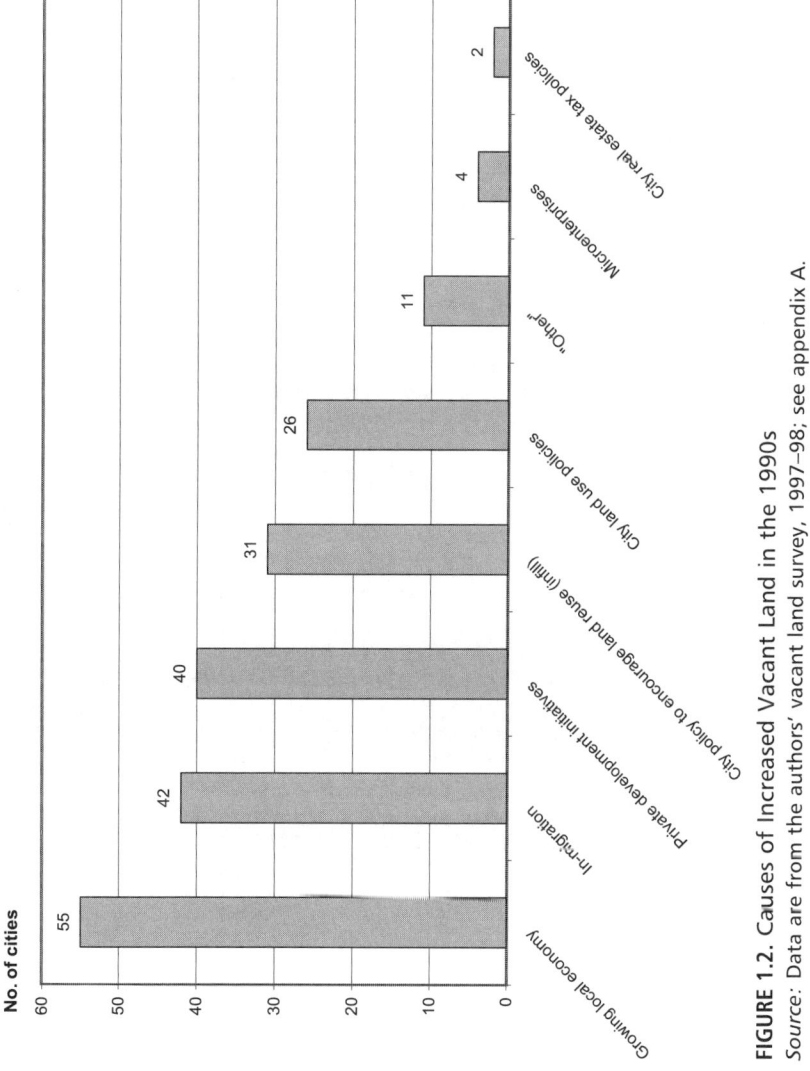

FIGURE 1.2. Causes of Increased Vacant Land in the 1990s

Source: Data are from the authors' vacant land survey, 1997–98; see appendix A.

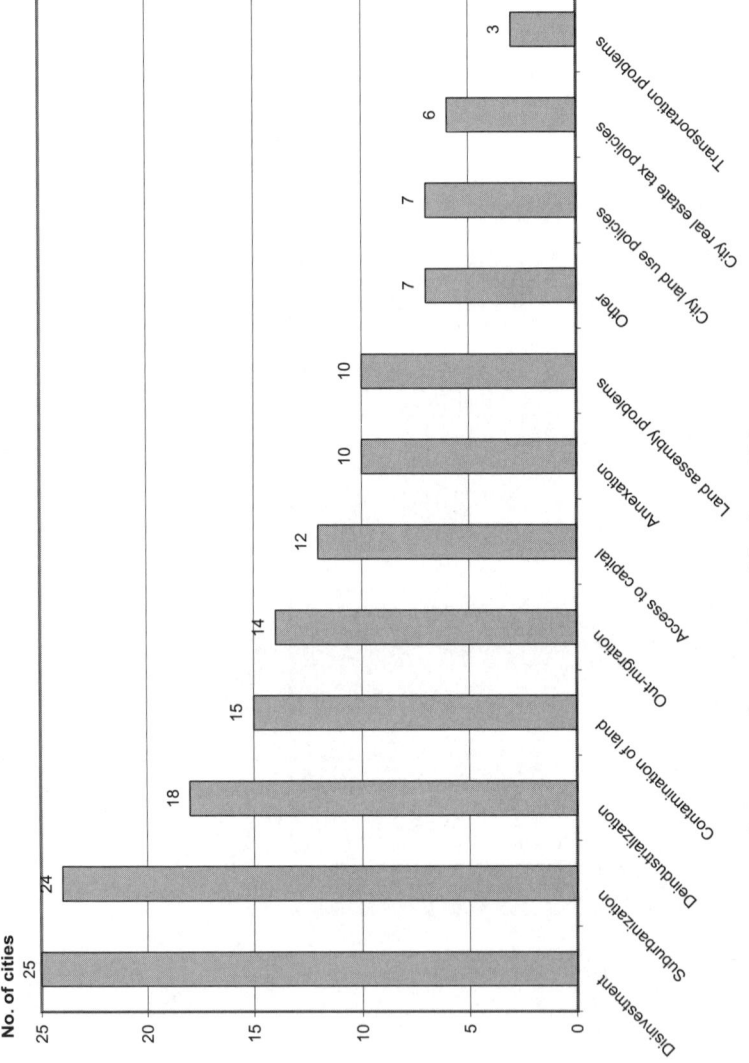

FIGURE 1.3. Causes of Decreased Vacant Land in the 1990s
Source: Data are from the authors' vacant land survey, 1997–98; see appendix A.

dominate: a growing local economy, increasing in-migration, and the use of private development initiatives. The first two of these items themselves are highly intercorrelated, both substantively and statistically ($r = 0.77$). Cities with growing local economies tend to be cities with increased in-migration. A decline in the availability of vacant land, especially in cities with a limited ability to annex additional territory, is a likely outcome.

Private development initiatives also play an important role in reducing supplies of vacant land. An aggressive private sector, operating in an expanding local economy, may make vacant land scarce. City government, in its land use and reuse policies, is identified as an important factor by more than half the cities with decreased vacant land stocks. Thus, although actions by the city are not thought to be linked to increases in vacant land, they are considered important in decreasing the amount of vacant land. This observation, however, is limited to land use and reuse policies; only two cities reported a city's real estate tax policies as causes of decreases in vacant land supply.

The relative lack of importance of real estate tax policies is surprising. Previous studies had suggested that a city's taxation of land and structures is directly tied to changes in the amount of vacant land.[31] Surely, adjustments to the tax system will have beneficial or detrimental effects on individual decisions to abandon or develop property. It is clear that real estate tax policies are deemed more important in cities with increases in vacant land than in cities with decreases. Still, compared with other explanations, real estate tax policies are reported to be of little consequence in most places. This curious finding will be explored more extensively in chapter 3.

CONTEXT MATTERS: VACANT LAND IN THREE METROPOLITAN AREAS

How do the various meanings of vacant land apply to real places, to actual jurisdictions? An examination of localities in three very different metropolitan areas—Phoenix, Seattle, and Philadelphia—provides some clarification. The contextual data on population trends, land areas, and economic bases for these jurisdictions appear in appendix B.

The Phoenix Metropolitan Area: Phoenix, Tempe, and Peoria

In the city of Phoenix, the question "What does the term 'vacant land' mean here?" generates many answers. In a descriptive sense, vacant land means virgin desert (especially to the north) and farmland (particularly in the southwestern part of the city). In other cases, it refers to underutilized land within the built city. For some neighborhoods, vacant land is a problem signifying dumping, weeds, trash, abandoned cars, and vagrants. In parts of Phoenix there are vacant industrial properties with real (or perceived) environmental contamination that complicates their reuse. Generally, however, the phrase "vacant land" means land, not abandoned structures. City-owned, dedicated open space such as South Mountain is typically not considered vacant land. City Council members tend to think about vacant land from their own district perspective, with some seeing it as redevelopment of underutilized space and others as new development of raw dirt. During the 1990s, the city intentionally created vacant land on occasion by razing dilapidated structures. Even when it is thought of as a problem, vacant land is often preferable to a previous use (e.g., an abandoned structure that had become a crack house). More peculiar to Phoenix is the presence of an extensive canal system that has created strips of vacant land adjacent to the waterways.

Although Phoenix has a relatively high proportion of vacant land compared with other cities of similar size, developers who work in the city's interior lament the loss of vacant land. Even at the fringes, vacant land is disappearing as ranches, farms, and desert are transformed into residential or commercial development. Figure 1.4 shows a new shopping area at the distant reaches of Phoenix's ever-expanding city limits.

The suburban cities of Tempe and Peoria, which share borders with Phoenix, have related but distinct definitions of vacant land. Tempe, given the constraints of a city with incorporated jurisdictions on all sides, has comparatively little vacant land. What it does consider as vacant land is actually "underutilized" land, that is, parcels that could be more intensely developed. Peoria, however, modeling Phoenix, has aggressively annexed desert land for future development. Thus its supply of vacant land is robust, and it tends to be of the raw dirt variety. In both communities, the problem of abandoned structures is fairly negligible and is concentrated in older residential or small-scale retailing areas.

The Seattle Metropolitan Area: Seattle, Bellevue, and Redmond

The land milieu for cities in the Seattle area is different from the Phoenix case. Washington's annexation laws are more restrictive than Arizona's and, more significantly, the state adopted a Growth Management Act in 1990. As a result, a city's supply of vacant land is more tightly controlled. In Seattle and the neighboring city of Belle-

FIGURE 1.4. New Shopping Area on Annexed Land, Phoenix, Northward along Interstate 17

vue across Lake Washington, vacant land, as variously defined, tends to be in short supply. Some land remains vacant by virtue of its physical characteristics, perhaps an undevelopable slope or terrain. For example, the City of Bellevue owns a ravine that is unbuildable. Other lands that may be considered vacant are those with particular natural resource value, such as wetlands or wildlife habitat. And the definition of vacant land is often extended to cover open space, including land dedicated for parks. Approximately 10 percent of the parceled area in Bellevue, for example, is parkland. (See figure 1.5, which shows parkland in the commercial heart of Bellevue.)

Given the demand for land in the area, there is little outright abandonment of property. In Bellevue, rarely is vacant land defined in terms of dilapidated structures or blight. The city's housing conditions surveys seldom show more than 1 percent of the structures as deteriorated. One might espy an unoccupied residential structure in the downtown area of the city only to find upon closer inspection that it is a redevelopment property destined to be replaced by an office tower. As a result, vacant land in Seattle and Bellevue is primarily a matter of underutilized land. Thus, an important goal in both cities is to redevelop existing parcels to intensify use. As one Bellevue planner stated, "The basic question here is how to use the land supply most efficiently."

FIGURE 1.5. Parkland in the Downtown Core of Bellevue, Washington

Because it has proportionately more undeveloped land than either Seattle or Bellevue, the City of Redmond tends to have a slightly different definition of vacant land. Vacant land includes not only redevelopment properties and open space (e.g., dedicated parkland and habitat preserve) but also land reclaimed from mining operations and former farm sites. To maintain a sufficient supply of vacant land, the city has annexed land under the guidelines of the state's Growth Management Act. Growth pressures are great, and the city has purchased land, some of it outside the city's limits, as open space, greenbelts, and parkland.

The Philadelphia Metropolitan Area: Philadelphia, Bucks County, and Camden

The Philadelphia area offers still another context. In the cities of Philadelphia and, across the Delaware River, Camden, New Jersey, vacant land is in great supply. It is also in great supply in nearby Bucks County, Pennsylvania, north of Philadelphia. But the abundant vacant land in the two cities is very different from the vacant land in the suburban county. In Philadelphia and Camden, much of the vacant land consists of abandoned or dilapidated buildings or land on which structures have been razed. Many of the vacant industrial sites are brownfields, including some toxic properties dangerous enough to be listed as Superfund sites. In Bucks County, however, vacant land is primarily farmland. Thus, the county faces a different set of challenges in managing its vacant land.

Given the intensive development patterns in both Philadelphia and Camden, vacant land is defined primarily in terms of abandonment, whether residential, commercial, or industrial. Figure 1.6 (with Philadelphia's distinctive City Hall visible in the distance) shows a vacant site in South Philadelphia, but it reflects the landscape of many sections of the city. Though some of the abandoned structures that posed particularly

FIGURE 1.6. Abandonment and Dilapidation in Philadelphia

serious threats to human health and safety have been razed, others continue to stand forlorn. Blighted properties and derelict land define much of what is vacant land in the two cities, which are reeling from decades of job loss and population exodus.

But in Bucks County, northeast of Philadelphia, it is a different story. There, the brownfield sites and blighted acres are few and far between. Instead, vacant land involves various types of open space, be it farm sites, wooded terrain, or meadows. Thus in Bucks County, the primary concern is not the accumulation of more vacant land but instead the rapid consumption of it. Bucolic scenes are giving way to subdivisions and malls indicative of farmland conversion, a phenomenon shown in figure 1.7.

All of the jurisdictions discussed in this section contain vacant land. However, the definition and image of vacant land is different from one place to another. State governments are responsible for creating at least part of the contextual variation, but even within a single state, the term "vacant land" has remarkable depth and range.

CONCLUSION

Vacant land is an elastic concept. It applies to an abandoned factory resting on toxic soil as well as to unbuilt land subject solely to the va-

FIGURE 1.7. Farmland Conversion: Construction of a Target Store in Bucks County, Pennsylvania

garies of nature. All cities have vacant land, although the supply, kind, and conditions vary. In one city, vacant land may symbolize despair, representing how far the city has fallen from its glory days. In another city, vacant land may symbolize hope, providing the opportunity for expansion and renewal. In its own way, vacant land tells the story of the city. Vacant land, then, offers a fresh perspective on cities—and on where they are headed.

One of the primary lessons of this chapter is that vacant land and abandoned structures reflect different situations. To expanding cities, vacant land represents an asset—a vast supply of potentially developable open space that can be harnessed to pursue a city's vision. To depopulating cities, vacant land is a red flag—an abundance of boarded-up buildings signaling neighborhoods in decline and a city in distress. Both types of settings call for the effective management of vacant land. And that is more easily said than done. A first step, however, is to reorient the concept of vacant land—to take a new perspective that sees it as an urban resource rather than problem. In the chapters that follow, we use a resource framework to explore urban vacant land and, therefore, the city.

Chapter 2, "Cities and Vacant Land: Data and a Model," answers the question "How much vacant land is there?" In addition, the chapter constructs a model for understanding the actions that cities take in regulating and reusing vacant land. Chapter 3, "City Policymaking: Exploring the Land–Tax Dynamic," then proceeds to analyze the "land–tax" dynamic, that is, city attempts to maximize the revenue-generating potential of vacant land contingent upon their access to a property, sales, or income tax. Chapter 4, "The Social Value of Vacant Land," explores the use of vacant land as a barrier or fence between income classes, land uses, and property values. Chapter 5, "The Development Potential of Vacant Land," examines city strategies in employing vacant land for development, introducing and exploring the importance of state policies in controlling local land use, especially in the arenas of annexation and growth management. Chapter 6, "Strategic Uses of Vacant Land," presents our thoughts about the characteristics of city policymaking that might inform policy reform and good practices. In that final chapter, we present a graphical depiction of our spatial model of vacant land—a three-dimensional cube that captures the interaction of the revenue, social, and development imperatives that constrain decisions about vacant land parcels.

NOTES

1. Henry G. Cisneros, "Urban Land and the Urban Prospect," *Cityscape: A Journal of Policy Development and Research* 3 (December 1996): 118.

2. Alice Coleman, "Dead Space in the Dying Inner City," *International Journal of Environmental Studies* 19 (1982): 103–7.

3. John A. Jakle and David Wilson, *Derelict Landscapes: The Wasting of America's Built Environment* (Savage, Md.: Rowman & Littlefield, 1992), 9.

4. Jakle and Wilson, *Derelict Landscapes*, 175.

5. The occupancy of abandoned structures by the homeless was moved tragically onto the public agenda in 2000 when a fire in an abandoned warehouse in Worcester, Massachusetts, killed six firefighters. The fire had been set accidentally by a homeless couple residing in the building.

6. John Accordino and Gary T. Johnson, "Addressing the Vacant and Abandoned Property Problem," *Journal of Urban Affairs* 22 (2000): 301–15.

7. Jakle and Wilson mention New York City's attempt to do something unconventional. The city once operated a program in which murals were painted on boarded-up buildings. The murals, an attempt to project a more positive image of a declining area, depicted family scenes. See Jakle and Wilson, *Derelict Landscapes*, 107.

8. In the 1980s, cities seeking to maintain the central business district's role as a retail center engaged in costly and often unsuccessful interventions, such as prohibiting vehicular traffic and creating pedestrian malls. However, vacant storefronts are vacant storefronts regardless of the mode of transportation.

9. Barbara Flanagan, "Good Design Creates Another Palm Beach Success Story," *New York Times,* June 12, 1997, B1, B8.

10. Mark Alan Hughes, "Dirt into Dollars: Converting Vacant Land into Valuable Development," *Brookings Review*, summer 2000, 34–37.

11. Civic Trust, *Urban Wasteland Now* (London: Civic Trust, 1988), 9.

12. Joseph Poracsky and Michael C. Houck, "The Metropolitan Portland Urban Natural Resource Program," in *The Ecological City*, ed. Rutherford H. Platt et al. (Amherst: University of Massachusetts Press, 1994), 251–67.

13. Michael Hough, "Design with City Nature: An Overview of Some Issues," in *Ecological City*, 40–48.

14. Neal Peirce, "Vacant Urban Land: Hidden Treasure?" *National Journal*, December 9, 1995, 3053.

15. For a broader discussion of how cities should manage their vacant land, see Paul Brophy and Jennifer Vey, *Seizing City Assets: Ten Steps to Urban Land Reform*, Survey Series (Washington, D.C.: Brookings Institution and CEOs for Cities, 2002).

16. William Fulton and Paul Shigley, "The Greening of the Brown," *Governing,* December 2000, 31.

17. Eric Price, as quoted in Jackie Spinner, "Decaying Buildings Targeted: D.C. to Acquire, Repair or Demolish 2,000 Properties," *Washington Post*, April 8, 2000, E1.

18. Barry Wood, *Vacant Land in Europe*, Working Paper (Cambridge, Mass.: Lincoln Institute of Land Policy, 1998), 99.

19. Wood, *Vacant Land in Europe*, 32.

20. Ray Northam, "Vacant Urban Land in the American City," *Land Economics* 47 (1971): 345–55.

21. David W. Jones, "Vacant Land Inventory and Development Assessment for the City of Greenville, S.C.," master's thesis, Clemson University, 1992.

22. Philip Kivell, *Land and the City: Patterns and Processes of Urban Change* (London: Routledge, 1993), 51.

23. U.S. General Accounting Office, *Superfund: Proposals to Remove Barriers to Brownfield Redevelopment*, GAO/T-RCED-97-87 (Washington, D.C.: U.S. General Accounting Office, 1997).

24. Michael R. Greenberg, Frank J. Popper, and Bernadette M. West, "The TOADS: A New American Urban Epidemic," *Urban Affairs Quarterly* 25 (March 1990): 435–54; Kumasi R. Hampton, "Land Use Controls and Temporarily Obsolete, Abandoned, and Derelict Sites (T.O.A.D.S.) in Cincinnati's Basin Area," master's thesis, University of Cincinnati, 1995.

25. Civic Trust, *Urban Wasteland Now.*

26. Survey respondents were asked to indicate which conditions were descriptive of the vacant land in their cities. No limit was imposed on the number selected, and no ranking was implied.

27. "Region" refers to the four major regional designations of the U.S. Bureau of the Census.

28. This was the conclusion of an early study of land use conducted by John H. Niedercorn and Edward F. R. Hearle, *Recent Land-Use Trends in Forty-Eight Large American Cities*, Memorandum RM-3664-1-FF (Santa Monica, Calif.: RAND Corporation, 1963).

29. An increase (or decrease) in the amount of vacant land is not the same as "oversupply" or "undersupply." First, assessments of oversupply and undersupply rely on the perceptions of the city official completing the survey. The increase-or-decrease question is based on empirical fact. Second, the characteristics are not necessarily parallel. The amount of vacant land in a city may have increased (or decreased) and an undersupply (or oversupply) could still exist.

30. Survey respondents could select as many causes as were applicable to their city.

31. Accordino and Johnson, "Addressing the Vacant and Abandoned Property Problem."

2

Cities and Vacant Land: Data and a Model

L and, especially its supply and its use, has been important in the political development of the United States. To Thomas Jefferson, tilling the soil—working the land—generated civic virtue and a sense of connection to place. Jefferson foresaw the triumph of republican principles, as he said in a letter to James Madison, "as long as agriculture is our principal object, which will be the case, while there remain vacant lands in any part of America."[1] To Madison and other framers of the Constitution, the vastness of the land offered a safety valve for political disputes. The massive size of the country, the huge expanse of open land, has structured the political landscape.[2]

Localities have also recognized the value of land. During the nineteenth century, Boston found that its relatively small size limited its growth and development. The city, which already was densely populated, allowed private developers to increase its landmass by filling in parts of rivers, marshes, and the harbor. Much of the area around Beacon Hill was created from land taken from the hill and deposited in the water at its base. This action had two positive effects: "It made level building sites on the hill . . . [and] also converted tidal flats at the base to new land."[3] The filling of the Back Bay area was a much larger and longer project. Using sand and garbage from Boston as well as gravel from a nearby town, acre after acre of new land was created over an almost forty-year period. The new vacant land allowed Boston to prosper.

Whereas landfilling is a physical means of increasing the amount of land, annexation offers a political and legal means. For instance, in 1950, the city of Atlanta encompassed 37 square miles. A decade later, the annexation of unincorporated adjacent land had pushed Atlanta's territorial size to 136 square miles. Oklahoma City offers even more evidence of the impact of annexation; the city leaders launched an unparalleled land expansion program from 1959 to 1963, annexing more than 550 square miles.[4] The ability to add more territory, to expand jurisdictional boundaries, is a powerful tool in a city's economic development arsenal.[5]

These days, land issues continue at the forefront of local public policy. To be sure, much attention is trained on the built environment not only for its empirical reality but also because of its symbolic representation. After all, the values of a polity are often embodied in the design and structures of the built environment.[6] But there is something to be learned from studying a different component of urban space: the "unbuilt"—or the "previously built"—environment. In other words, rather than focusing on the dazzling new glass and steel office tower as an embodiment of power relations in a city, consider the vacant lot next to it. It also represents power relations—and much more. Gary McDonough goes so far as to contend that it is through studies of empty spaces rather than the built environment that one learns about a city, its culture, and its values.[7]

As was discussed in chapter 1, vacant land may be the ultimate urban resource. That empty space may represent hope or, as has been the case in many places, it may symbolize despair. It is something that city governments respond to; some types of vacant land are to be maximized, and other types are to be minimized. Vacant land offers a tabula rasa to a city intent upon reconfiguring itself. It has development potential; and more specifically for the city, it has fiscal value and it both reflects and structures social relations. Further, a community's natural resources are quite often found on its vacant land. To quote McDonough: "Whether vacant, reserved, open, or razed, empty spaces thus play crucial roles in the fabric of the city."[8]

Until recently, vacant land has been terra incognita, both literally and figuratively. This book is devoted to reducing the "incognita" condition of vacant land. The preceding chapter emphasized the diversity of vacant land, ranging from the raw dirt depicted in figure 2.1 to the pile of rubble shown in in figure 2.2. The next section of this chapter explores a related topic: the amount of vacant land in cities.

THE AMOUNT OF VACANT LAND IN U.S. CITIES

Just how prevalent is vacant land in a typical city? Are a few parcels scattered here and there, or is it a widespread phenomenon, dominating the cityscape? The survey data provide estimates of the amount of usable va-

FIGURE 2.1.   Vacant Land: The Unbuilt Environment

cant land (thus excluding unusable land such as streets, rights of way, submerged land, wetlands, and so on) within corporate boundaries.[9]

Vacant Land in the Aggregate

On average, less than one-sixth (15.4 percent) of a city's land area is vacant land.[10] This figure includes widely varying types of land, ranging

FIGURE 2.2.   Vacant Land: The Previously Built Environment

from undisturbed open space to abandoned, contaminated brownfields. The 15.4 percent figure reflects a decline in vacant urban land from estimates reported during the 1960s, the last time that national studies were conducted. One 1960 study of forty-eight large cities put the average figure at 20.7 percent.[11]

Earlier studies opined that then-current levels of vacant land were perilously close to a minimum level that might reduce the potential economic growth rates of cities.[12] Whether the new data showing a decrease in usable vacant land should warrant a general or even faint alarm is unclear. The horizontal factory space that was so important for manufacturing enterprises shaped earlier perspectives about the need for vacant land. Without adequate vacant land, economic growth would be stifled. But the so-called new economy requires a different kind of land mix. For example, the Seattle metropolitan area, with precious little vacant land supply in the late 1990s, was teeming with job opportunities and growth. The City of Seattle, in fact, estimated its available vacant land at under 4 percent of its total area. Indeed, as any city's vacant land supply diminishes to zero, economic repercussions will follow. Whether they are dire for the economic survival of a municipality, however, is another question.

Eight cities with populations greater than a quarter-million reported a higher percentage of vacant land than the survey average: Albuquerque, Charlotte, Fort Worth, Mesa, Nashville, Phoenix, San Antonio, and Virginia Beach. In these cities, vacant land made up at least 20 percent of the total land area. Large cities with substantially less vacant land than the survey average included Atlanta, Baltimore, Cincinnati, Jacksonville, Kansas City, Louisville, New York, San Jose, and Seattle. None of these cities had more than 10 percent of their land area vacant. In terms of the prevalence of vacant land within their territorial limits, these two groups of major U.S. cities are quite different.

The average land area of the surveyed cities was approximately 64,426 acres (roughly 101 square miles), with much variation. These cities contained an average 12,367 acres of usable vacant land, although these figures also vary considerably. A subset of cities with large amounts of vacant land—Phoenix reported about 128,000 acres of vacant land; Fort Worth, 83,000; and Nashville, 82,000—skews the average. Another measure of central tendency, the median, provides perspective on the vacant figures; it shows the amount of usable vacant land to be just under 4,500 acres. (The data on vacant land and abandoned structures are given in appendix C.)

Vacant land figures are broken down by census region in table 2.1. Cities in the South reported the highest proportionate amount of vacant land (19.3 percent), whereas Western cities reported vacant land pro-

TABLE 2.1.   The Amount of Vacant Urban Land

Census Region	No. of Cities	Average Population, 1995	Average City Area (acres)	Average Vacant Land (acres)	Average Percentage of Vacant Land Relative to Total Land Area	Median Percentage of Vacant Land Relative to Total Land Area
Total survey	70	346,639	64,426	12,367	15.4	12.7
South	23	326,167	103,869	20,011	19.3	18.0
West	30	274,183	47,232	10,349	14.8	7.8
Midwest	11	240,798	59,433	5,904	12.2	12.4
Northeast	6	1,345,612	55,122	5,004	9.6	9.7

Sources: Data on land are from the authors' vacant land survey, 1997–98; see appendix A. Data on population and area are from the U.S. Census Bureau.

portions similar to the survey average (14.8 percent). Of the twenty-five cities reporting higher proportionate amounts of vacant land than the survey average, twenty-one (84 percent) are located either in the South or West. Cities in the Midwest report less vacant land than these two regions (12.2 percent), but it is among Northeastern cities that the proportionate amount of vacant land is the lowest (9.6 percent). No Northeastern city reported vacant land figures higher than the survey average. It should be noted, however, that the averages mask wide variation in the proportion of vacant land across cities. The figures in the last column of table 2.1, for example, demonstrate that the median Western city contains proportionately less vacant land than cities in the other census regions.

As is shown in table 2.1, Southern cities reported an average gross vacant land supply that is four times as large as reported by cities in the Northeast (20,011 vs. 5,004 acres). As a proportion of total land area, the difference in reported vacant land between Southern cities and their Northeastern counterparts is a factor of two (19.3 vs. 9.6 percent). These regional extremes are noteworthy, suggesting that the issue of vacant land is far from uniform throughout the country.

Vacant Land: Changes in Population and Land Area

To probe the regional patterns further, we look at changes in population and land area between 1980 and 1995. Of interest are subsets of cities at the high and low ends of the population and land area changes. Nineteen cities in the study increased their populations by at least 50 percent between 1980 and 1995. Table 2.2 classifies these fast-growing cities by census region and shows that eighteen of the nineteen cities (94.7 percent) are located in either the West or South. Using these growth parameters, no Northeastern city and only one Midwestern city (Naperville, Ill.) among survey respondents could be classified as a fast-growth city. The average growth rate among this subset of cities was 113 percent, fueled by a few cities that had unprecedented growth (e.g., Moreno Valley, Calif.; Pembroke Pines, Fla.; Plano, Tex.; Naperville, Ill.; and Mesa, Ariz.).

Cities that experienced population losses from 1980 to 1995 are grouped regionally in table 2.3. No Western city responding to the survey lost population during this fifteen-year period. Although the average population change for "declining" cities was –6.0 percent, cities such as Baltimore (classified as a Southern city by the census) and Cincinnati lost sizable portions of their population base during the fifteen-year period.

TABLE 2.2.   Vacant Land in Cities with Growing Populations

Census Region	No. of Cities with More than 50% Change in Population	Average Change in Population 1980–95 (percent)	Average Percentage of Vacant Land Relative to Total Land Area	Median Percentage of Vacant Land Relative to to Total Land Area
West	10	115.4	24.4	24.7
South	8	101.9	20.2	19.7
Midwest	1	181.7	13.0	13.0
Northeast	0	—	—	—
Cities with more than 50% change in population	**19**	**113.2**	**22.0**	**17.4**
Total survey	**70**	**43.6**	**15.4**	**12.7**

Sources: Data on land are from the authors' vacant land survey, 1997–98; see appendix A. Data on population and area are from the U.S. Census Bureau.

A comparison of the data in tables 2.2 and 2.3 shows that growing cities contain more vacant land than their nongrowing counterparts. The nineteen growing cities reported 22 percent of their land as vacant, nearly four times the amount reported by cities that lost population (6.04 percent) and 7 percentage points higher than the survey average. Nine of the nineteen cities (47 percent) reported more than 20 percent vacant land, whereas no cities that lost population contained more than 20 percent vacant land within their borders. Cities that lost population averaged less than half the vacant land within their borders as the

TABLE 2.3.   Vacant Land in Cities with Declining Populations

Census Region	No. of Cities with Population Loss	Average Percentage Change in Population, 1980–95	Average Percentage of Vacant Land Relative to Total Land Area
Midwest	4	−5.3	8.2
Northeast	2	−5.6	4.2
South	2	−7.1	4.4
West	0	—	—
Cities with population loss	**8**	**−6.0**	**6.6**
Total survey	**70**	**43.6**	**15.4**

Sources: Data on land are from the authors' vacant land survey, 1997–98; see appendix A. Data on population and area are from the U.S. Census Bureau.

survey average (6.04 vs. 15.4 percent). On the surface, this may seem counterintuitive. One would expect cities with population growth to have less vacant land, as a simple function of demand. After all, one of the primary characteristics of the urban sprawl phenomenon is the comparatively greater consumption of land relative to population increases. The findings reported here suggest that other forces are at work.

Especially important among those other forces is the rate of land expansion, primarily through annexation, that the cities experienced during the 1980–95 period. Disaggregating the cities by their rate of land area change provides another perspective on regional differences. Sixteen cities (we label them "expanding cities") had a 25 percent or greater increase in land area between 1980 and 1995 (see table 2.4). Fourteen of these sixteen cities (87.5 percent) are located in either the West or South; the other two are in the Midwest. (No Northeastern could be classified as an expanding city.)

The proportionate amount of vacant land in expanding cities is, on average, nearly one-quarter of their total land area. This figure is 8 percentage points higher than the survey average (23.3 vs. 15.4 percent). Ten of the sixteen expanding cities (62.5 percent) report more vacant land within their borders than the survey average. Expanding cities, by definition, annex land, and it appears that the territory being annexed adds more undeveloped land (or "raw dirt," as it is often called) to the city's land area.[13]

Twenty cities ("fixed-boundary cities") from all four census regions reported a negligible land area change (no more than 2 percent) between 1980 and 1995 (table 2.5 presents the data). Although fixed-boundary cities contain vacant land, they report less vacant land than the survey average and substantially less than expanding cities (8.8 vs. 23.3 percent). Of the twenty fixed-boundary cities, only three have a higher percentage of vacant land than the survey average, and only among Western cities does the vacant land average reach double digits. Midwestern cities with fixed boundaries have the least amount of vacant land on average; however, their Southern counterparts have the lowest median levels of vacant land.

This comparison of expanding and fixed-boundary cities suggests that territorial growth accounts for at least some of the vacant land in many cities. Annexation provides a means through which jurisdictions can augment their supply of developable land. Further, the small amount of vacant land in fixed-boundary cities resurrects the question of whether a minimum supply is needed to accommodate future development.

TABLE 2.4.   Vacant Land in Expanding Cities

Census Region	No. of Cities with More than 25% Change in Land Area	Average Percentage Change in City Land Area (1980–95)	Average Percentage of Vacant Land Relative to Total Land Area	Median Percentage of Vacant Land Relative to Total Land Area
West	6	45.4	24.9	28.3
South	8	74.3	23.1	21.0
Midwest	2	33.7	19.0	19.0
Northeast	0	—	—	—
Cities with more than 25% increase in land area	**16**	**58.4**	**23.3**	**23.0**
Total survey	**70**	**18.0**	**15.4**	**12.7**

Sources: Data on land are from the authors' vacant land survey, 1997–98; see appendix A. Data on population and area are from the U.S. Census Bureau.

Abandoned Structures

Cities' ordinances define "abandonment" of structures differently. For example, some cities contend that a structure is abandoned (and therefore presents an "imminent danger" to the community or threatens the city's "health and safety") if it has been unoccupied for 60 days; others use 120 days or longer as the threshold. Some cities

TABLE 2.5.   Vacant Land in Cities with Fixed Boundaries

Census Region	No. of Cities with Negligible or No Change in Land Area	Average Percentage Change in City Land Area (1980–95)	Average Percentage of Vacant Land Relative to Total Land Area	Median Percentage of Vacant Land Relative to Total Land Area
West	8	+0.35	11.5	5.8
Northeast	4	+0.21	8.3	7.5
South	5	+0.39	7.5	3.4
Midwest	3	−0.41	4.4	6.0
Cities with fixed boundaries	**20**	**0.22**	**8.8**	**5.7**
Total survey	**70**	**18.0**	**15.4**	**12.7**

Sources: Data on land are from the authors' vacant land survey, 1997–98; see appendix A. Data on population and area are from the U.S. Census Bureau.

criminalize the abandoning of a structure unless the owner registers it with the city. The survey asked respondents to estimate the number of abandoned structures in the city; it did not request a disaggregation of abandoned structures by use (i.e., single-family residential, multifamily residential, commercial, industrial), nor the square footage of the abandoned structures.

Sixty cities provided data on abandoned structures within their borders. As table 2.6 shows, those cities average more than 2.5 abandoned structures per 1,000 inhabitants (2.63).[14] The Northeast—the region with the lowest reported percentage of vacant land and the lowest average percentage change in city land area—reports the highest average number of abandoned structures per 1,000 inhabitants (7.47). Cities in the West, where population growth was high, report the lowest number of abandoned structures per 1,000 inhabitants (0.62). Northeastern cities average approximately twelve times the number of abandoned structures per 1,000 residents than cities in the West, and about two to three times more than cities in the South and Midwest.

Caution should be exercised in comparing abandoned structure figures across regions. The presence of a few jurisdictions with exceptionally high numbers of abandoned structures skews the regional average. For instance, Philadelphia, with a reported 36.5 abandoned structures per 1,000 population, dramatically increases the Northeastern average. Baltimore, at 22.2 abandoned structures per 1,000 inhabitants, has a similar impact on the Southern regional average. Thus in these instances, it may be more useful to speak in terms of median numbers rather than averages. Indeed, the median statistic for the Northeast is much smaller than the regional average, or 3.1 abandoned structures per 1,000 inhabitants, although it is still higher than the median figures for the other census regions. The median figure for both the South and Midwest is 1.4 abandoned structures per 1,000 residents.

The cities with large supplies of vacant land do not necessarily have disproportionately large stocks of abandoned structures. In fact, table 2.6 suggests an inverse relationship between the two situations. Thus, the presence of vacant land and the existence of abandoned structures may be separable conditions calling for different policy solutions.[15]

A Closer Look

The vacant land figures displayed in the preceding tables provide a good overview of the situation in U.S. cities. By unpacking the aggregate data for three cities that provided detailed information on their vacant land conditions in 1998—Columbus, Ohio; Orlando, Florida;

TABLE 2.6.   The Number of Abandoned Structures

Region	No. of Cities Reporting Abandoned Property Data	Average Change in Population, 1980–95 (percent)	Average Change in City Land Area, 1980–95 (percent)	Average Percentage of Vacant Land Relative to Total Land Area	Average No. of Abandoned Structures per 1,000 Inhabitants	Median No. of Abandoned Structures per 1,000 Inhabitants
Northeast	7	−3.1	1.9	8.3	7.47	3.13
Midwest	10	23.7	9.2	11.3	3.16	1.43
South	20	43.7	27.7	17.1	2.98	1.38
West	23	59.1	15.2	15.7	0.62	0.14
Cities reporting abandoned structures data	**60**	**40.5**	**16.7**	**14.8**	**2.63**	**0.74**

Sources: Data on land are from the authors' vacant land survey, 1997–98; see appendix A. Data on population and area are from the U.S. Census Bureau.

and Greenville, South Carolina—we can take a closer look at the vacant land phenomenon.

The city of Columbus occupies a land area of 210 square miles. Of that, approximately 12 percent is usable vacant land; there are approximately 1,000 abandoned structures. Almost three-quarters of the city's vacant land is privately owned; one-quarter is publicly owned. Although commercially zoned property makes up roughly 12 percent of the city's land usage, more of this property is vacant than is industrial or residential property. The City of Columbus owns nearly half of the publicly held vacant land; other local governments, such as the county and the school district, own the next largest amounts (more than the state or federal governments). The location of vacant land is relatively balanced between the core of the built city and its fringe (8,800 acres in the core, 8,100 acres on the fringe.) The ratio of three-quarters privately owned to one-quarter publicly owned is maintained regardless of core or fringe location.

Orlando presents a different picture. The city is less than half the territorial size of Columbus (95 square miles), with vacant land representing a larger proportion (29 percent) of the city's total land area. The number of abandoned structures is estimated to be 400. Two-thirds of Orlando's vacant land is privately owned; one-third is publicly owned. The location of vacant land is split fairly evenly between the core and the fringe areas of Orlando; however, the ownership patterns shift slightly from one area to the other. The ownership of 77 percent of the vacant land in the city's core is in private hands; at the fringe, private ownership is approximately 60 percent.

Nineteen percent of the land in Greenville, a city of 19 square miles, is vacant. The vast majority (94 percent) of vacant land in the city is held privately. Of that, the proportion of industrially zoned land that is vacant is 24 percent; commercially zoned land is 9 percent, and residentially zoned land is 9 percent. Of the approximately 6 percent of the vacant land that is publicly owned, the greatest proportion is held by local governments other than the city. Less than 10 percent of the publicly owned land in Greenville is vacant, although the pattern varies from one level of government to another. For example, 52 percent of the federally owned land is vacant; 6 percent of the city owned land is vacant. Less than 1 percent of the vacant land at the fringe of the city is held publicly; however, at the city's core, the proportion increases to 13 percent.

These three cities make it clear that although we can talk comfortably about national trends and about the patterns in particular groups of cities, important city-specific distinctions remain. Several compelling variations complicate the development of a uniform set of policy prescriptions. Some cities own a large amount of vacant land; others own very little. What drives a city's decision to own vacant land or, alternatively, to eschew it? Is city ownership the sign of a jurisdiction that is taking charge of its destiny? Or is it an indicator of a moribund real estate market in which city ownership occurs as a last resort? The question of why cities do what they do with vacant land and what it might mean is taken up in the next section.

TERRA INCOGNITA: UNDERSTANDING CITY ACTIONS

A city's landmass, its territory, is one of its most fundamental characteristics. In many important ways, land—size and shape, location, physical features, quality, and utilization—defines a city. Land is a resource that city governments regulate, manage, develop, and preserve. As was noted above, vacant land has been terra incognita, both literally and figuratively. The data presented in chapter 1 and thus far in chapter 2 open up this unknown land to scrutiny. The next step is to shine a light on the actions and behaviors of city governments with respect to vacant land. Ultimately, of course, vacant land is more than images, conditions, and amounts. We contend that vacant land can be a lens through which to view the political, fiscal, and social policy choices of cities. The next subsection sketches the argument.

Mapping City Strategic Behavior

Given the decentralized, competitive context in which cities function in the U.S. federal system, three imperatives predominate:

1. the need to enhance the fiscal condition of the city;
2. the need to minimize social disruption and protect property values in the city; and
3. the need to augment or, at a minimum, maintain the economic vitality of the community and to sustain or enhance its image.

Within this context, the principal goal of city officials is to maximize citizens' individual and collective well-being, that is, to do what they think is best for the city. To be sure, much of the motivation for elected officials is their desire to retain their offices.[16] Their actions are further structured and influenced by any number of constraints, both internal and external to city government.

Because the political risks of failing associated with new public policies or experimental actions are often perceived as high, municipal corporations (following Isaac Newton's First Law of Motion) prefer to stay at rest unless forced to change. The political comfort of policy stasis is preferable to the uncertainties associated with policy change. But cities do change and create new policies in response to or in anticipation of certain factors. These factors include a perceived or actual threat to a city's tax/service equilibrium within a competitive federal system,[17] an aspiration to be a player in a certain "orbit" of a market-based economic system, and a response to changing citizen demands and preferences.

More specifically, these factors can come in the form of (1) shifts to a city's underlying economic or fiscal base; (2) policies, programs, grants, and mandates from state or federal agencies; (3) policy actions of neighboring or overlapping local governments; (4) changes in the supply and demand of production factors; and (5) changes in citizen preferences, needs, and wants. In response to, or in anticipation of, these changing environmental factors, city officials act on behalf of their citizenry.[18] Our interest is in those actions that involve land use, particularly vacant land use and reuse.

Strategic Behavior and Vacant Land

As with policy actions in general, a political logic produces city strategies toward the use and reuse of vacant land. In other words, concerns of fiscal condition, of social disruption and property values, of economic vitality and image enhancement overlay city officials' land use choices. The interaction of these imperatives plays out in a city's formal decision-making and rule-making powers guiding the use or reuse vacant land. City governments zone areas for desired uses, invest public funds to purchase land, regulate allowable activities on privately held land, and promote certain parcels of land for development.

For example, a city might decide to purchase a particular vacant lot as part of a downtown redevelopment strategy. Once the land has been purchased, the city might choose to either dedicate it as open space or develop it into multifamily housing. On another parcel near its border, a city might decide to approve a landowner's petition to rezone a parcel to allow the conversion of abandoned residential structures into retail space.

These actions are neither random nor inconsequential. Instead, they are purposive actions designed to accomplish the goal of enhancing the community's well-being. As such, they form part of a city's land development strategy. What complicates the strategy is that a city operates in a multi-jurisdictional milieu.

In this milieu, strategic behavior in developing a vacant land parcel requires city officials in, say, Myhometown to think about what the neighboring jurisdiction of Neartown would do in response to the expected actions of Myhometown officials, actions that in turn are premised on the probable behavior of Neartown officials—and on and on in a cascade of connected actions.

In pursuing this question about the strategic development of vacant land, we happened on a quite logical and defensible answer: City boundaries matter and frame the vacant land actions of city officials. Why, we speculated, would it not be in the city's best interest to develop a parcel of vacant land at or near the city's fringe or boundary rather than at its core, given the opportunity to choose between two locations? The effects of fringe development of vacant land in the form of, say, a public park would surely spill over to the neighboring city, an externality with little immediate benefit to the investor city. The neighboring city, knowing that a park will be constructed near its boundary by the investor city, would surely be induced to encourage residential development near the park, which would in turn maximize some utility for the city, while being grateful and gracious to the investor city for enhancing a residential neighborhood at little or no cost.

Yet, surely cities do at times, when given the choice, choose to develop the vacant parcel at the fringe location even if the cost burden falls on only the developing city and not on the free-rider city. If, say, the investor city were to develop a vacant land parcel for commercial purposes, would not the neighboring city bear some negative (and certainly positive) spillovers with increased levels of traffic, congestion, and other costs that tend to spread out from the commercial development site? The neighboring city could conceivably share some of the development costs.

Why would a city engage in such counterintuitive and potentially "unstrategic" behavior by developing open space at the fringe? Should not the investing city expect something in return from the other, free-riding city? Would a cooperative development strategy be preferable to a go-it-alone approach in vacant land development? Why would the neighboring city cooperate with the investor city, if the costs of a commercial development site were not totally internalized within the investor city's framework?

In our journey through cities and their vacant land conversion reports and through both geographical and mental maps on the approaches to vacant land use and reuse, we found the pattern of vacant land decisions to inhere in at least three principles. First, because cities must pursue policies that enhance their fiscal condition, policy officials are motivated to consider vacant land options that either maximize revenues or minimize costs. Second, because cities must pursue policies that minimize social disruption and protect property values, policy officials are encouraged to assemble, zone, and dedicate vacant land for the purpose of simulating natural barriers and protecting property values. Third, because cities must pursue policies that augment or, at a minimum, maintain the economic vitality and enhance the image of the community, policy officials are induced to use or reuse vacant land to its highest and best use. At certain times, the principles work in harmony, producing salubrious effects from the investor city's perspective. At others, one principle trumps another.

Figure 2.3 maps the land uses for a section of the city of Bellevue, Washington. Vacant parcels, outlined on the land use map, tend to be widely scattered across the city. There is vacant land located near existing parkland (to the west of Interstate 405), adjacent to residential areas (appearing on this map on the north), in industrial areas (north of Interstate 90), and abutting commercial uses (on the east side). Much of the vacant land is privately owned. Why will city officials promote the development of one parcel over another? Part of the explanation in Bellevue involves the vacant land actions that adjacent cities (Redmond, Kirkland, and Issaquah) have taken and are likely to take in the future.

These factors influence the strategies that a city considers in managing the use and reuse of vacant land. The development of some parcels is allowed (or disallowed), encouraged (discouraged), and in some instances, subsidized (not subsidized). Strategies pursued by cities are designed to achieve particular ends and to meet the preference structures of the decision makers.[19] City officials, as actors anointed by the state's constitutional and legal system with the responsibility to make decisions for the community, clearly have preferred outcomes in the political process. Certainly, their preferences may be thwarted at times by private market forces. For instance, choices made by large landowners to sell parcels or by land speculators to hold property can confound a city's plans. But it is city officials who have the power to transform the landscape—or not.

THE THREE IMPERATIVES AND VACANT LAND

Cities' strategic behavior to maximize community well-being derives from the three principal imperatives of municipalities in a federal sys-

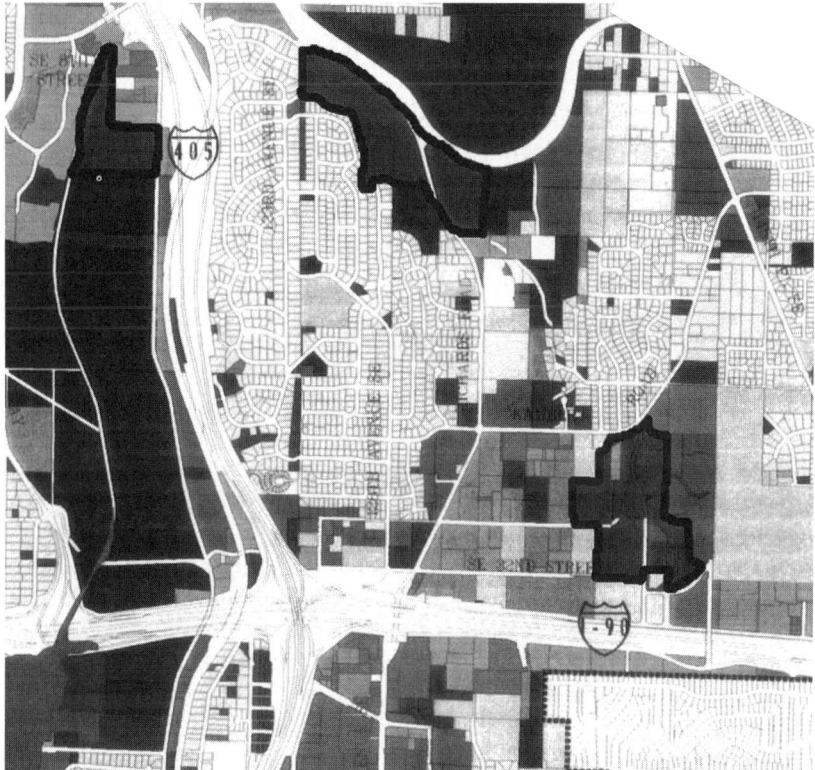

FIGURE 2.3. Land Use Map for Bellevue, Washington
Source: City of Bellevue, *Current Land Use (12/29/98)*. Reprinted by permission of the City of Bellevue.

tem. Although each vacant land imperative is pursued in the subsequent chapters, we preview their importance here.

The Fiscal Imperative

One political strategy that cities employ to reach their goal of enhancing their residents' quality of life resides in their general taxing authority. Cities' revenue-generating systems for public services, which are authorized by their states, usually depend on either the property tax or on a combination of property and sales (or income) taxes. Each of these general tax sources is site specific (although this is not so obvious with the income tax), meaning that a city's revenue system has a spatial dimension. High-end properties, especially expensive multistory commercial or residential buildings or large industrial concerns, generate a disproportionately large amount of revenue compared with similarly sized lots with structures appraised for much less (figure 2.4).[20] Similarly, commercial establishments that sell expensive commodities, such as automobiles, generate more sales tax revenue per unit or per lot than a local hardware store.

Private firms in a competitive market economy attempt to minimize costs and maximize profits and thus locate, when possible, where factor costs are the lowest. Among the key factors of land, labor, and capital is a spatial marker for firms to consider—that is, their proximity to factors and to markets. In most cases, the spatial costs are factored into cost calculations through the costs of transportation. Just as private firms' strategies for survival and growth hinge on cost minimization, municipal governments in a federal system engage in a competition that induces a spatial revenue-maximization strategy.[21]

One of the most powerful conditioners of city strategic behavior is what we refer to as the "land–tax dynamic," by which we understand municipal governments in a federal system to engage in a competition that induces a spatial revenue-maximization strategy. The strategic choice of encouraging or facilitating the development of vacant land at one site or at another depends in large part on the general taxing authority of the municipality. The spatial derivation of municipal tax rev-

FIGURE 2.4. The Fiscal Imperative: High-Value Residential Development on Vacant Land

enues shapes decision makers' political strategies on vacant land poɪ.
cies. Different tax structures should produce different land use choices.

The conceptual framework suggests the following: (1) property-tax-
dependent cities think strategically about the pattern of vacant land use
based on the market value of the development and on the possibility of
shifting service-delivery costs to other jurisdictions (fiscal externalities);
(2) sales-tax-dependent cities think strategically about the temporal development of vacant land based on their mental constructs of "shopping
sheds" and on which transactions are taxable; and (3) income-tax-dependent cities think strategically about vacant land use based on their assessment of the income growth potential of the individual or firm.
Knowing a city's revenue structure, then, should allow us to predict, ceteris paribus, which vacant land parcels ought to be developed for the
purpose of maximizing revenues or minimizing costs, so that the city's
goal of enhancing the quality of life for its citizens might be better at-
tained. The land development patterns in property-tax-dependent cities
generally differ from those in a sales-tax-dependent city, which in turn
differ from those in an income-tax-dependent city. For example, a sales-
tax-dependent city is predicted to encourage vacant land conversion to
commercial purposes at the city's borders, whereas an income-tax-dependent city is expected to encourage vacant land conversion to professional office purposes.

The location and use of these revenue-producing activities structure
the political strategy of a city. Because cities' fiscal policies compete
with those of neighboring cities, cities try to maximize their revenue
without increasing the tax burden on their residents. The consequence
is that cities not only are constantly challenged to manage their services
effectively and efficiently but are also encouraged to seek out mechanisms for ensuring that service-delivery costs are borne by users. Besides the enormous explosion in user-fee financed services by municipalities during the past quarter-century, there has been the constant
search for ways to export tax costs to nonresidents. Land, especially vacant land, is a key component in a city's revenue maximization strategy. Thus, the development of vacant land will be pursued by cities
with the intent of maximizing revenues for the city fisc.

The Social Imperative

The mental image of a city that is described as "depressed," "in decline,"
or "unsafe" is of an urban wasteland and shuttered factories. The piles of
rubble in war-torn and bombed-out cities in the pages of history text-
books and on the nightly television news are only marginally worse than
the caved-in tenements, cyclone-fenced lots, or desolate Kafkaesque

landscapes of some inner cities (figure 2.5). The visual image of vacant land sends messages about the city. Do city officials intentionally neglect certain areas of the city? Does the land possess no more value in the marketplace? Might other uses, or any uses for that matter, improve the "feel" of the city?

Although any and all of these questions might be entertained, unused and vacant land serves other interests as well. Just as the "peace line" (in reality, a wall) in Belfast and the "green line" drawn through neighborhoods in Nicosia respectively serve the purposes of separating religious and ethnic groups, vacant land and abandoned structures can serve a similar purpose: Though they separate and segregate, they also protect. In the case of vacant land, property values are protected.

Cities decide how land should be utilized. Even though the development of a parcel of land has immediate revenue-generating potential, the well-being of the broader neighborhood and society might be augmented by not improving the land with residential, commercial, or industrial structures. The value of a parcel of vacant land to neighboring residential communities might be greater if the land were to remain vacant, either as a well-manicured urban park or as a stark reminder that one is leaving a particular neighborhood and entering another. Open space—whether in the form of public parks that impose public costs on

FIGURE 2.5.   The Social Imperative: Abandoned Structures as Barriers and Buffers

all the city's taxpayers or in the state of unkempt vacant lots that concentrate costs on the immediate neighbors through lower property values—serves a social purpose by defining areas and neighborhoods along income and class lines. The property values associated with higher-priced residential housing and commercial structures are protected by barriers.

In some cities, such barriers are natural (cliffs, mountains, streams); in others, they are created by city actions and policies. The salutary effect of New York City's Central Park on the property values of abutting properties is a case in point.[22] Parks, open space, and even transportation corridors are planned and built or left alone by the city, serving the purpose of protecting the property values of certain areas and, intentionally or not, clustering groups and individuals by class and income. These vacant spaces, in effect, function as fences or walls and, as such, influence the city's social landscape. City officials thus consider social consequences as they make decisions about the use or reuse of particular vacant parcels.

The Development Imperative

Vacant land, then, can serve to create social barriers and protect property values. Yet cities also take purposive actions to augment the value of land through deliberate developmental activities. In a seminal work on the reach of city policies,[23] Paul Peterson argues that the development function is the only arena that can be effectively influenced by city actions. Subsidizing development costs, creating a good investment climate for developers, providing an adequate and appropriate public infrastructure, and promoting other development-related programs can enhance the city as a locus of economic activity. Cities mobilize public resources for the purpose of enhancing and capturing economic vitality. Vacant land, an important resource in encouraging and promoting development, is regulated by city policies, and it can be offered up by the city to lure developers (figure 2.6).

An example of the development imperative at work can be seen in the redevelopment of the vacant land that until 1995 had been Denver's Stapleton Airport. The massive tract (4,700 acres) offered an array of redevelopment possibilities. The city eventually settled on a fifteen-year plan intended to transform the old airport property into 10 million square feet of commercial, research and development, and industrial space; 3 million square feet of retail space; more than 12,000 residential units; and more than 1,000 acres of parkland.[24] The employment potential of the project has been pegged at 35,000 new jobs.

FIGURE 2.6.   The Development Imperative: The Reality of (and the Symbols for) Economic Vitality

Cities do not have carte blanche authority. Just as states define cities' revenue-raising authority, which structures their fiscal fortunes in important ways, states also to a considerable extent control cities' capacities to influence and control economic growth and development. "Smart growth"—as growth management initiatives have become known, especially since the 1985 passage of Florida's Growth Management Act—imposes important constraints on city strategic behavior. Indeed, the overriding purpose of smart growth strategies is to rein in sprawl, reduce the costs of expensive infrastructure, and increase density for a state's municipalities and other local governments.[25] Yet these state laws result in vastly different development plans for cities across states. City inducements to convert vacant land to another use are influenced by state-imposed constraints.

Another aspect of the development imperative is more perceptual or symbolic. City leaders may pursue the development of vacant land because it will improve the city's image, its perception by outsiders—most important, outside investors. Development of a formerly blighted site may provide an immediate economic boost, but it may also have longer-term effects. If city leaders aspire to move their city to a different, "higher" level of economic competition, the development of vacant land can be an important first step.[26] An improved cityscape upgrades a city's image, and with an enhanced image, the city is better able to compete economically with a different set of cities. Furthermore, elected city officials benefit. Political dividends await a mayor or city councillor who can take credit for revitalizing his or her city.

Interactive Effects of the Fiscal, Social, and Development Imperatives

The strategic policy choices of cities toward vacant land and abandoned structures are influenced to a greater or lesser extent by an interaction of these three imperatives, namely, a fiscal need to generate resources and to keep the city's fiscal position strong, a social need to create stable neighborhoods and sectors and to protect property values, and a development need to ensure and enhance the economic vitality of the community. The predominance of any one of these in structuring a city's policy depends on the environment at the time of the decision.

Moreover, the woof and warp of these three imperatives are often woven so closely together in the political fabric of a city that it is nearly impossible to separate them. Their influence is structured in important ways by state statutory and constitutional provisions. Indeed, states control municipal land use and zoning regulations, local taxing authority, debt issuances and finance for public infrastructure, subsidies, annexation powers, and a host of other tools that influence and possibly determine a city's strategic behavior in designing policies that directly or indirectly affect vacant land use and reuse. Although we contend that, among the three, the fiscal imperative is usually primus inter pares, by also including the development and the social values one gains a robust explanation of city strategic behavior toward vacant land.

CONCLUSION

About 15 percent of the average large city's landmass is vacant. Some might ask whether that proportion is too high or too low, but such a question misses the point. The pivotal issue is what city government chooses to do with that 15 percent. As this chapter has argued, cities are constrained by three imperatives in their efforts to make strategic decisions regarding the use and reuse of vacant land. A strong fiscal imperative may predispose city officials toward a particular option for a specific parcel; the pressure of the other two imperatives may modify the preferred option. And the need to "do something" with vacant land varies also by its condition. A 15 percent that is raw dirt is quite different from a 15 percent that is blight and decay.

Furthermore, the 15 percent figure masks the tremendous range in vacant land supply from one city to another. Compare, for example, two Southern cities: Atlanta with an estimated 7 percent of its land vacant, and Nashville with slightly more than 24 percent vacant. Is one city significantly advantaged over the other? If so, which one? If one pursues the "vacant land as a resource" line of thinking, then Nashville is the winner. Yet it depends on how the city manages its resource. In that regard, Atlanta has taken an important step with its Fulton County–City of Atlanta Land Bank Authority. The authority, which was established through an interlocal agreement in 1991, converts derelict land and buildings into marketable properties.[27] Social and development imperatives have driven the authority's efforts.

Abandoned structures offer a different slant on the vacant land situation. Northeastern cities lead other sections of the country in the number of dilapidated, blighted structures, even though the region's cities have substantially lower amounts of vacant land than cities elsewhere. Abandoned structures have costs associated with them that vacant land without structures does not. The notion of these properties as assets is more difficult to fathom. Further, a preponderance of abandoned structures suggests a comparatively weak real estate market, and therefore a low probability of an infusion of private capital. In these settings, city officials play a central role in identifying certain strategically located structures for rehabilitation or razing and redevelopment.

The involvement of city government does not stop there, however. In the absence of private capital, the conversion of these abandoned eyesores into assets is the task of city government. As the respondents to the survey indicated, city land use policies can go a long way in reducing the amount of vacant land. The fiscal, social, and development imperatives influence these actions in a variety of ways. The next three chapters take up these imperatives.

NOTES

1. Thomas Jefferson, as quoted in Daniel Kemmis, *Community and the Politics of Place* (Norman: University of Oklahoma Press, 1990), 22.
2. See, e.g., Frederick Jackson Turner, *The Frontier in American History* (New York, H. Holt & Co., 1920).
3. Ann Whiston Spirn, *The Granite Garden* (New York: Basic Books, 1984), 18.
4. Richard M. Bernard, "Oklahoma City: Booming Sooner," in *Sunbelt Cities: Politics and Growth since World War II*, ed. Richard M. Bernard and Bradley R. Rice (Austin: University of Texas Press, 1983), 213–34.

5. See the discussion in David Rusk, *Cities without Suburbs*, 2nd ed. (Baltimore: Johns Hopkins University Press, 1995). Rusk contends that a city's degree of elasticity strongly influences its economic health.

6. Dolores Hayden, *The Power of Place: Urban Landscapes as Public History* (Cambridge, Mass.: MIT Press, 1995); Sharon Zukin, *Landscapes of Power* (Berkeley: University of California Press, 1991).

7. Gary McDonough, "The Geography of Emptiness," in *The Cultural Meaning of Urban Space*, ed. Robert Rotenberg and Gary McDonough (Westport, Conn.: Bergin & Garvey, 1993), 3–15.

8. McDonough, "Geography of Emptiness," 15.

9. The survey contained this definition of vacant land: "Vacant land includes not only unused or abandoned land or land that once had structures on it, but also the land that supports structures that have been abandoned, derelict, boarded up, partially destroyed or razed, etc."

10. To make meaningful comparisons across cities with different territorial sizes, total vacant land by acres was converted to a proportion of the city's total land area. This variable, the proportion of usable vacant land to total land area, provides a better indicator of the magnitude of the vacant land situation in a given city than does the absolute "vacant land acreage" figure.

11. Neidercorn and Hearle estimated vacant land in 48 "large" cities at 20.7 percent of cities' land area. Manvel's 1968 study found that for cities with populations greater than 250,000, the amount of undeveloped land was 12.5 percent; the median amount of undeveloped privately held land in those large cities was only 119 acres. See John H. Niedercorn and Edward F. R. Hearle, *Recent Land-Use Trends in Forty-Eight Large American Cities*, Memorandum RM-3664–1-FF (Santa Monica, Calif.: RAND Corporation, 1963); and A. D. Manvel, "Land Use in 106 Large Cities," in *Three Land Research Studies*, Research Report 12 (Washington, D.C.: Prepared for the consideration of the National Commission on Urban Problems, 1968).

12. Neidercorn and Hearle, *Recent Land-Use Trends*.

13. Recall, however, that in only ten cities was annexation reported as a cause for increased vacant land. The empirical data suggest otherwise.

14. Because cities with more people are likely to have more structures, a standardized measure of abandoned structures was created. Of the responding cities, only two-thirds could estimate the number of abandoned structures. Much of the difficulty in obtaining an accurate count of abandoned structures resides in the rapid turnover of properties, the definitions imposed by municipalities as to what constitutes an abandoned structure, and the city's administrative capacity to count—and therefore to know about—the number of abandoned structures.

15. Ann O'M. Bowman and Michael A. Pagano, "Transforming America's Cities: Policies and Conditions of Vacant Land," *Urban Affairs Review* 35 (March 2000): 559–81.

16. Anthony Downs, *An Economic Theory of Democracy* (New York: Harper & Row, 1957).

17. This argument is developed more fully in Michael A. Pagano and Ann O'M. Bowman, *Cityscapes and Capital* (Baltimore: Johns Hopkins University Press, 1995).

18. Exactly what constitutes the collective well-being of the community may not necessarily be agreed upon by all residents or by all cities. For example, a report of a major city addressed the problems and opportunities of its future with reference to its collective well being. The City of Philadelphia's 2000 "Transition Team" of Mayor John Street identified the well- being of its citizens under the rubric "Quality of Life," which included (1) the presence of a civil society and a sense of collective responsibility; (2) opportunities for cultural, intellectual and spiritual growth; (3) economic development/ streetscape; (4) community control and enforcement; (5) safety; and (6) the availability of essentials which are present and affordable (City of Philadelphia, Quality of Life, 2000; www.phila.gov/transition/QualityOfLife.htm [June 2000]).

19. Strategic behavior is extensively examined in social science literature. See, e.g., Kenneth A. Shepsle and Mark S. Bonchek, *Analyzing Politics: Rationality, Behavior, and Institutions* (New York: W. W. Norton, 1997); Avinash K. Dixit and Barry J. Nalebuss, *Thinking Strategically* (New York: W. W. Norton, 1991); David A. Lake and Robert Powell, eds., *Strategic Choice and International Relations* (Princeton, N.J.: Princeton University Press, 1999); Roy Meyers, *Strategic Budgeting* (Ann Arbor: University of Michigan Press, 1994); David Weimer and Aidan R. Vining, *Policy Analysis*, 3rd ed. (Upper Saddle River, N.J.: Prentice Hall, 1999).

20. In cities with site value tax systems, the revenue-generating disparities would be much less pronounced.

21. See, e.g., the findings of Mark Schneider in *The Competitive City* (Pittsburgh: University of Pittsburgh Press, 1989).

22. Blaine Harden, "Neighbors Give Central Park a Wealthy Glow," *New York Times*, November 22, 1999, A1, A29.

23. Paul Peterson, *City Limits* (Chicago: University of Chicago Press, 1981).

24. Diane Kittower, "Turning an Airport into an Urban Village," *Governing*, May 2000, 90.

25. Patricia E. Salkin, "Political Strategies for Modernizing State Land Use Statutes to Address Sprawl," paper presented at the Who Owns America? II Conference, Madison, Wisc., 1998.

26. Pagano and Bowman, *Cityscapes and Capital*.

27. Paul C. Brophy and Jennifer Vey, *Seizing City Assets: Ten Steps to Urban Land Reform*, Survey Series (Washington, D.C.: Brookings Institution and CEOs for Cities, 2002).

3

City Policymaking: Exploring the Land–Tax Dynamic

The purpose of this chapter is to explore the links between a city's political strategy of vacant land development and its revenue structure. We contend that a city's revenue structure influences, and possibly determines, its development of vacant land. We examine the taxing authority of U.S. cities, focusing on three city tax types: property, sales, and income. The general taxing authority ought to be of extraordinary importance in understanding and predicting which vacant land parcel will be considered in the collective interest of the municipality and, therefore, possibly supported, subsidized, and otherwise promoted by the municipal government.

CONSTRAINTS AND OPPORTUNITIES OF GENERAL TAXING AUTHORITY

Municipalities as legally incorporated governmental organizations are granted certain legislative, judicial, and service-delivery responsibilities. Their jurisdictional survival depends on access to certain general sources of taxation. Although the number and extent of user fees and charges and of specialized or specific taxes varies by municipality across the nation, all municipalities are granted access to the property tax (although Oklahoma's municipalities do not levy it for operating purposes) and many have been granted some form of retail sales taxing authority or an income (earnings, wages, or payroll) taxing authority. Very few cities are allowed access to all three forms of general taxes (e.g., New York City; Yonkers, Philadelphia; Saint

Louis; and Kansas City, Missouri). Of the approximately 555 U.S. cities with populations greater than 50,000, about 34 percent have access to the property tax only, 8 percent have access to the income tax, and nearly 58 percent have some retail sales taxing authority.[1]

Cities promote vacant land conversion and other development projects for a variety of reasons (e.g., to enhance the employment and income base of the city, to stimulate neighborhood or community development, to increase city revenue collections), but rarely is city investment in development projects encouraged with the purpose of enhancing the employment or fiscal profile of a *neighboring* city. Cities invest in projects with the expectation that the return on investment will redound to the benefit of the investor city. If this perspective influences city selection of vacant land conversion projects, it is not unreasonable to expect cities to channel their scarce development dollars to projects in which the benefits can be fully captured by the investor city. Indeed, economists argue that inefficiencies may arise from government provision of services because it is often difficult, if not impossible, to match the "consumer" of city government services with the "payer."[2] As a consequence, the fiscal policy of one jurisdiction may end up subsidizing citizens or residents of another jurisdiction.

A city with property taxing authority has a fiscal incentive to invest resources in the reuse of vacant land parcels. The more valuable the land becomes, the more property tax revenue the city collects. If the conversion of vacant land into productive use is successful, the adjacent parcels' values will also increase and the city will have benefited from its investment. Moreover, if the adjacent parcels are all located within the city's jurisdiction, the city reaps all the rewards of its investment. It stands to reason, then, that the city would be motivated to invest in vacant land parcels that, when fully developed, maximize property tax revenue production for the city. Investment in vacant land parcels at the city's edge reduces the return on investment to the investor because the neighboring municipalities claim some of the benefits, such as enhanced property values and more employment opportunities.

Yet cities' revenue structures are not unidimensional. Through an array of pricing mechanisms, from general taxes and fees to permits and special assessments, both residents and nonresidents provide revenue to cities for some services, although not always in equal amounts. Water fees, for example, are charged to all users, even if the user is a nonresident who rents office space in the city. Building permits are charged to anyone, resident or nonresident, who builds within the city's limits. Sales tax revenue is collected at the point of transaction, rather than on the basis of one's residency status.[3] And because cities are in a state of perpetual competition with their neighbors to provide an appropriate bundle of services at a politically acceptable tax price, any opportunity to export taxes to nonresidents and thereby hold down residents' tax burden is sought and embraced.

Cities continually explore mechanisms to augment the well-being of their citizens, in part by ensuring that the costs of services are spread among users and not borne solely by residents. As the nation's migratory impulse pushes concentrations of people outside the original jurisdictions of municipalities even as they continue to be consumers of city services, cities search for ways to stretch both the legal boundaries of their landmass and the fiscal reach of their taxing powers.[4]

The political logic undergirding most municipalities' inducement of vacant land use and reuse is to stretch their property tax base in order to finance city services (e.g., Texas' extraterritorial jurisdiction). In other cities, the political logic behind vacant land reuse is to stretch their sales tax base, which provides the bulk of municipal revenues (e.g., Oklahoma City). Ohio's municipalities derive the majority of their own-source revenues from the income tax, and therefore pursue policies to reuse vacant land to stretch their income tax base. The strategic choice of encouraging or facilitating the development of vacant land at one site or at another depends, we argue, in large part on the general taxing authority of the municipality.[5] The spatial derivation of municipal tax revenues shapes the decision makers' political strategies on vacant land policies. Therefore, different tax structures induce and produce different land development choices.

Property Tax Cities

An ad valorem real estate tax is a tax on land and structures, which are place specific. Owners of real property pay taxes on the assessed value of the property; state and municipal laws determine the tax rate. If the owner is also the resident, then the taxpayer-citizen pays property taxes to the municipality in exchange for services. If the owner is a nonresident who rents a facility, the costs of providing city services are potentially borne by the owner, although they might be shifted at least partly to the tenant, depending on demand for rental property (i.e., the higher the demand, the more likely the owner can shift tax costs to the renter). Studies of the property tax burden suggest that the ability to export taxes to nonresidents is greater among cities with more commercial and industrial property than among cities with more residential property.[6]

Because commercial and industrial concerns capitalize at least some of their property tax liabilities into the price of their commodities or services, consumers of those products absorb some of the property tax burden. Suburban or bedroom communities, conversely, are less able to shift the property tax burden to nonresidents because most residents own their homes. This argument hinges on the perspective that commercial property taxes are probably shifted to the consumers of the products that are produced or distributed by the firm. Those consumers are assumed to be distributed across the metropolitan area (or beyond) and not just across the city's residents. Estimates of the exporting capacity of the property tax by the nation's major cities average about $0.52, meaning that for every $1.00 of property tax contributed by resident property owners, $0.52 can be raised from nonresidents in property taxes.[7]

Sales Tax Cities

Municipalities that have the authority to impose a tax on retail sales or on other commercial transactions cannot easily distinguish between consumers who are residents of the municipality and consumers who are not.[8] It is quite likely, in fact, that sales tax payers do not always reside in the jurisdiction within which the purchase is made. Some sales taxes, then, are shifted or exported to nonresidents in municipalities that are centers of commerce and retail sales, reducing the effective sales tax burden on residents. It should be noted that residents of cities that are centers of commerce and retail sales are also purchasers of goods and services in other jurisdictions. As a result, municipalities with the authority to impose a sales tax shift or export taxes to nonresidents; but residents of those municipalities also often pay sales taxes to other jurisdictions. The net effect of these tax transfers for major cities, according to estimates by Helen Ladd and John Yinger, is that for every $1.00 raised in sales tax revenues from residents of a municipality, another $0.21 is collected from nonresidents.[9]

State laws governing the imposition, use, and rate of sales taxes vary dramatically. Seventeen states give their municipalities the authority to directly levy a sales tax, whereas California shares a portion of the state sales tax with its cities.[10] Idaho gives three cities a sales tax authority, whereas in Pennsylvania, only Philadelphia has a sales tax.

Other states require cities and counties to share a sales tax. Tennessee, for example, allows municipalities to impose up to a one-cent tax if the county has not already claimed the one-cent local-option sales tax. In other words, where a county sales tax is levied, it preempts the city tax and the city can only levy the difference between the maximum local tax rate and the rate levied by the county, assuming the county does not levy the top rate. Ten Tennessee cities levy a sales tax. Cities also receive a portion of the county sales tax based on origination. In North Carolina, all counties are authorized to levy, and in fact do levy, a 2 percent local sales tax. Cities within each county receive a portion of the sales tax revenue based on origination and/or population (depending on county formula). Minnesota cities need both state and municipal approval before a sales tax can be levied. Currently, nine cities have temporary sales tax authority, and one city (Duluth) has permanent authority. Sales tax authority is granted through special state legislation and subsequent voter approval. It is generally authorized for regionally significant projects, and the authority ends with project completion. Seven additional cities have sales tax authorization, pending voter approval.

The definition of what exactly constitutes taxable sales varies across states. Some states exempt food and prescription drugs, others clothing, and others very little at all. The revenues generated from the municipal retail sales tax, then, are not uniform. Adding to the complexity is state revenue sharing, which in many states does include the state's sales tax. Although the state might be motivated to export the sales and use tax to nonresidents (especially to residents of cities located in other states but near the state's border), we do not include the state sales tax as an exogenous factor in vacant land development policy.

Income Tax Cities

The third general tax form is the income tax, or variants of the income tax sometimes called an earnings, wage, or payroll tax. This tax instrument allows municipalities to tax the income of individuals or some portion of an individual's income (e.g., payroll, earnings, stock options). Few states allow all of their municipalities to have access to this revenue source.[11] Indeed, municipalities in Ohio and Pennsylvania account for more than 90 percent of all income-taxing local governments. Whether nonresident workers of a municipality pay income taxes to the place of work or to the place of residence or some combination is dependent on state law. For example, Pennsylvania municipalities are authorized to tax residents' earnings (and net profits) up to 1 percent. Ohio's municipalities can impose an income tax on individuals (persons and firms) and on nonresident workers in their cities. Some municipalities in Ohio allow their residents to credit all or a portion of their income tax payments made to the cities in which they work against income tax liabilities owed to their city of residence.[12]

Only two cities in New York State are permitted to levy an income tax (Yonkers and New York City). The high court of New York State ruled that a 1999 state law prohibits the City of New York from collecting income taxes from commuters, resulting in a loss of more than $210 million from New York State commuters and $150 million loss from commuters outside the state. Like New York, some states permit only select cities to implement an income tax, including Wilmington, Delaware; Baltimore (as a city-county); Saint Louis; and Kansas City. Alabama and Michigan permit their municipalities to levy an income tax; eighteen cities in Alabama and twenty-six in Michigan have opted for the tax. Georgia allows municipalities to impose an income tax with the approval of a majority of all *registered* voters. With voter turnout often falling below half of registered voters, no city has sought the tax.

The potential of the income tax to export tax burden to nonresidents is the most substantial of the three general tax forms. Ladd and Yinger find that a city that can impose an earnings tax is likely to raise $1.27 from nonresidents for every $1.00 raised from residents.[13]

The definition of "income" for those municipalities with the authority to levy an income tax varies. The cities of Ohio and Pennsylvania are restricted to taxing wages primarily, and not capital gains. The explosive growth in state income tax revenues during the 1990s outpaced growth in municipal tax revenues because the latter's taxable base excludes nonwage income.[14] New York City, however, includes capital gains in its income tax base and saw an extraordinary growth in income tax collections in the late 1990s. One report noted that "nearly 80 percent surge in city PIT [the city-collected personal income tax] revenues in recent years [1994–97] results from an increase in the tax liability of upper-income residents. . . . The increasing PIT shares of wealthy and very wealthy for the most part reflect these groups' growing share of income as opposed to changes in tax policy."[15] The report estimates that the increase in income on the part of the city's millionaires was "fueled by a 162 percent surge in income from capital gains from 1994 to 1997."[16] Wage growth, conversely, is what fuels the tax collections of the nation's other income tax cities.

Idealized Patterns of Vacant Land Use and Reuse

No city generates all of its own-source revenues from one form of general taxation. In addition to the increasing prevalence of user fees and charges as the "own-source revenue of choice" of the past three decades, cities also employ a host of other specific or targeted taxes. Building permits, taxes on inventory, business privilege taxes, occupancy taxes, entertainment and food taxes, and a host of others provide cities with a substantial—though not a majority—of own-source revenues. The lion's share of cities' own-source revenues is derived from a general tax source, or a combination of general tax sources. These general sources of taxation then are (1) a tax on real estate or personal property, (2) a tax on consumption, and (3) a tax on earnings, payroll, or income.

For the sake of simplicity, however, we present an idealized vision of city land use, assuming a city has access to one and only one tax source. In the real world of numerous specific taxes and city access to two general tax sources (and in a few cases to all three tax sources, e.g., Philadelphia, New York City, Saint Louis, Kansas City), the hypothetical distribution of land use would not necessarily conform. Moreover, our model excludes the contribution of other specialized taxes to the land use strategies of cities. We present below a hypothetical argument for a city's strategy to encourage the use and reuse of vacant land as if only one general form of taxation were available to the city.

Assuming that the vacant land parcels are distributed homogeneously across the city's jurisdiction and not concentrated in any one neighborhood or sector of the city, and given scarce public investment resources, the city will be induced to promote vacant land conversion away from the city's edge and closer to its geographical center, at least in the early evolution of the city, so that the full benefits of its investment can be captured. In turn, the probability of fiscal externalities diminishes. The potential effect of a fiscal externality that derives from property tax considerations is only one consideration in city investment in vacant land conversion. No city is fully dependent on the property tax as its only source of revenue. Consequently, the fiscal externality potential of other taxes weighs on the city's decisions to convert vacant land. For example, a common strategy pursued by cities with broad sales taxing authority is to encourage commercial development near the edge of the city in order to export tax burdens to nonresidents. This form of fiscal externality benefits the investor city because the tax revenue is derived from other taxpayers who do not live in the city.

This would have the potential effect of imposing a relatively higher tax rate on non resident sales tax payers and a lower tax rate on residents of the sales-taxing jurisdiction, while granting both sets of consumers or taxpayers the opportunity to consume the service. Provision of police or public safety services to a nonresident worker is an illustration of this kind of fiscal externality. Some central cities, then, tax residents at a nonoptimal rate, given the consumption preferences of those residents, and provide more public safety than is actually demanded. Cities have adapted to this problem by securing the authority to collect taxes and fees from nonresident users of city-provided services. Indeed, cities have adeptly diversified their tax structures during the past half-century by charging users for consumption of a specific service (e.g., water, transit, trash collection) and by imposing taxlike charges on services that benefit individuals (e.g., special assessment taxes).

The probability that the fiscal action of one municipality might spill over jurisdictional boundaries and benefit residents of another municipality, then, should certainly be considered in city decisions to promote vacant land use or reuse. But this consideration has little impact on private developers' decisions to invest in land development or to cooperate with city development initiatives. Developers respond to market signals, giving them mobility to invest in vacant land projects throughout a region regardless of the jurisdiction within which the project lays. Because of the private developer's territorial freedom, city promotion of urban land is attractive only *in comparison* to myriad other market forces and government policies that influence the developer's decision to invest in vacant land conversion.

In contrast, municipal corporations are often hemmed in by the corporate boundaries of neighboring cities or are discouraged from expanding borders by state statutes. Indeed, the argument that cities can only legally control activities or efforts that take place on their soil is the reason, according to some urban observers, that cities should focus their resources on enhancing their economic base.[17] Chicago has been landlocked for the better part of a century and, except for its eastern border on Lake Michigan, is surrounded by incorporated municipalities. City officials' perspectives on the "developability" of a vacant land parcel, therefore, might be infused with a sense of potential fiscal externalities, a consideration absent from the developers' perspective on a potentially "developable" parcel.

THE STRATEGIC BEHAVIOR OF PROPERTY TAX CITIES

Property tax cities think strategically about the pattern of development of vacant land based on the market value of the development and on the possibility of shifting service-delivery costs to other jurisdictions (fiscal externalities).

"Enhance real estate values!" Property-tax-dependent cities think strategically about the temporal development of vacant land based on the improvements to real estate, especially to structures that have a high tax value.[18] Cities without a uniform tax assessment system on all forms of property usually place a higher real estate tax rate on industrial or utility property. Policymakers for cities with high-valued industrial, commercial, and utility properties, then, are expected to zone key sections of their city for such purposes to concentrate the revenue-generation potential.

City officials are also encouraged to develop land that will recruit as many high-income residential structures as possible on the assumption that owners of those structures will become net contributors of tax revenue to the city (net of public service consumption). The development of vacant land is expected to be undertaken in an orderly manner that maximizes revenue collection from high-valued real estate prior to developing vacant land for other purposes (e.g., open space, residential housing for low-to moderate-income people). To the extent that there is a market for lower-valued structures in any city, the placement of such structures should occur near the edges of the city and the placement of high-end structures should be near the center. Figure 3.1 displays the likely spatial pattern.

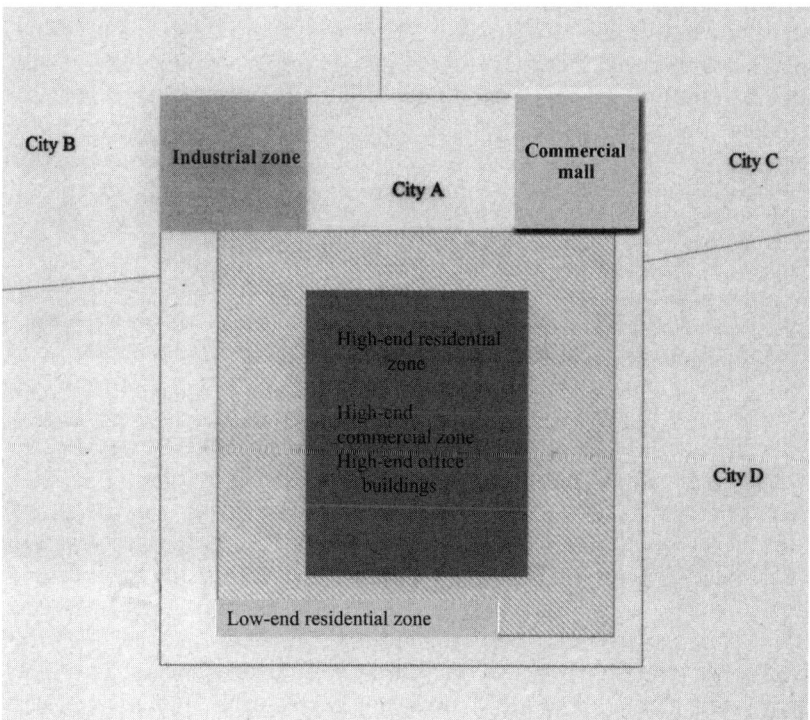

FIGURE 3.1. Hypothetical Spatial Distribution of Land Uses in a Property Tax City

City A is expected to capture the upward pressure of high-valued structures by concentrating them in the center of the city. A property value isobar is expected to be concentric from the center of the city in which more highly valued properties and structures are located near the center and properties and structures with a lower value are at the fringe. This expectation applies principally to residential and commercial structures and not to industrial structures, because the city's revenue imperative on the industrial side is slightly different.

Cities' attempts to maximize property tax revenue collections promote the development of high-end residential housing or high-valued commercial or industrial structures because the full value of those investments is captured by the property tax authority of the city. Yet those developments tend to require public investments, often in the form of spending on infrastructure and increased service levels. Streets, sidewalks, street lighting as well as police and fire protection need to be augmented by the city for the newly developed areas. Cities' attempts to minimize expenditures encourage a strategy of shifting costs of development to neighboring municipalities or other governments, when possible. A commercial enterprise—a mall, for example—would generate automobile traffic. Streets, signaling, and other transportation-related costs are typically borne by the city government (City A). Yet, placement of such development near the boundary of the City A might increase the transportation (feeder) costs of neighboring City B and City C.

Columbia, South Carolina: Development and Property Values

Columbia does not have a local-option general sales tax or a local-option income tax. The property tax, then, is the only general tax to which the city has access. Its property tax reliance is considered high compared with the national average. The property tax rate for the city hovered around 99 mills throughout most of the 1990s, then dropped to 92 mills in 2000 due to increased assessed valuations on existing properties.[19] Although the property tax generated nearly three-fourths of the city's own-source revenues in 1967, the city's mix of own-source revenues changed dramatically during the intervening thirty years. By 1997, the surge in user charges and fees had eclipsed the steady growth in property tax revenues and had become the principal own-source revenue for Columbia. User charges and fees amounted to 54.1 percent of own-source revenues (compared with the national average of 40.7 percent), while the property tax figure slipped to 27.3 percent. Nevertheless, the property tax incentive to encourage vacant land reuse in Columbia should not be underestimated. As a source of general tax revenue for Columbia, the property tax is the only tax game in town.

The development of vacant land and abandoned structures in Columbia reflects the city's balancing act between investing in residential neighborhoods and in the commercial and industrial areas of the city. According to the city manager, these projects were undertaken with the express purpose of reducing blight, encouraging revitalization, and enhancing property values.[20] The Columbia Industrial Park project, for example, expanded an existing industrial park and required the city to invest in infrastructure expansion. Eight new industries eventually located at the long-vacant site located at the southern edge of the city. Extensive investment in the downtown area was intended to revitalize the 100-block area surrounding the state capitol and other state office buildings as well as the older commercial establishments. Abandonment by longtime tenants, such as Macy's department store in the city's downtown business district, encouraged active involvement by the city to revitalize it. The investment activities are designed to entice residents to newly renovated buildings and to enhance the commercial appeal of the downtown area by encouraging restaurants, museums, retailing, and other activities and to create "twenty-four-hour life" in the heart of the city. As suggested in figure 3.1, the historic center of the city is the favored target for city investment.

The goals and projects of the City of Columbia would certainly not be antithetical to those of other cities. Reducing blight, encouraging revitalization, and enhancing property values figure prominently among the foci of economic development programs of not just Columbia but also of municipalities nationwide. The goal of the city, as the city manager emphasized, is to preserve property values citywide. Yet little mention was made by the city officials involved in these development projects of the direct impact on retail sales or jobs and income growth. This omission is not to suggest these potential goals are unimportant. Rather, the city's need to protect its fiscal position motivates concerns that are more directly connected with enhancing property values than with some other goal, such as augmenting retail sales.

This observation cannot be emphasized enough. Columbia's officials understand that the city's property values will be threatened if it does not take action to enhance its commercial and employment base. City development efforts would be stymied in the absence of this "balanced" public policy approach. Nevertheless, the fiscal well-being of the city is tied closely and explicitly to its property values. And investment activities by the city in commercial, industrial, or residential development keep the property value implications of land redevelopment activities uppermost in Columbia's economic development decision calculus.

Columbia's actions reflect the property tax logic. The fiscal incentive for Columbia as it approaches land conversion projects is ultimately to enhance property values. Land development projects for commercial and industrial projects are indeed promoted by the city because they meet the city's goals of "balanced development" and "protect property values." Without the property tax revenue flowing from the city's investment in those projects, its fiscal position and certainly its quality of life might be compromised.

Disinvestment and State Aid in Camden, New Jersey

Across the Delaware River from Philadelphia lies the city of Camden, New Jersey, which like Columbia is a property-tax-reliant municipality. It is an old city that served as an industrial employment center during much of the twentieth century. However, since the 1950s, Camden has experienced a substantial exodus of jobs and residents.[21] The city's private-sector employment base declined by more than 60 percent from 1950 to 1997, and its population decreased by one-third during the same period.[22] Real estate values are among the lowest in the state. Camden, like other New Jersey cities, has relied heavily on the property tax for own-source revenues.[23] Its tax base, already strained due to the city's limited land area (less than 10 square miles) and the amount of tax-exempt property (an estimated one-third of its land), has suffered as a result of the devaluation of real estate.

As the city's economic decline intensified, the tax base problem worsened with high rates of tax delinquency and correspondingly low rates of tax collection. By the late 1990s, the State of New Jersey had, in effect, taken control of the city's finances. In addition, the city has an unusually large amount of vacant land, much of it with cluttered with abandoned structures. These fiscal and economic conditions complicate Camden as a test of the property tax city model.[24] Yet despite the special circumstances of the Camden case, at least some of the predicted land development patterns can be discerned; others however, are absent.

The city is located in the southwestern part of Camden County. Historically, Camden has concentrated much of its industrial zoning along the riverfront, at the city's border, as expected. (Many of the industrially zoned tracts are now vacant.) The riverfront is where the state chose to locate two of its major investments, the state aquarium and a state prison; the other, a state university, is in the city's central core. As anticipated in a city with a property tax logic, there is a relatively small amount of open space, whether recreational or wooded. But Camden does not conform to expectations in several important ways. One deviation is the lack of high-end residential and office facilities near the center of the city. The city center is awash in low-end commercial enterprises and low-value multifamily dwellings. Also contrary to expectations for a property-tax-reliant city, the more highly valued housing in Camden is found at the outer edges of the city.

In interviews, city leaders acknowledged their interest in redeveloping interior tracts of vacant land as higher-end housing and offices.[25] Indeed, pockets of redevelopment in the city's center reflect these preferences. Further, the city has created a new zoning category, the center city flexible development district, as a means of stimulating mixed-use development. Thus, it is apparent that city officials are pursuing a strategy derived from a property tax logic, even though the city's reliance on property tax revenue has decreased amid massive infusions of state aid. However, despite the efforts, Camden's land development patterns remain stubbornly resistant to the guiding hand of city government. Assuming eventual economic improvement and the renewal of the property tax base, the predicted land use patterns may emerge.

In 2000, the State of New Jersey provided funding to transform a major cross-city roadway lined with decaying warehouses, empty lots, and boarded-up buildings into a tree-lined greenway. Tree-lined vistas may not generate any direct revenue effects, but they are preferable to visible indicators of decline. And they have the potential to shore up real estate values and, perhaps, generate additional investment with positive revenue consequences. However, the depressed local economy and the city's fiscal woes have muted the spin-off effect of these efforts.

In the final analysis, as suggested above, Camden does not fit the strategic behavior of a property-tax-dependent city. The city's dire economic straits and the role of state financial aid have altered the predicted land–tax dynamic. The fact that Camden's current land tax situation is at variance with the hypothetical spatial development pattern owes to its status as a deviant case among the constellation of U.S. cities. During the 1990s, as most cities improved and enhanced their fiscal positions, Camden's fiscal structure was collapsing and state intervention was imminent. The property-tax model in figure 3.1 is premised on an ideal type of tax reliance that is less applicable to Camden's contemporary situation. New Jersey's declaration in 1998 that Camden was in a "state of imminent peril" not only reduced the city's property tax reliance but also diminished the importance of the property tax logic in explaining its spatial evolution.[26]

THE STRATEGIC BEHAVIOR OF SALES TAX CITIES

Sales tax cities think strategically about the temporal development of vacant land on the basis of their mental constructs of "shopping sheds" and on which market transactions are taxable.

"Develop commercially, not residentially!" The political strategy of sales-tax-dependent cities is to promote land development in areas that stretch the fiscal reach of the city beyond its borders. A city can maximize sales tax receipts and hold down the tax burden on its own residents by encouraging and supporting the development of vacant land close to the city's border and to transportation corridors that cater to visitors. The location and development of automobile malls, retail malls, and other centers of sales tax generation is vital to maximizing revenue collection and the collective well-being of the community.[27]

If transportation costs are the primary cost imposed on consumers and shoppers, their choice of a retail center is expected to minimize those costs. Cities that rely on retail sales tax revenues to finance the delivery of services should encourage commercial development of land areas that are at the corners of the city (to maximize tax exporting as well as to saturate the "shopping shed" to which the retail center caters) and between the corners at a location that would capture residents' shopping needs.

Figure 3.2 illustrates the hypothetical placement of six retail centers within the borders of City A; each shopping center is denoted by a circle. Each retail center services residents within its shopping shed, denoted by the hexagon, and each shopping shed captures not only the consumption needs of the residents (within the dotted line) but also the consumption needs of nonresidents. Each retail center is situated within a shopping shed designed to satisfy the (majority of) consumption needs of the shed's residents and to minimize transportation costs. Consequently, although the revenue imperative of sales-tax-dependent cities is to "develop commercially," municipal governments must also assure that the city caters to the residents' service needs. But because these governments rely more on sales tax revenue than on property tax revenue, the revenue strategy of property-tax-dependent cities ("enhance real estate values!") is somewhat muted.

It is clear from this diagram that there is little or no political-revenue logic to encourage commercial development within the center of the city. And there is an overriding logic to develop land for retail centers at the city's edge. The strategy for City A is to encourage the development of each of the retail districts, A through F, which capture both residents

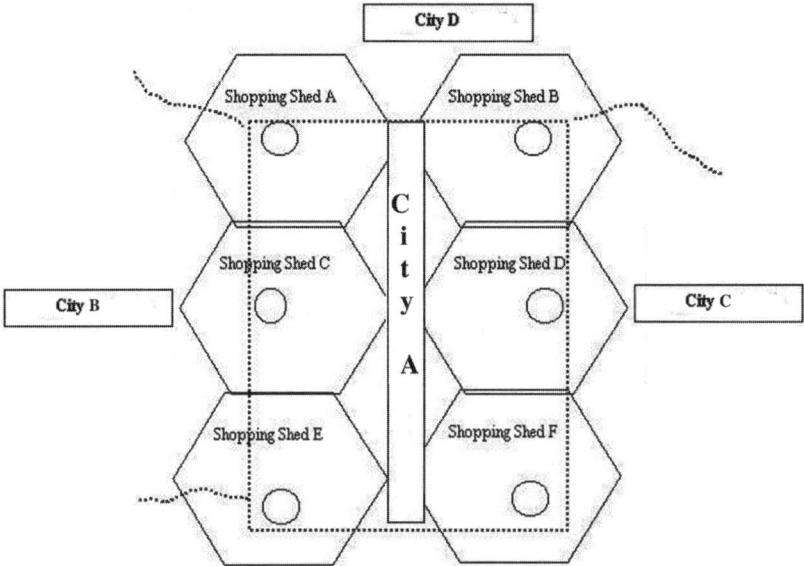

FIGURE 3.2. Hypothetical Spatial Distribution of Shopping Areas in a Sales Tax City Surrounded by Incorporated Municipalities

and nonresidents in each of the respective shopping sheds. Moreover, each of those exports sales tax burdens to nonresidents and, in this hypothetical example, denies other retailers in City B, C, or D access to the consumers in City A. A's preference for not only capturing tax revenues from residents but also from nonresidents (lowering the actual tax burden on A's residents) is realized. Moreover, in this case, A's strategy of supporting or subsidizing the retail development at those six locations is preferable to subsidizing other locations between A and B, C and D, or E and F.

The political strategy for vacant land policies adopted by sales tax cities that are *not surrounded by incorporated municipalities* is different from the situation described above. City strategies are pursued in response to the perceived (or actual) policy reactions of neighboring municipalities. The situation in which the fringe of the city does not border another city (or, in the case of Texas municipalities, in which the city has extraterritorial jurisdiction authority, allowing the city land use control over neighboring unincorporated territory) creates the environment for a different land use logic. Figure 3.3 suggests that City A's vacant land strategy is to encourage commercial development at the city's fringe with the expectation that the shopping shed will eventually be contained within City A as it annexes unincorporated land. City A would encourage development

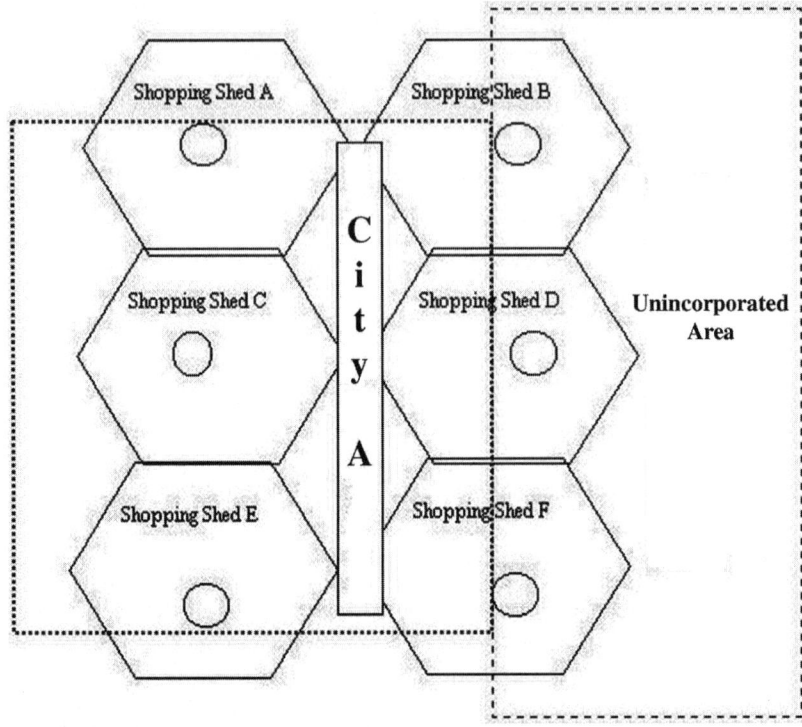

FIGURE 3.3. Hypothetical Spatial Distribution of Shopping Areas in a Sales Tax City Surrounded by Unincorporated Land

beyond, say, Shopping Shed A's boundaries, even if it means subsidizing (e.g., transportation corridors for residential housing) vacant land conversion in what will become Shopping Shed B. Shopping Shed B becomes the next frontier of the city and City A then promotes commercial development beyond Shopping Shed's B boundaries, encouraging more annexation.

Tempe, Arizona: Surrounded by Other Cities

Arizona allows municipalities to tax real estate, but the primary source of income is the retail sales tax. Property tax collections per household, according to officials in Tempe and Phoenix, cover less than half the public-service costs for the typical home. Residential development advantages school districts, but schools are not general governments and cannot offer inducements. Cities can offer abatements and appear to offer a sales tax abatement frequently to retail developers, a policy pursued to attract high-end retailers such as automobile malls. But because retail sales depend on a critical mass of consumers, either easy access from neighboring communities via transportation corridors or residential development near the retail center (or both) is encouraged by the municipalities.

Tempe's strategy, then, would argue for encouraging retail development at the fringe of the city's borders. The advantage of fringe development over core development hinges on the expectation that retail shoppers would include nonresidents as well as residents. Some of the costs of service provision would effectively be exported to nonresidents, thus reducing the net tax burden on residents. Of course, Tempe residents are expected to purchase taxable retail items in other (non-Tempe) locations, thus sending part of Tempe's residents' tax burden to non-Tempe jurisdictions. But the city's strategy should be premised on the assumption that the majority of taxable consumer purchases will be realized within the city's borders, especially if the placement and development of retail centers are on the city's edge. The "core" residents would be expected to do most of their shopping within the city because the costs of transportation would make travel to other centers less likely. And by encouraging retail development along the city's fringe, residents of neighboring towns, who minimize transportation costs when deciding where to shop, should also choose retail centers that are close to their residences and therefore at Tempe's fringe.

The political logic argues against cooperation with neighboring municipalities in rationally allocating commercial zoning, unless the municipality finds it in its best interest to do so. Competition, in other words, can force temporary alliances among municipalities, allowing them to concentrate their development incentives and efforts in other areas. Much like international alliances, which may allow "competitors" or "enemies" to bury the hatchet on borders that at one time prompted battles in order to concentrate their resources on other unprotected flanks, cities in Arizona (and elsewhere, presumably, where the sales tax predominates and annexation encourages competition) likewise undertake policies that resemble players' strategies of the board game Risk.

This hypothetical spatial distribution of retail centers in figure 3.2 resembles the actual situation in Tempe (figure 3.4). One difference, however, is that the city's major retail centers are in the southwest corner and close to the southeast corner, extending toward the west. The northeast corner has mostly university-related buildings and commercial concerns, as does the northwest corner. The central portions of Tempe (corresponding to Shopping Sheds C and D) at one time housed the strip shopping commercial development, until a major eight-lane

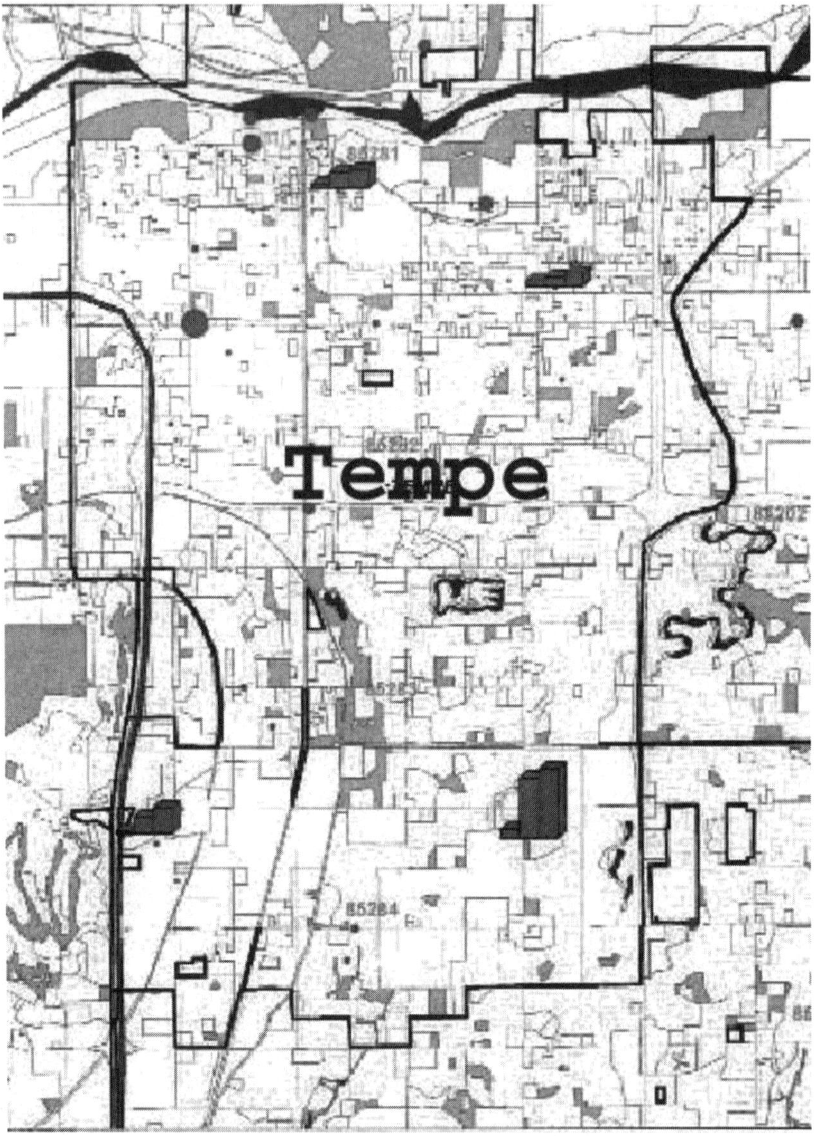

FIGURE 3.4.   The Growth in Tempe's Sales Tax Revenues from 1992 through 1999 (Estimated) According to Location
Note: The dark circles refer to vacant land in 1999 (scaled by value).
Source: Data from the City of Tempe. Map by the authors.

freeway was relocated several miles to the south. Nevertheless, the primary shopping sheds in Tempe appear to conform to theoretical expectations (corresponding to Shopping Sheds A, B, E, and F). The city is investing in its central corridor area, in which quite a few abandoned structures are located, through a redevelopment process. The southwest quadrant, which contained the last large parcels of vacant land, has been developed since the early to middle 1990s for commercial concerns, as was land in the southeast corner.

The success of this strategy in maximizing revenues by encouraging development of vacant land at the fringes is demonstrable. In 1992, sales tax revenues from four commercial locations (the northwest, Tempe's main business district; the southwest corner; the southeast section; and the central corridor along the now-abandoned state highway)—denoted by the first bar of each of the four histograms in figure 3.4—generated approximately 14 percent of the city's retail tax collection. The third bar of each histogram denotes 1999 sales tax revenues from each of the major shopping sheds and the second bar the 1998 contributions. By 1999, those four shopping sheds generated more than a third (36 percent) of the total sales tax collection of the city.

The shaded circles identify the location of vacant land in Tempe, according to the city's planning department. The assessed value of the vacant land is denoted by the size of the circle (the larger the circle, the higher the value). These days, few parcels of vacant land in Tempe have significant value. Most have been reused in the city's reinvestment strategy of promoting the commercial development potential of the city's vacant land.

Annexation and an Abundance of Vacant Land in Peoria, Arizona

Peoria's annexation strategy closely follows the political logic for sales tax cities that are not surrounded by incorporated municipalities. The strategy appears to be twofold. First, Peoria's tax base until the late 1980s was residential. Most of Peoria residents' retail shopping was done in a neighboring city, Glendale. To grow and thrive, Peoria needed to expand its tax base. (It could also tap the potential consumer purchases of retired residents in the unincorporated place of Sun City, to the west.) In the 1990s, Peoria began an aggressive annexation program of the surrounding farmland for commercial purposes. (The subsequent luring, with sales tax abatement, of an auto mall located just over the city boundary in Peoria from Glendale was a major coup.) Then Peoria encouraged the development of a strip mall on the south side of an avenue that bordered Glendale, which had just seen a large shopping mall completed.

Second, fearing that Glendale might take adjoining available land for more retail outlets and, more important, fearing that Phoenix's rapid annexation north along Interstate 17 might also double back into unincorporated land to the north of Peoria, the city raced to the north. It annexed a huge swath of vacant land at such a rate that the city increased its area threefold. This aggressive annexation, essentially walling off Phoenix's westward expansion and Glendale's possible northwesterly drive, was designed as a purely defensive strategy—it blocked Phoenix (and to a lesser extent, Glendale) from getting the land first. Peoria's northward expansion took in a lake situated in a neighboring county that was intended to meet the city's long-term planning needs to develop a recreation and tourist industry. The revenue-related hope in annexing the land around a boating lake was that commercial and retail development would eventually surround the lake and the roads leading to the lake would become strips of retail land. Subsequently, additional sales tax revenue would be generated from high-priced items (e.g., boating equipment) and shifted to nonresidents for the most part. Peoria's actions mirror the strategic behavior of a sales-tax-reliant city with access to annexable land, as depicted in figure 3.3.

Enhancing the Retail Sales Tax Base in Oklahoma City

Sales and use tax revenue constitutes nearly all of Oklahoma City's general tax collection, except for a relatively small amount of property tax revenue that is dedicated to capital improvements. In 1967, Oklahoma City collected nearly one-third of its own-source revenues from the property tax and slightly less than 20 percent from the general sales tax, according to census data. By 1992, property tax revenues had dropped below 8 percent of own-source revenues. By the end of the decade, the city did not fund any of its general operations from the property tax at all, relying instead on sales tax collections. Of the city's $264 million general fund budget for 2001–2, 61 percent was generated from retail sales and use taxes; $143 million was collected from the sales tax and another $18 million from use taxes.[28] The fiscal incentive for Oklahoma City's land reuse projects differs significantly from a property-tax-dependent city's. If land values are not capitalized into property tax revenue, the city's fiscal incentive to support land development projects resides in the project's sales tax-generating potential.

An illustration of the kind of vacant land conversion project the city supports is its negotiated agreement with Bass Pro Shops, which involved the construction of a major specialty retail store in the downtown's Bricktown redevelopment area. It serves to draw specialty retail to the previously underutilized parts of the downtown area and to draw customers from the region. By early 2002, the city's efforts to redevelop downtown had mainly been in the entertainment sphere to complement public-sector projects such as the arena and performing arts theater. The construction of this 110,000-square-foot retail store that is projected to attract 950,000 customers a year was an effort to revitalize downtown as a retail center. The city agreed to finance and construct the building and lease the facility to Bass Pro Shops. The major costs were paid for with tax increment financing, a tool that had only recently cleared legal hurdles for use in Oklahoma. The project is also in an empowerment zone.

The Bass Pro Shops project illustrates the power of the underlying fiscal incentives of a sales tax city as well as an innovative approach to development, one that might be considered unusual if it were adopted by a city with high property tax reliance. This project required the city to finance the construction of the building to be leased to Bass Pro Shops. The city retains ownership of the property, meaning Bass Pro Shops has no property ownership and pays no property taxes to other governments (or the relatively low assessment for the city's capital improvement programs). However, the city's fiscal imperative of promoting the taxable base of the city is accomplished because Bass Pro Shops, as a specialty retail operation, was expected to service nearly 1 million customers each year. The loss in forgone property tax revenues (the city-owned property is exempt from property taxation) is minuscule compared with the enhanced retail sales revenue base.

Oklahoma City's approach to promoting economic development is underscored by the city manager's comment, "what motivates us is the sales tax." The jurisdictional area of Oklahoma City is very large, encompassing 607.8 square miles. It feels the pressures of economic competition along the city's edges and it has targeted the revitalization of its center as a critical goal in bringing attention to the city's core and deflecting the economic tugs to the outskirts. Competition for big-box retail centers creates what one city official labeled "Wal-Mart Wars" near the city's borders. But revitalizing and energizing the downtown area is an equally important goal, as the Bass Pro Shops project emphasizes.

The broad land development strategy of Oklahoma City, then, is one of encouraging retail sales centers at the borders of the city, while the city builds a critical mass of cultural, entertainment, and nightlife attractions at its center. The $400 million downtown development projects, including a performing arts center and an arena, are designed to focus pedestrian and consumer traffic on the downtown area and augment the retail sales base of the city. The city voted to increase sales taxes by one cent for the purpose of funding more than $300 million in infrastructure and capital improvement projects designed to promote the redevelopment of downtown Oklahoma City. This strategy is part of the city's Metropolitan Area Projects (MAPs). Not only is the city's commitment to advancing its downtown interests demonstrated in its MAPs and the dedicated one-cent sales tax; it also illustrates the fiscal imperative to promote retail sales.

THE STRATEGIC BEHAVIOR OF INCOME TAX CITIES

Income tax cities think strategically about vacant land use on the basis of their assessment of the income growth potential of the individual or firm.

"Recruit high-income individuals and big payroll firms!" The political strategy of income tax cities is one of two distinct types, depending on how cities are authorized to collect income taxes. For those cities with an earnings tax that can be imposed on individuals at the place of employment, the revenue logic is to promote the transformation of vacant land into places of work for high wage earners (e.g., corporate headquarters, legal, medical, finance, insurance, and real estate buildings). For those with the authority to tax the income of its residents, the logic is to transform vacant land into residential facilities and into office towers (in which employees are both residents and high salaried).

Several scenarios can be represented. First, assume a city that imposes an income tax on residents (not on employees or commuters) and the tax is higher than the neighboring cities' residential income tax. In these central cities, we would expect the central core of the city to be zoned for office space, such as corporate headquarters. The closer these office towers are to the fringe of the city, the more likely high wage earners will encourage the office's relocation to the (low-income tax) neighboring cities. Furthermore, the city would be encouraged to zone the land around the office towers for high-valued residential structures on the assumption that high-wage earners would reside there. Because property values are not capitalized into city revenues in income tax cities, individuals choose residential locations to maximize their own wealth. Cities can reduce commuting costs by zoning residential neighborhoods near places of employment. Because individuals are also attempting to maximize their own welfare, an income tax city would be motivated to induce high-income earners into living within the city's borders. Individuals would have to trade off the increased income tax costs to their personal welfare against the increased transit costs and costs of other public services.

In figure 3.5, City A can, for example, reduce transit costs by zoning high-income residential areas close to the professional office towers. High-income neighborhoods are expected to be found near office towers that employ highly paid individuals. The political strategy that these cities logically develop promotes the zoning and development of vacant land that would attract and retain high-income residents. The strategy of Cities B, C, and D is to develop vacant land for residential purposes as close to City A's boundaries as possible. The optimal use of those cities' vacant land would be to concentrate as many high-income wage earners as possible along the border of City A. This strategy would allow those cities to enhance their revenue profiles by taxing their residents' incomes. To counter the effectiveness of such a strategy, City A's political strategy might be to encourage the concentration of

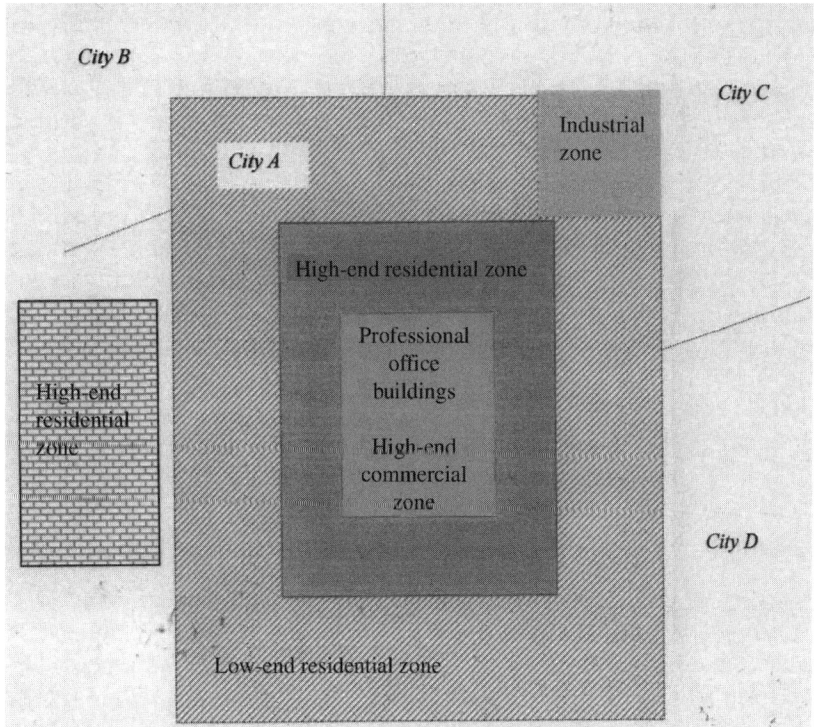

FIGURE 3.5. Hypothetical Spatial Distribution of Land Uses in an Income Tax City without a Commuter Tax

professional office buildings and to enhance the residential zone surrounding the structures.

Next, assume that a city imposes an income tax at the place of employment. The incentive for the city is to ensure that corporations are assisted in developing vacant land anywhere in the city, not just in the central core. The incentive to attract high-income residents by zoning property for expensive structures is muted. It is not the residents' wealth that is capitalized into city revenues in these cities; rather, it is the income of people who work within the city's borders. This revenue imperative influences the behavior of city officials. For example, if earnings are taxed but pension income and capital gains are not, developing vacant land for retirement communities would not be a wise strategy. Indeed, the retirement growth centers of Arizona, Florida, and Texas do not allow municipalities the authority to tax income. Income tax cities, then, would prefer their "high-end residential" neighborhoods to be turned over from retirees to highly paid professionals.

Nevertheless, because the political strategy of a city is not only to maximize revenue but also to minimize costs, the city may be encouraged to ensure a mix of residents, unlike the city that taxes only its residents. Residents who build expensive homes would not be induced to construct the home outside the city's limits because their tax burden would not be appreciably decreased (because it is the city of employment, not the city of residence, that collects the income tax). Cities would not have an incentive to develop vacant land into residential property unless it was the only mechanism to keep individuals working in the city. The city has every incentive to subsidize and otherwise encourage the use or reuse of vacant land as places of employment. If the neighboring city's income tax rate does not differ from the central city's, this form of taxation would most likely have no impact on location decisions. Consequently, the decision to support the use or reuse of vacant land would have to be thought of as a cost-minimization strategy as well as a revenue-maximization one.

Seattle: Vacant Land and the Business and Occupancy Tax

Seattle's principal own-source tax revenues are the retail sales tax, the business and occupancy (B&O) tax, and the property tax. The B&O tax is levied on the gross receipts of businesses that operate or perform any work within the city, including services, which makes it very similar to a corporate income tax. Retail trade, wholesaling, printing, and publishing are taxed at 0.215 percent of their gross receipts, whereas personal professional services (e.g., financial institutions, physicians, accountants, and lawyers) are taxed at a 0.415 percent rate. The state allows municipalities to impose a retail sales and use tax at 0.5 or 1 percent (excluding food). Seattle imposes a 1 percent sales tax but is required to send 15 percent of its collections to King County. The net sales tax rate, then, is 0.85 percent.

The largest and most important category for Seattle's revenue stream is the B&O tax, which, along with the retail tax, grows more rapidly "during periods of strong economic growth and more slowly during periods of decline or stagnation."[29] The B&O tax increased 11.3 percent in fiscal 1997, while retail sales tax revenue grew by 8.8 percent. The property tax contributed $157 million in fiscal 1997, or 33 percent of the city's tax revenues, which signifies a decline in its contribution to total tax revenues from its 1988 level of 37 percent. In 1997, property tax revenues grew to $157 million, 5.7 percent over 1996 levels.[30]

Figure 3.6 traces the changes during the decade in the city's major tax sources. The growth in the property tax levy is capped by the state at 6 percent a year (excluding new construction), but it can be exceeded if approved by 60 percent of the voters. All properties are taxed at a uniform rate and at full market value. In 1998, the property tax rate was limited to 0.369 percent (or $3.693 per $1,000 of fair market value). With high demand in the land market and the rapid addition of new and renovated structures, near-term projections for property tax

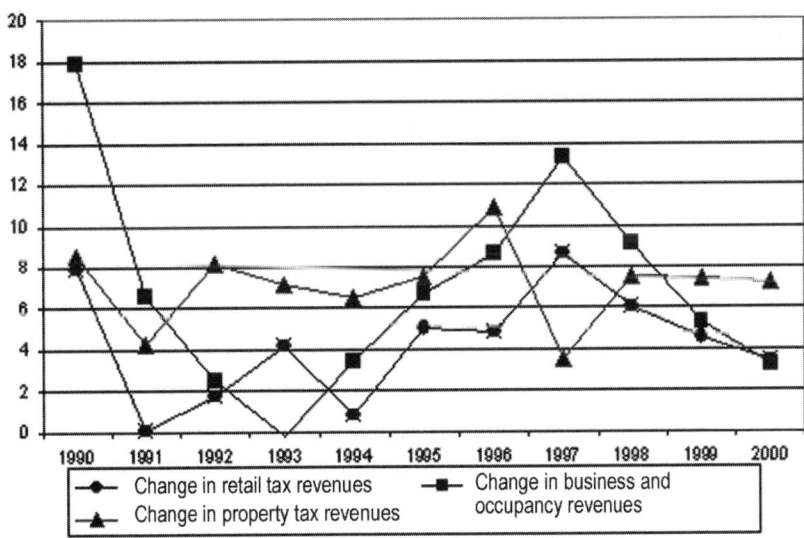

FIGURE 3.6.   Annual Percentage Change in Seattle's Revenue Collection from Major Tax Sources, 1990–2000
Source: Data from the City of Seattle.

revenues exceeded those of the retail and B&O taxes. Booming population and employment growth in the area—coupled with growth boundaries' restricting expansion of the land supply—have benefited the city's revenue stream and reduced its supply of vacant land to 4 percent of its usable land.

Like Phoenix, Seattle receives nearly two-thirds of its general tax revenues in the form of nonproperty taxes, but the similarities between the two cities end there. The logic undergirding Seattle's use and reuse of vacant land is quite different from the annexation-cum-shopping-mall strategy of Phoenix and other Arizona cities. Seattle is landlocked with no (or very little) possibility of annexation. The B&O and sales taxes encourage the city to zone commercial as much land as possible. (Seattle cannot offer financial incentives, except for a property tax abatement on multifamily structures that was implemented for the first time in 1999.) Yet, because of the uniform property tax law, the city has a very strong interest in increasing the number of office towers and amount of commercial property in its downtown and in its designated urban centers and villages, which are scattered around the city fairly evenly.

The B&O tax, because it is a tax on both residents and nonresidents and because it applies to services that include high-end services, may have much the same effect on political strategies as cities that levy an income tax on nonresidents. That is to say, it is at least as important to keep high-income (or high B&O) firms in the city as it is to encourage high-value property construction. Indeed, the city's revenue system is more dependent on the B&O and retail taxes than on the property tax, pushing political actors' policy focus toward the spatial location of commercial and professional services rather than on a nonspatial growth policy (which would be expected of income tax cities).

Like most major central cities, Seattle provides general services to nonresident employees in the city (e.g., fire protection, public safety, street lighting, sidewalks). Many cities adopt policies designed to capture tax support from nonresidents, often including an income tax on nonresidents or a sales tax. The B&O tax is levied on any commercial activity (including professional services), and its prospects for exporting the city's tax burden to nonresidents are quite good. For example, the city's Office of Management and Planning estimated that more than 12 percent of the firms that paid a B&O tax were not domiciled in the city, including many out-of-state companies.

The B&O tax in combination with the city's retail sales tax establishes an incentive for political officials to encourage the growth of commercial centers not only in the traditional central business district (CBD) but also on the fringes of the city. Commercial centers on the city's fringe attract consumers who are not only residents of the city but also nonresident neighbors. Nonresident consumers, then, contribute to the (retail) tax base of the central city. A senior city official noted that city service-delivery costs exceed the property tax stream from residential areas in all but the high-end cities: "Unless you have 'Gold Coast' homes in your city, cities need the B&O and sales tax; revenues are insufficient otherwise." The city estimates that approximately a third of its revenues is derived from the three major taxes in downtown Seattle and that another third is derived from the several commercial and industrial centers.

B&O and retail sales tax data for the city's four major hubs of commercial activity that border the city on the north and south (the east and west borders are Lake Washington and Puget Sound, respectively) are expected to support a political strategy on vacant land use and reuse. Figure 3.7 presents estimates of the origins of B&O tax revenues in the CBD, the Northgate area (northeastern corner), and the "rest of the city"; figure 3.8 presents estimates of origins of retail sales tax revenues in the four commercial centers near the northern and southern borders of the city. The B&O revenue data from the city's budget office were apportioned across the city's census tracts on the basis of their employment contribution (for estimates of the B&O tax) and of their population (for estimates of the retail tax).[31]

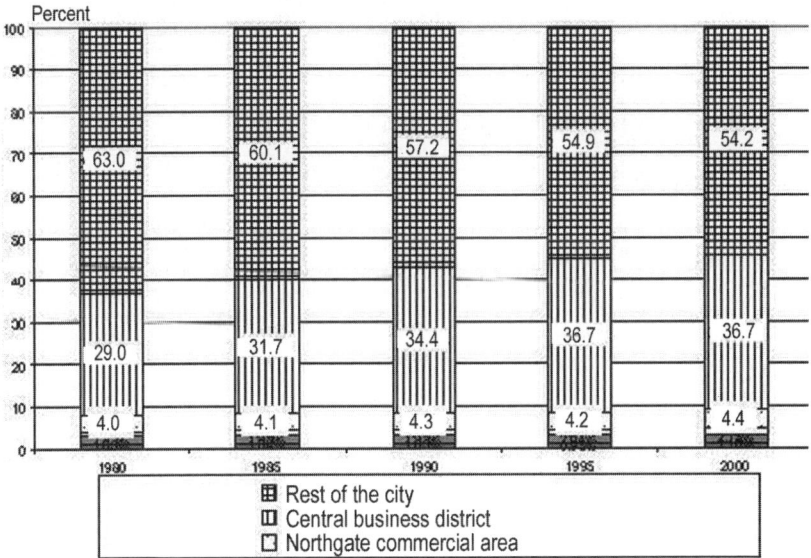

FIGURE 3.7.   Seattle's Business and Occupancy Tax Revenue by Census Tract as Percentage of City Total
Source: Data from the City of Seattle. Regional estimates by the authors.

Figures 3.7 and 3.8 show that these border commercial zones have increased ever so slightly their relative revenue-generating contribution to the city's treasury since 1980. Although the increase in the relative contributions from the four corners has been modest, it has come during a time when the growth in Seattle's downtown has been remarkably strong. To register any relative increase in revenue-generating importance, then, suggests that the four corners have performed quite well. Indeed, the growth centers of the city have been in the Capitol Hill–First Hill urban center, due to the high concentration of health-related services, and the two urban centers in the traditional central area (downtown Seattle and Seattle Center). These areas contained 178,373 of Seattle's 309,438 jobs in 1980, or a 57.6 percent share. By 1990, they housed 230,744 jobs of the city's 386,187 (or a 59.7 percent

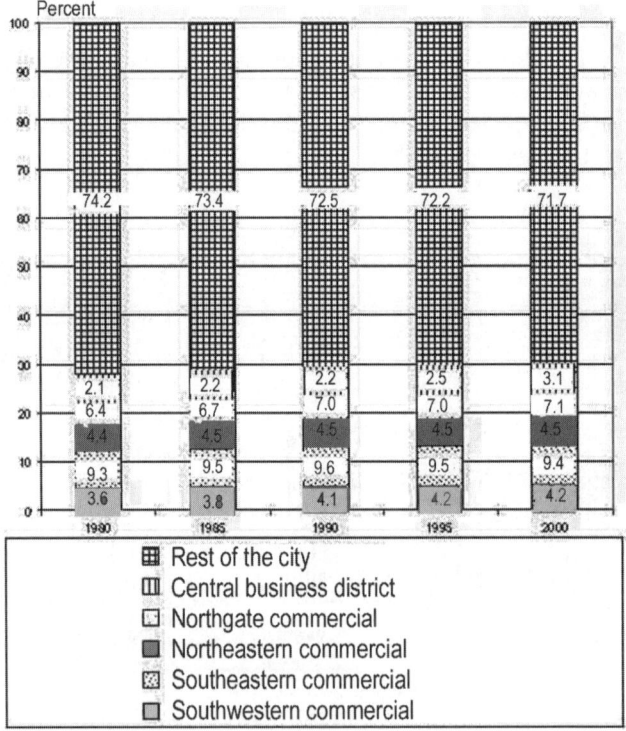

FIGURE 3.8.   Seattle's Sales Tax Revenues by Census Tract as Percentage of City Total
Source: Data from the City of Seattle. Regional estimates by the authors.

share), and the data for 2000 indicated that 260,659 jobs of the city's 431,491 jobs were in these areas (60.4 percent).

The employment opportunities in the city's central area are expected to continue to fuel the growth in B&O tax revenues. The city's budget office estimated that $30 million in B&O revenue was collected from the services sector in 1998 (approximately 32 percent of total B&O collections), up from 25 percent in 1988. If the contribution of the city's central area is removed from the revenue list, the border areas have improved their relative positions as revenue contributors to the city's treasury.

Figure 3.9 presents the data from the histograms in figures 3.7 and 3.8 (excluding the "rest of the city" data) in a spatial format and overlays these data on the city's per capita income data by census tract. The establishment of retail centers at the city's four corners conforms to expectations for sales tax cities that are surrounded by incorporated municipalities. Moreover, the high-end residential areas are generally situated in the central and northern sections of the city, whereas the south end contains residents with more modest incomes. The hybrid nature of the Seattle case makes a less pure example (compared with the Phoenix area) of the land–tax dynamic. The distribution of residents by income does not match the hypothetical model entirely (lower-income residents are predicted to be located at the northern end of the city as well as the southern end).

As a consequence, strategies to reuse vacant land in the city reflect the hybrid revenue system. The city encourages professional office buildings and high-end commercial establishments in the center, which is illustrated by the growth in B&O tax revenue collection in the city's CBD during the twenty-year period (figure 3.7). The histogram demonstrates that B&O collections in the CBD since 1980 have increased dramatically as a proportion of the city's total B&O collections. Figure 3.9 maps the city's census tracts by income groupings and also layers the B&O and retail sales tax proportions from 1980, 1990, and 2000, derived from figures 3.7 and 3.8, at the five spatial centers of employment and retailing (i.e., the four corners of the city and the CBD). The height of each histogram represents a proportion of the total city sales tax collection or the total B&O tax collection for 1980, 1990, and 2000. The map illustrates that retail development at the four corners has remained quite strong during the twenty-year period, even though their relative contribution to the city's retail tax collections has not changed much during the period. Further, the size of the retail tax histograms at the four corners is quite large compared with the relatively small retail sales tax collections in Seattle's CBD, an issue we discuss further in chapter 5.

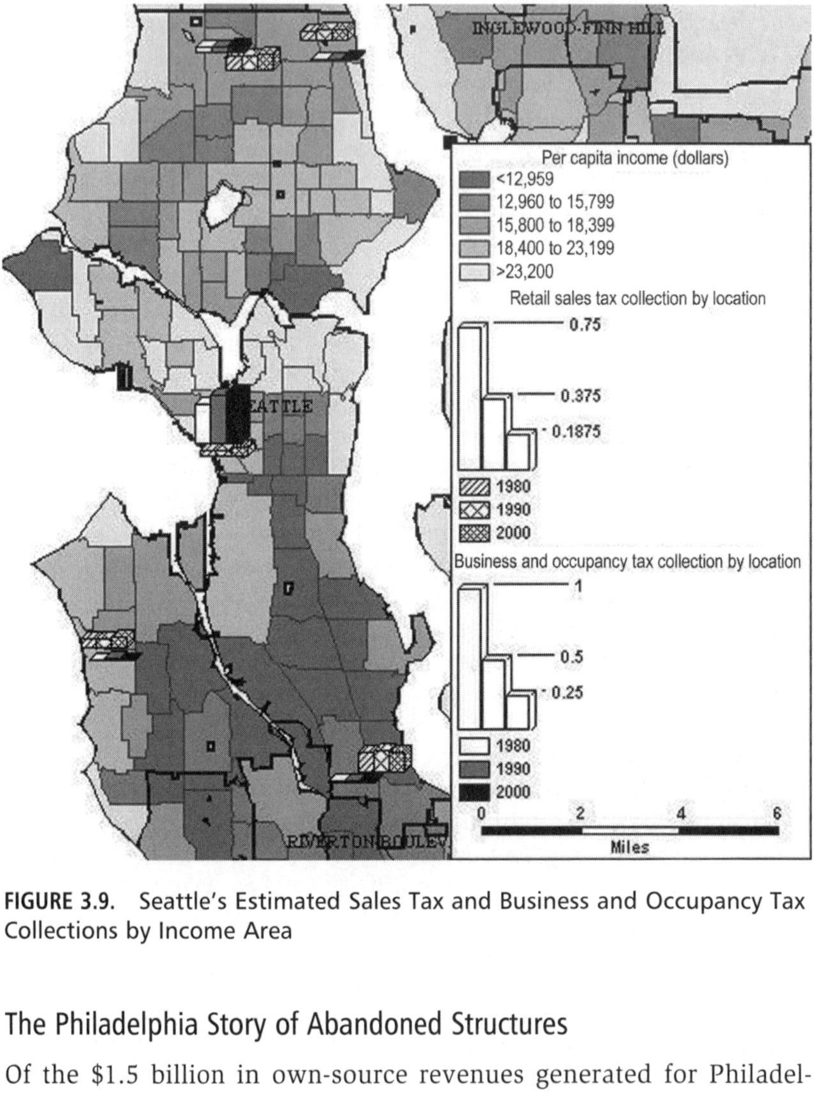

FIGURE 3.9.   Seattle's Estimated Sales Tax and Business and Occupancy Tax Collections by Income Area

The Philadelphia Story of Abandoned Structures

Of the $1.5 billion in own-source revenues generated for Philadelphia's General Fund in 2000, more than $1 billion was derived from the income tax on both residents and nonresidents (the "wage, earnings, and net profits tax"). The executive director of the city's Revenue Commission estimated that nearly 38 percent of the income tax was collected from nonresidents. The property tax contributed nearly $350 million to the General Fund and the sales tax generated more than $100 million in 2000.[32]

Philadelphia's heavy reliance on the income tax, then, should encourage a development strategy to attract high-income employees. Because the sales tax provides much less revenue to the city than the income tax, the city's political strategy should probably reflect the comparative strength of the income tax. Retail and commercial development is a less productive use of vacant land than professional offices. The best situation for the city is to develop professional office buildings for high-income employees who will also live in expensive housing (given the property tax of 3.7 percent of assessed value, which is approximately 24 percent of market value).

The City of Philadelphia estimates that there are nearly 31,000 vacant parcels within its borders. The reuse of the vacant lots, we argue, should be influenced by the city's principal revenue structure, that is, by its income tax reliance. Because the city exports such a substantial share of its taxes to nonresidents, the city's revenue-maximization strategy ought to be one of encouraging vacant land reuse for high-income occupants. Supporting the construction or occupancy of professional office buildings would, for example, be an appropriate political strategy for Philadelphia. Indeed, during his term in office, Mayor Edward Rendell encouraged an infill strategy aimed at developing the office space in downtown Philadelphia. The strategy pursued in the low-income residential areas is not to maximize revenues (the market demand for vacant lots in the city's residential section is quite low) but to minimize costs.

Vacant residential side lots generate very little in property taxes (forgone tax revenues, therefore, are small) and are unlikely to house high-income individuals, who tend to live in the northwest and northeast sections of the city, not in areas where vacant lots have become a concern. With the continuing abandonment of the city's residences (mostly rowhouses), more land has become available and suburban-like housing is replacing the high rises, most of which are scheduled for razing. The city encourages neighbors to purchase the side lots as a side yard or parking space.[33] Most of these lots are tax delinquent and require the city to "clean and secure" the structure or vacant lot, resulting in a lien on the property for those costs. Most liens are not collectible, and the city loses money. Because transferring property to owners might generate property tax revenue of only $80 or so, according to estimates by Fairmount Ventures, the strategy is not revenue maximization but expenditure minimization. The city estimates that it costs nearly $1.8 million a year to keep vacant lots clean, excluding the more than $8 million the city spends annually to raze dilapidated housing.[34] The other solution to the vacant side lot problem is the gardening approach, a topic discussed more fully in chapter 4. The Pennsylvania Horticultural Society encourages gardening on vacant lots and has successfully transformed hundreds of the city's unused parcels into gardens. This "beautify the city" approach not only enhances the image of the city but is also expected to reduce property deterioration and maintain property values in the neighboring area.

Figure 3.10 presents a map of the city of Philadelphia and its vacant lots in 1999, at the end of Mayor Rendell's eight-year administration, during which much of his development emphasis centered on the CBD.[35] The sizes of the dots are scaled to the market value of the lots. Notice the preponderance of high-valued vacant land located in the city's downtown business district between the two rivers. In conformance with the model set out in figure 3.5, much of the vacant land downtown has been developed for professional offices and for the performing arts. The city's revenue strategy is served by encouraging the development of vacant land into enterprises that will hire high-income individuals. Moreover, the tens of thousands of tiny dots in figure 3.10

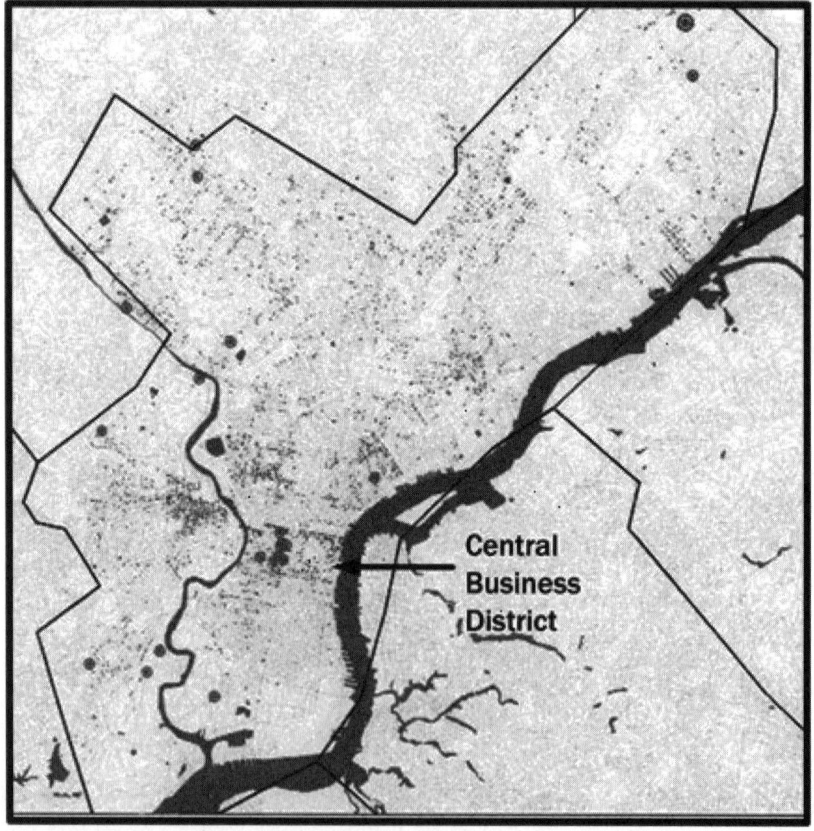

FIGURE 3.10.   Location and Market Value of Philadelphia's Vacant Lots

are in most cases very small and low-valued vacant lots, razed row houses, or vacant lots with gardens in residential neighborhoods.

Office towers, high-end residential developments, or other reuses of vacant land would be in the city's revenue-maximizing interest. Because more than 95 percent of the vacant lots are "small" and usually not contiguous to other vacant lots, the city has authorized their use for "art work" or side yards to adjacent row houses. Office towers would require larger parcels, which tend to be located in the center of the city and are indeed being developed as such.

The Vacant Land Logic in Columbus

Columbus, as well as 540 other municipalities in the State of Ohio, collects a tax on earning compensation and net profits of all businesses within the city, of all persons' income who work within the city's borders regardless of their place of residence, and on residents' income even if they work outside the city. All cities may impose a 1 percent income tax rate on earnings and net profits by a vote of the city council; increases to the rate must be approved by a vote of the people.

In 1967, income tax revenues contributed less than 46 percent of Columbus's own-source revenues.[36] By 2000, the city's income tax levy (the current income tax rate is 2 percent) generated $318 million for the city's general fund in 2000, or 63 percent of its total general fund revenues. The city estimated that income tax collections from nonresident commuters reached nearly $140 million in 1999.[37] The property tax, which amounts to a minuscule amount, contributed $37 million or less than 10 percent of its general fund revenues in 2000.[38] The fiscal incentive to undertake land reuse projects in Columbus, then, derives only marginally from the revenue-generating potential of the land and structures but principally from the revenue gains associated with employment creation.

Columbus is the state capital and the home of the state's largest university. As noted in chapter 2, it has a substantial amount of tax-exempt land and structures within its jurisdictions. The fiscal impact to Columbus of removing state-owned, tax-exempt land from its tax base is minor, even though the estimated value of the tax-exempt land in Columbus is $6.6 billion. Indeed, the promotion and expansion of state buildings, university and hospital facilities, and other tax-exempt organizations are applauded and supported by city development officials if such development brings with it more jobs, more employees, and higher incomes.

As expected in an income-tax-reliant city, a key element of Columbus's approach to land conversion centers on preventing decay in the city's central core and promoting job creation. For example, the city was engaged in the downtown's Nationwide Arena and Nationwide Entertainment District projects by creating a tax increment financing (TIF) district for infrastructure improvements. Even though the city relies very little on property tax revenues, other local governments (especially the school district) are heavily dependent on the property tax base. The potentially high revenue loss for the school district was politically unacceptable, and the TIF district that was created for this project did not abate school district property tax revenues. The entire cost of the project was privately financed, except for the TIF-financed infrastructure. It converted a 95-acre parcel of vacant land into projects with more than 300,000 square feet of retail and entertainment space and 1.3 million square feet of office space. The project enhanced the employment base of the city and rejuvenated an area for entertainment purposes, yielding a healthy tax return to the city.

Interest in promoting employment opportunities does not mean that other types of activities are unimportant. All cities must balance residential neighborhood integrity with commercial and employment concerns. Columbus also invests in projects that improve blighted areas or promote employment opportunities, such as, respectively, the West Edge Business Park and Easton Town Center. In these projects, the city's investment is not predicated on enhancing the land value as much as it is on enhancing commercial and employment opportunities and improving the "livability" of neighborhoods. The Easton Town Center project, which is located on the eastern edge of the city, is an extension of an existing office complex and includes restaurants and retail centers. The 1,700-acre project, begun in 1987, involved creation of a TIF district in addition to property tax abatements for the nonretail establishments. Nearly 10,000 employees work in Easton Town Center. The West Edge Business Park is on the site of a former public housing project 1 mile south of downtown. The neighborhood and the city sought to strengthen the neighborhood by converting the newly created vacant land into employment opportunities. The project, which was financed in part by the city's revolving loan program, also received tax abatements for its 42-acre site, and it resulted in the creation of approximately 1,000 new jobs.

Just as property-tax-dependent cities have a fiscal imperative to improve neighborhoods, so do Columbus and income-tax-dependent cities. Nevertheless, Columbus' imperative is principally focused on job creation, and preferably on high-paying job creation. Higher-income citizens tend to contribute more revenues to city coffers than they consume in services. But the salience of the strategy to attract high-income persons differs across the urban landscape. In cities that are fiscally dependent on a property tax, a high-income person is especially attractive from cities' fiscal-generating perspective if he or she also owns property with a high valuation. That is to say, a corporate executive who works in the city and lives in the suburbs is less desirable from the city's fiscal imperative than one who owns property in the city. The city's direct fiscal impact is linked to heightened property values.

But for cities with commuter taxes, such as Columbus with its income tax, the fiscal imperative to both house and employ high-income persons is diminished. Columbus need not worry itself about the executive who lives in the suburb because her high salary is taxed at the place of employment. The issues are de-coupled; whether she owns property or resides in the city becomes a secondary issue to the fiscal imperative of the city. The overriding fiscal imperative is that she work in Columbus; thus, vacant land conversion for employment uses is preferred.

REFLECTIONS ON THE LAND–TAX DYNAMIC

In setting up the land–tax dynamic, we began with a basic contention: Cities adopt political strategies to maximize revenues or minimize costs to meet the collective and individual needs of their residents. Successfully doing so increases the likelihood that elected officials will achieve one of their central objectives: reelection to office. Decisions about developing vacant land are some of the political strategies available to cities as they seek their preferred ends. Vacant land represents an opportunity for cities. We have argued that how (and whether) a city decides to develop the vacant land is dependent to a large degree on its revenue structure.

In this chapter, we have analyzed three general city tax systems: property, sales, and income. Admittedly, none of the cities presented here is a pure type—all of them have mixed revenue systems, as do all cities within the U.S. constellation of cities. However, cities are distinct in that they vary in their dependence on various tax sources and offer reasonable approximations of the types. These different revenue systems have structured, we contend, different political strategies for the development of vacant land.

The difficulty of collecting revenue data by their spatial origins rendered a more thorough test of the model problematic. Nevertheless, although a true test of the posited relationship requires diachronic analysis

with more cities, the spatial-revenue data that were collected are sugges-
tive of a vacant land development logic that closely parallels the hypothesized patterns. The land development patterns in Columbia and Camden
differ from those in Tempe, Peoria, and Oklahoma City. And those cities
are different from Seattle, Philadelphia, and Columbus. If we are correct
about the linkage, knowing a city's revenue structure should allow us to
predict, ceteris paribus, which vacant land parcels ought to be developed
for the purpose of maximizing revenues or minimizing costs, so that the
city's goal of enhancing the quality of life for its citizens might be better
accomplished.

Although an underlying land–tax (or spatial–revenue) political logic
appears to be an important determinant in explaining the use and reuse
of certain parcels of vacant land, cities' behavior does not always
match hypothesized expectations. For example, why would a sales-tax-
dependent city not develop, or support development of, a parcel of vacant land for retail purposes, and instead set it aside for recreation uses,
thus reducing forgone sales tax revenues from that site? Although the
city strategy of revenue maximization or expenditure minimization is a
powerful predictor of city behavior toward the vacant land use and reuse that best maximize community welfare, cities' vacant land and
land use policies are constrained by two other key factors. First, a city
seeks to minimize social disruption and protect the property values of
its residents and firms. Second, a city needs to maintain and augment
its economic vitality. We now turn to these constraints on cities' revenue-maximization strategies in chapters 4 and 5.

NOTES

1. The calculations were done by the authors. The material on general taxing
   authority is derived from Michael A. Pagano, *City Fiscal Conditions in 1999*
   (Washington, D.C.: National League of Cities, 1999), appendix A, and revised by the authors; city population figures are from the U.S. Bureau of the
   Census, 1990.
2. See, e.g., David Weimer and Aidan Vining, *Policy Analysis* 3rd ed. (Upper
   Saddle River, N.J.: Prentice Hall, 1999).
3. In the case of catalog sales, the customer pays the sales tax rate of his or her
   place of residence because the transaction is deemed to have occurred
   there.
4. Fiscal and political stretching policies are discussed in Michael A. Pagano,
   "Metropolitan Limits: Intrametropolitan Disparities and Governance in US
   Laboratories of Democracy," in *Governance and Opportunity in Metropolitan America,* ed. Alan Altshuler, William Morrill, Harold Wolman, and
   Faith Mitchell (Washington, D.C.: National Academy Press, 1999), 253–92.
5. For a discussion of the fiscalization of land use, see Paul G. Lewis, "Retail
   Politics: Local Sales Taxes and the Fiscalization of Land Use," *Economic De-*

velopment Quarterly 15, no. 1 (February 2001): 21–35; and Robert W. Wassmer, "Influences of the 'Fiscalization of Land Use' and Urban-Growth Boundaries," California Senate Office of Research, Sacramento, August 2001 (revised).

6. See, e.g., Helen Ladd and John Yinger, *America's Ailing Cities* (Baltimore: Johns Hopkins University Press, 1989).

7. Ladd and Yinger, *America's Ailing Cities*, 51.

8. Use taxes do require consumers to identify their location in order to collect the tax. These use taxes, however, are most effectively collected on large ticket items.

9. Ladd and Yinger, *America's Ailing Cities*, 54.

10. California returns one cent to the city in which the sale originated.

11. See, e.g., Nonna Noto, "Local Income Taxes on Nonresidents in the Nation's 25 Largest Cities," Congressional Research Service memorandum, March 4, 2002 (draft).

12. Michael A. Pagano and Richard G. Forgette, "Regionalism and Municipal Tax Structures: Assessing Tax-Base Sharing in Ohio Metropolitan Areas," paper presented at the annual meeting of the Association for Budgeting and Financial Management, Kansas City, October 10, 2002.

13. Ladd and Yinger, *America's Ailing Cities*, 54.

14. National Association of State Budget Officers, *Fiscal Survey of the States, December 2000* (Washington, D.C.: National Association of State Budget Officers, 2000).

15. New York City Independent Budget Office, *Big City, Big Bucks: NYC's Changing Income Distribution"* (New York: New York City Independent Budget Office, 2000), 5.

16. New York City Independent Budget Office, *Big City, Big Bucks*, 1.

17. Paul Peterson, *City Limits* (Chicago: University of Chicago Press 1981).

18. The political strategy adopted by two-tiered land tax systems would not be expected to follow such a logic. Owners of vacant land or improved land under this type of property tax system would both pay a high tax premium to own the land. Municipal governments would have a much-muted incentive to encourage development of vacant land or the reutilization of vacant buildings, except that these usually require more services in the form of "health and safety" (e.g., police). A cost-minimizing incentive, then, might induce dual-tax systems to encourage the reuse of vacant land, rather than a revenue-enhancing incentive.

19. City of Columbia, Planning and Development Services, *Columbia, SC Demographics, Development and Growth*, March 2001; www.columbiasc.net/city/adobeforms/grfinl01.pdf (May 2002).

20. Interview with City Manager Leona Plaugh, January 2002.

21. Neil Smith, Paul Caris, and Elvin Wyly, "The 'Camden Syndrome' and the Menace of Suburban Decline: Residential Disinvestment and Its Discontents in Camden County, New Jersey," *Urban Affairs Review* 36 (March 2001): 497–531.

22. Camden Department of Development and Planning, *Overall Economic Development Program 1998–2004* (Camden, N.J.: City of Camden, Department of Development and Planning, 1998).

23. Unlike many other New Jersey cities, however, Camden's weak tax base makes it especially dependent on state aid to finance the delivery of basic public services. In 1994, for example, almost two-thirds of the city's revenues came from state funds. The property tax was the single largest *other* source of revenue for the city.

24. The economy is not Camden's only concern. The city has experienced a series of governance problems that have led to the intervention of a state oversight board. See Judith Havemann, "A City that Good Times Forgot: Blighted Camden, N.J. Reflects Inner Cities' Resistance to Renewal," *Washington Post,* April 1, 1999, A3.

25. See Camden Department of Development and Planning, *Overall Economic Development Program 1998–2004.*

26. A report noted: "Although real estate taxes comprise over two-thirds of locally generated revenues, the City does not rigorously enforce collection, with the result that it receives only about 77% of its levy on a current basis. Out of the 26,668 parcels of land in the city, nearly three out of ten (7,786) are in serious tax arrears. Delinquent taxes increased steadily in the 1990s, and there is now more than a full year's municipal taxes in arrears" (City of Camden, *Multi-Year Recovery Plan, Fiscal Years 2001–2003,* 2001, p. 3; www.state.nj.us/dca/camdensummary.pdf [June 1, 2003]) The report goes further and claims that roughly 65 percent of Camden's 2001 operating budget is supported by state aid. In effect, then, the strategic behavior of the City of Camden in reusing its vacant land appears not to support the expected strategic behavior of cities that depend on the property tax, as it comes to depend less on the property tax and more on state aid.

27. For a fascinating description of the importance of luring sales-tax-generating activities into a city, and creating a "Sales Tax Canyon," see William Fulton, *The Reluctant Metropolis: The Politics of Urban Growth in Los Angeles* (Baltimore: Johns Hopkins University Press, 1997).

28. City of Oklahoma City, Department of Finance, *FY2001–2002 Budget Revenue Summary,* 2002; www.okc-cityhall.org/ (May 2002).

29. City of Seattle, *Comprehensive Annual Financial Report, 1997* (Seattle: City of Seattle, 1997), 19.

30. Data are derived from the City of Seattle, *1999–2000 Proposed Budget;* www.ci.seattle.wa.us/budget/99_00bud/REVENUE.htm (March 2001).

31. Apportioning B&O and retail sales tax derivation is imprecise and crude. Discussions with analysts in the city's finance department suggested that place of employment is an adequate surrogate for B&O tax origins, though imprecise. Employment data are from the Puget Sound Regional Council (PSRC). Data on retail sales tax originations are not collected. On the basis of an assumption that most sales are correlated with place of residence, retail sales tax revenues were apportioned across census tracts according to population data. Population data and estimates are derived from PSRC.

32. City of Philadelphia, *Comprehensive Annual Financial Report,* 2000; www.phila.gov/atservice/reports/annual99 (June 2000).

33. The problem, of course, is incredible bureaucratic red tape. Mark Allan Hughes notes that fifteen public agencies are responsible for vacant property in Philadelphia ("Dirt Into Dollars," *Brookings Review,* summer 2000,

36–39). The time delay in transferring blighted structures to the Redevelopment Authority was reduced from two years to six months under the Commonwealth of Pennsylvania's "spot condemnation" law (Act 94/39), which allows the Redevelopment Authority to acquire vacant, tax-delinquent, and blighted properties. Yet the spot condemnation law tends to be invoked only when a buyer or a community development corporation has expressed interest; otherwise, the city would take title. Horror stories of bureaucratic inefficiency resulting in delays of up to twenty-five years in transferring vacant land to neighboring owners are legion (Stephen Seplow, "Too Many Houses, Too Few Residents," *Philadelphia Inquirer*, May 10, 1999, 1).

34. Seplow, "Too Many Houses," 1.
35. The data for more than 630,000 lots were provided by the City of Philadelphia's Board of Revision of Taxes.
36. The 1966–67 city finances report of the Bureau of the Census did not segregate "income tax" revenue from "other" tax revenue. The 46 percent figure reported here assumes all "other" tax revenue pertains to the income tax, which clearly overestimates the actual amount because the city also levies a hotel/motel tax and other taxes that are included in the census's "other taxes" category.
37. Richard Forgette and Michael Pagano, "Fiscal Structures and Metropolitan Tax Base Sharing," paper presented at the annual meeting of the American Political Science Association, San Francisco, September 1, 2001.
38. City of Columbus, *City of Columbus 2002 Budget*, 2002; http://mayor.ci .columbus.oh.us/2002Budget/PDF/Financialoverview.pdf (June 1, 2003).

4

The Social Value of Vacant Land

The fiscal imperative of cities relative to land use is important, perhaps the most important of the three imperatives. In this chapter, the focus shifts to a different imperative, specifically the social value of vacant land. As was posited in chapter 2, cities need to minimize social disruption and protect property values. Vacant land can be utilized in various ways in an effort to achieve this social imperative. Take, for example, a wetland or a steep slope. These parcels of land have physical characteristics that make them unbuildable, and thus they remain vacant in perpetuity.

Yet even though these parcels lack direct developmental value, at least in a conventional sense,[1] they possess high social value. Wetlands and steep slopes can serve as barriers or fences, and therefore they preserve land values by separating one type of land use from another. Similarly, a city may convert a tract of vacant land into a public park that acts as buffer between two areas. Once dedicated as open space, formal zoning locks out the potential for land-value-reducing activities. The use of vacant land to create social boundaries and barriers, and even an occasional social benefit, has been little explored thus far—a condition that this chapter seeks to remedy.

Using vacant land for social purposes involves fundamental questions about property ownership. Economists and political scientists have long explored the interaction between city fiscal policy and individual or firm location decisions. Charles Tiebout's half-century-old argument indicates that intercity competition would encourage a fair tax price for a bundle of goods.[2] Private property owners would "vote with their feet" if dissatisfaction with tax rates or service quality reached some critical threshold.[3] Cities also compete with one another in protecting private property values, as William Fischel documents in a recent important refinement of Tiebout's hypothesis.[4] Individual voting behavior is influenced by the knowledge that, as a property owner, the "home voter" can take actions to protect her asset and also by the fear that she cannot protect against collective neighborhood effects. Consequently, property owners take action to reduce the variance in adverse outcomes of neighborhood effects. In other words, home voters engage in individual and collective action to protect their own property values.

Our argument extends the individual-level motivation undergirding the home voter hypothesis to city policies and actions toward the use and reuse of vacant land. Nominal land banking by city governments, especially in anticipation of future city facilities such as parks, is fairly common. However, as a general rule, most city governments are reluctant to amass an extensive supply of vacant land, whether through market purchase, takings procedures, or tax foreclosures. For example, the City of San Diego reported in our 1998 survey that it did not own a single vacant lot. The City of Detroit, however, held title to about 30,000 vacant lots and abandoned structures.[5]

Cities also vary in how they acquire vacant land. For instance, city acquisition of land and structures through tax foreclosures ranged from nearly 100 percent in Rochester to less than 5 percent in Riverside, California, and less than 1 percent in Portland, Oregon. Nearly 55 percent of the large cities (more than 100,000 population) responding to the survey indicated that they lacked the authority to seize property in tax arrears. In many states, it is county government that is empowered to do so, thereby creating a situation of county-owned vacant land located within the corporate limits of a city. Thus, from one city to another, a range of contextual issues affects the use of vacant land for social objectives. Furthermore, the choices for cities are many: using vacant land as a buffer or fence to separate land uses, or instead using it as a bridge to link disparate areas; adopting a policy of infilling to increase density, or contrarily pursuing a policy of de-densification; developing open space for its economic value, or conserving open space for its natural resource value. The remainder of the chapter addresses these topics.

MENTAL MAPS

Vacant land not only affects the physical form of the city; it also affects the image of the city. After all, the cityscape as a whole carries meaning and evokes reactions from viewers.[6] These meanings and reactions vary across locations and observers. "The city landscape may have value as a source of delight to people and a possible restoration from the stresses of everyday life."[7] By the same token, the cityscape may be a source of distress. Vacant land factors into both the positive and negative reactions to the cityscape. It is in its distress-inducing role that it is most familiar.

Thinking about Vacant Land

The term "vacant land" frequently carries a negative connotation—abandoned, empty, dangerous—and has often come to symbolize disinvestment, blight and decay.[8] This type of vacant land is perceived by observers to be a pernicious destroyer of community. A report by the *Detroit Free Press* located Detroit's city-owned vacant land and, as the map in figure 4.1 shows, the areas of high concentration are very nearly contiguous. At best, they are surrounded by blocks in which city ownership of vacant land is moderately high and increasing. Much of this vacant property is of the boarded-up buildings and

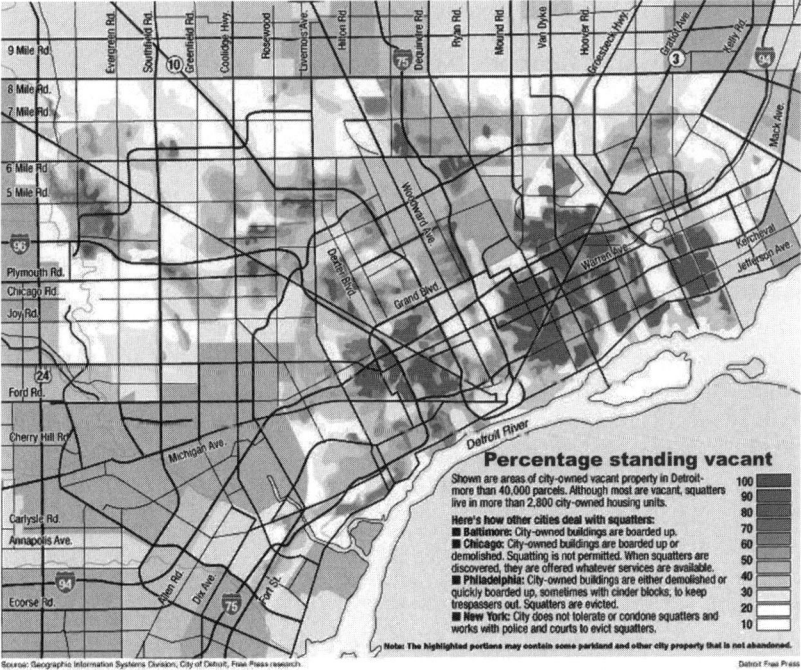

FIGURE 4.1. The Location of City-Owned Vacant Land in Detroit
Source: Detroit Free Press, July 7, 2000. Reprinted by permission of the *Detroit Free Press*.

trash-strewn lots variety, the type of vacant land that sends clear signals of decay and distress warnings to passersby. For instance, a Philadelphia council member explained that the visual problem of abandoned structures and unkempt vacant lots was "the 'red flag' that a neighborhood's become undesirable."

City officials in Seattle's Department of Construction and Land Use (DCLU), which is charged with ensuring the safety of residential and commercial structures, refer to the visual image of decay as the "Broken Window Theory."[9] Neighbors report broken windows, unkempt buildings, safety violations, and other problems to DCLU, which then investigates the complaint. Upon notification that the structure is in violation of the city's safety code, the owner is given the opportunity to correct the deficiency. If it is not corrected immediately, the structure is placed in the Vacant Building Monitoring Program and revisited every three months. The owners pay a fee as a consequence of their property's listing in the monitoring program. After three quarters of no violation, the owner's name is removed from the system. In Seattle, almost all the complaints are registered for single-family, detached dwellings. One city analysis of program data found that of the 778 properties that were placed on the Monitoring Program for a three-and-a-half-year period between 1996 and 1999, only 300 were still vacant at the end of the period (although no longer in violation), and fewer than 65 were still on the monitoring list.

Phoenix is another city that has grappled with vacant land safety and security issues. When officials of the city's Neighborhood Services Department sponsored a citywide series of forums in 1992, participants zeroed in on several concerns, among them the condition of vacant land. In one neighborhood after another, residents demanded that absentee landlords be held accountable for the upkeep of their property, that the city take more aggressive action to remove graffiti, and that, where possible, empty buildings be used for community functions.[10] The general consensus was that the presence of vacant lots and abandoned structures diminished the sense of community. In transitional neighborhoods, the concern was that more vacancy and abandonment would lead to full-scale blight.

One of the components of a city's physical form is its edges, or boundaries. These are linear elements that represent breaks in continuity. In Kevin Lynch's words, "Such edges may be barriers, more or less penetrable, which close one region off from another; or they may be seams, lines along which two regions are related and joined together."[11] Edges isolate, but they can also unite. Vacant lots and abandoned structures assume the mantle of the proverbial "railroad tracks" that separate people by income, class, and race. That is, vacant land often sets apart neighborhoods, creating boundaries between human settlements.

A physical landscape of abandoned structures and vacant land informs our mental map of these socioeconomic divisions. These form part of what Hughes and Loizillon refer to as "settlement structures," by which they mean "both the physical landscape of buildings and streets and the social landscape of boundaries and routes."[12] The settlement structure shapes our understanding of fences and barriers, both physical and social. Vacant land with much development potential does not convey the same sense of urgency and despair as the vacant lots littered with hypodermic needles, broken-down shopping carts, and trash. Indeed, the more prominent mental map of urban vacant land is the one of despair, not of hope.

In studies of landscapes in Tennessee cities, people responded positively to areas that were clean and well kept, had abundant greenery and open space, and provided scenic views. [13] They reacted negatively to sections that were dilapidated and dirty, had poor upkeep, and were crowded. An open-ended question about what should be done to improve a city's appearance yielded especially interesting results. Among the five most frequently mentioned actions were the renovation or replacement of old buildings, the clean up of litter, and an increase in the amount of public green space. These findings have substantial implications for city policies regarding vacant land and abandoned structures. Ideally, cities can use vacant land to maximize the positive values while minimizing the negative ones, thereby transforming the mental map to a more hopeful status.

Vacant land contextualizes settlement structures in many cities by delineating neighborhoods and microcommunities. The debate between consolidationists and fragmentationists in the literature on metropolitan governance hinges on the same ideas expressed here. Whereas the metropolitan governance debate is over the legal drawing of political boundaries, which in turn determines who has the authority to articulate interests to which government, the settlement structures—of which vacant land is a part—refer in particular to intramunicipality boundaries. [14] Nevertheless, the boundaries and barriers created by vacant land can serve the same kinds of ends that are considered problematic to both the fragmentationists and the consolidationists with respect to political boundaries. That is to say, individuals choose residential locations to maximize their own personal or familial needs, in many cases, the schooling needs of their children. In the process, however, segregation by income and race results.

Whether segregated housing and neighborhoods reflect purposive race consciousness or whether segregation is a by-product of individuals' maximizing their own welfare,[15] recent census tract data demonstrate that individuals with similar income, race, ethnicity, and education continue to cluster in neighborhoods or microcommunities within cities. City governments, then, are placed in the position of regulating land use to ensure that the property values of various relatively homogenous microcommunities are not threatened. Policies designed to protect property values, in turn, may (inadvertently or intentionally) reinforce the racial or income or class or ethnic homogeneity of those microcommunities.

City policies toward (re)using vacant land or creating vacant land (open space) serve the purpose of protecting or enhancing property values by demarcating neighborhoods. Although barriers and boundaries other than vacant land (e.g., roads and waterways) perform similar functions of separating or segregating, vacant land also serves to isolate and protect communities' property values. It should not be surprising, then, that cities are not always eager to reuse vacant land for seemingly "productive" or revenue-generating purposes (e.g., construction or placement of multifamily dwelling units), if the land in its "vacant" or unused state serves a value-enhancing or value–maintaining purpose. Nor should it be unexpected that vacant land in the form of open space, greenways, parks, and playgrounds can create one of the more effective fences between classes or races of city residents.

In this light, the role of urban parks as "green walls," or perhaps "green magnets," rather than as open-air recreation sites, is worthy of closer examination. For instance, does New York City's Morningside Park serve as a barrier between the poor, predominantly minority neighborhood of West Harlem and the middle-class, primarily white neighborhood of Morningside Heights? Or does the park provide a link between the two neighborhoods? Research suggests that the former is a more apt characterization of the park's function—that little interaction occurs between the neighborhoods and that the park therefore serves as a mechanism of social control.[16] A study of four parks in Boston develops a similar argument. There, the parks effectively created green walls between different neighborhoods.[17]

However, research in Chicago offers an alternative perspective.[18] Gobster's study suggests that while Warren Park on the city's Far North Side serves as a boundary between white and nonwhite neighborhoods, it is not a barrier. Rather, it functions as a magnet, drawing in residents from the surrounding area, promoting social and cultural diversity. A set of internal and external conditions (e.g., stable community groups and active park management) has fostered this integrative role for Warren Park. The Chicago findings point to the fact that open space or green space boundaries are not inevitably barriers. Nevertheless, if our thesis is accurate, promoting green space as barrier is a strategic city policy that is and will be pursued at the insistence of microcommunities, even in places such as Warren Park, if individuals' property values become threatened.

Dividing Lines and Social Buffers

The canals in the Phoenix metropolitan area, although not particularly wide, provide a physical barrier in that they can be traversed only at specific crossings. In a sense, the city is divided into canal-defined segments. Further, the canals create a social buffer because they separate neighborhoods and define land uses. They can serve as starting and ending points for development activities. More pernicious by their ubiquity are the fences within neighborhoods, further dividing neighborhoods into smaller microcommunities. Figures 4.2 and 4.3 capture the phenomena of canals and fences. Figure 4.2 shows one of the canals and the strips of vacant land that line both sides of the canals. Figure 4.3 displays a moderately priced subdivision walled off from the lower-value housing across the street. The combination of canals and fences is often visually startling; the high walls of Phoenix's subdivisions demarcate neighborhoods according to housing values that are al-

FIGURE 4.2.   Canals and Vacant Land in Phoenix

FIGURE 4.3.   Walls and Income Classes in Peoria, Arizona

most invariably promoted by developers as Community Residential Associations, or gated communities.[19] In the instances in which high
walls separate income classes, vacant land often does not serve to segregate. The segregation function has already been performed by the
narrow housing-value variation in gated communities. Nevertheless,
the demand to ensure property value protection or enhancement of
those gated communities pushes conversion of vacant land into park
space or open space.

Cities take action designed to influence their settlement structures by
deliberately setting aside land for open space, green space, and park
space. Open spaces—often thought of as influencing the "physical
landscape" of cities—often contribute to forming the "social landscape" as well. In effect, open spaces can protect and enhance adjacent property values. A land use and income map from the Tempe
area of Maricopa County, Arizona (figure 4.4), illustrates the importance of canals, railroads, and public parks (open spaces) in separating
income classes. The public park in the center of the map parallels the
canal and acts as a natural barrier between the higher-income residents to the east of the park and the lower-income residents to the
west. Because the census tract includes properties on both sides of the
park, the stark visual difference between the two communities is not
well illustrated in figure 4.4. Suffice it to say that the average per capita income on the east side of the park is substantially higher than
that on the west side.

Further, the western parcels are separated by three important barriers: railroad tracks, the canal, and the park. The triangular-shaped lot
in the center of the map is an industrial concern, separated from the

FIGURE 4.4. Fences and Canals in Tempe, Maricopa County, Arizona, 1998

higher-income neighborhoods by both the park and the canal. Both establish a distinct and impenetrable boundary preventing the industrial firm from expanding eastward. As such, the remaining parcels of vacant land west of the canal and railroad tracks are not likely to be considered candidates for creating social barriers. Rather, their use or reuse will conform to more traditional conventions of residential housing, albeit low- to moderate-income housing, and possibly industrial use, in particular the adjacent vacant land to the west of the industrial firm.

The three maps that follow are of Philadelphia and its census tracts. The city's boundaries are outlined in black and bounded on the east by the Delaware River. Figures 4.5 and 4.6 are coded so that each dot rep-

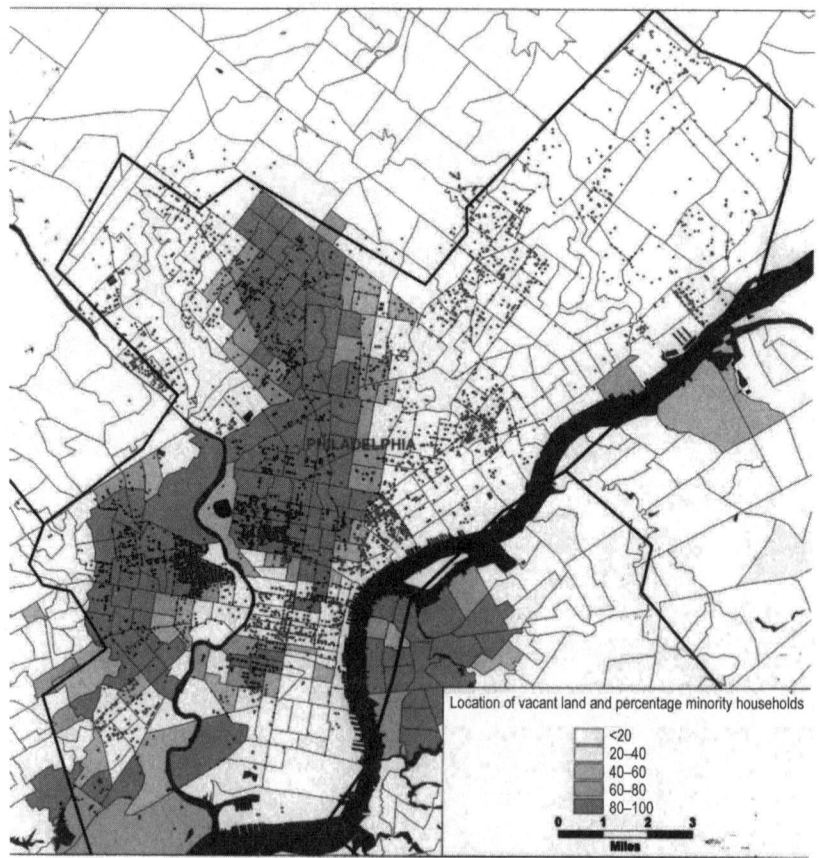

FIGURE 4.5. Vacant Parcels and Minority Households, Philadelphia, 1999

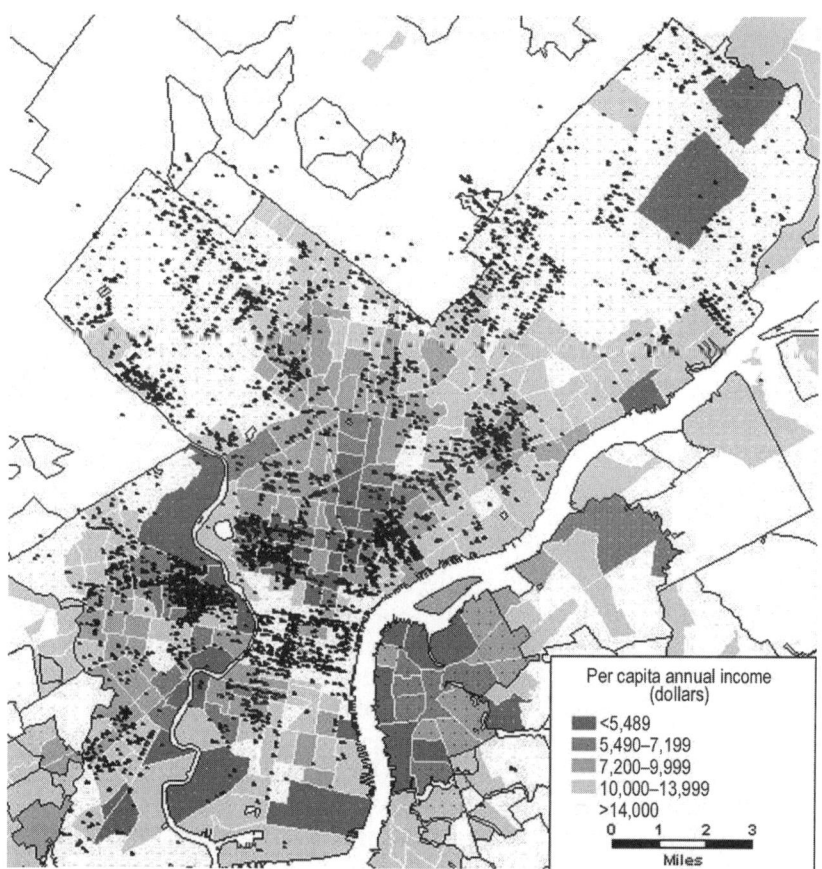

FIGURE 4.6. Vacant Parcels and Per Capita Income, Philadelphia, 1999

resents a vacant parcel, of which there were more than 31,000 in 1999 (of the more than 600,000 total parcels in the city). In the western and central sections of the city, the dots are so numerous (i.e., the vacant lots so prevalent) that it seems that an Impressionist artist's paintbrush was at work. Figure 4.5 maps the location of the city's vacant lots and the percentage of minority households by census tract. A look at the map shows that although vacant lots are found throughout the city of Philadelphia, tracts with high percentages of minority households appear to be especially hard hit. In those communities, vacant land is not an occasional parcel but, instead, nearly an uninterrupted series.

The map in figure 4.6 displays vacant lots and per capita income by census tract. The pattern suggests that most of the vacant lots in

Philadelphia are found in tracts with lower per capita income. However, there is a considerable number of vacant lots in high-income areas in the center of the city. To the west of the Schuylkill River (the westernmost river in the city), the cluster of dots reflects a university student sector of the city where little income is reported, even if the wealth is much more substantial. The narrow neck of the city between the two rivers is the central city, which has a higher per capita income than the neighborhoods to the south or to the north. Vacant lots in the city's central business district hold substantial market value. Nearly all the remaining dots on the map refer to vacant lots with values under $2,000, and in some cases, the values are much less. To the north and to the northeast of the central business district are some of the city's poorest residential neighborhoods, where vacancy stretches for blocks, as in the Kensington area of the city.

Figure 4.7 offers a different view of the distribution of vacant land and income levels. The map scales the market value of the city's vacant lots and plots them within the coded census tracts reflecting gradations of per capita income. The smaller dots on this map denote, in most cases, vacant lots in residential areas, often resulting from razed row house structures. Clusters of such low-valued (and small) vacant lots appear to the north of the darker shaded areas and to the west. As was noted above, the area immediately north of the central business district is home to some of the poorest families in the city, whereas, to the west, is the city's university section. The larger dark squares in the central city denote high-valued vacant land in areas zoned for commercial use, which in many cases is being reused and the area revitalized.

Vacant Land and Preserving Value

The abandonment of a structure, whether residential or commercial, disrupts a neighborhood. If other abandonment follows, the neighborhood's character changes commensurately. The area may survive in its new form and function, but the built environment no longer represents its past. The past exists only in memory. Dolores Hayden refers to "the power of place," which she defines as the power of ordinary urban landscapes to nurture citizens' public memory, to encompass shared time in the form of shared territory."[20]

Abandoned structures rob an area of its past, giving a neighborhood a forlorn look, a sense of neglect. Blighted areas eventually become targets of the wrecking ball, and the demolition sweeps away the history of a place, its social history as well as its architectural past. The cultural landscape, and often the natural landscape, is obscured. Hayden argues

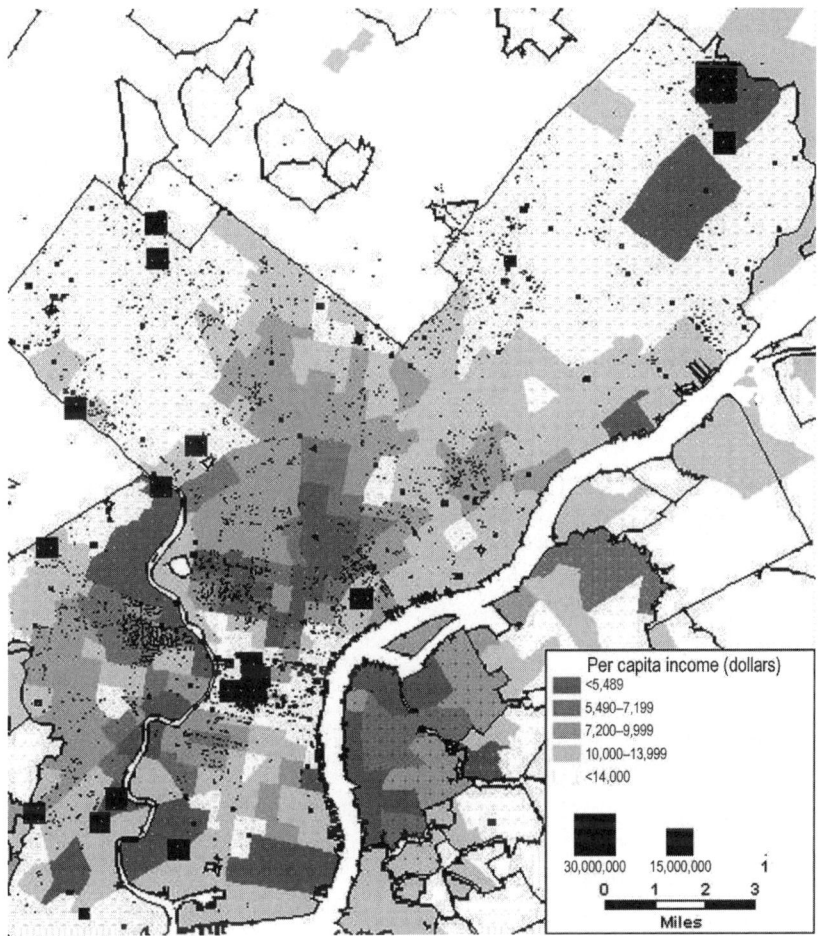

FIGURE 4.7. The Value of Vacant Land and Per Capita Income, Philadelphia, 1999

for preserving traces of the ordinary landscape to provide a truer picture of the past. In instances in which vacant sites now mask what had been important structures, she suggests creating new public art or open space designs to commemorate the past.

Philadelphia's City Mural Arts program does some of what Hayden has called for. The program funds the painting of murals on the sides of structures that have become exposed due to an adjacent abandoned lot. Professor Lilly Yeh of the University of the Arts has been instrumental in creating murals and in placing artwork in North Philadelphia vacant lots. (Figure 4.8 provides an eye-catching example of the work done through the Mural Arts program.) The expectation by city officials is that the Mural Arts program will send a signal to neighbors and potential in-migrants that the residents care about the cleanliness and safety of their neighborhood. Property values will stabilize, neighbors might be encouraged to invest not only in their own homes but also in adjacent side yards, and neighborhoods will enjoy increased security. Indeed, the Mural Arts program, together with the Pennsylvania Horticultural Society's urban garden program, have been designed in the hope of preserving communities and neighborhoods. But property values must be stabilized for the projects to be successful.

Squatters and Abandoned Structures

One of the social issues embedded in the vacant land and abandoned structures situation is the presence of squatters. Detroit offers one of the most extreme cases. There are more than 40,000 parcels owned by the city of Detroit—many of them vacant lots and unoccupied buildings.[21] By all accounts, the management of these parcels is a nightmare for the city. Particularly troublesome are the nearly 3,000 city-owned buildings occupied by squatters. Some of squatters lost their homes through tax foreclosure but never moved out of them; others broke into nominally secured buildings. Some of the squatters pay rent to bogus landlords who present themselves as lawful own-

FIGURE 4.8.   An Example from Philadelphia's City Mural Arts Program

ers. Conditions are squalid in many of the occupied buildings, due to a lack of running water and electricity.

However, because of a City Council–imposed moratorium on most evictions,[22] officials have had only limited success in dealing with the problem. In the meantime, some advocates for poor people defend squatting, contending that it meets a social need. Detroit has an estimated 5,300 homeless people, and evicting squatters would likely put more people on the streets. In 2000, officials in Detroit's Planning Department launched an amnesty sales program, in which they gave squatters an opportunity to purchase city-owned property. To provide an incentive to purchase, the department had hoped to convince the City Council to reconsider its moratorium on evictions.

Few cities face the magnitude of the Detroit situation, but the issue remains salient for them as well. Should squatting be legitimized? Would cities be well served to convert some of the unoccupied structures they own into homeless shelters? Answering these questions requires rethinking the social imperative, with its emphasis on minimizing disruption and protecting property values. Perhaps when applied to vacant land and abandoned structures, the social imperative can be stretched to cover broader conceptions of social benefit.

INFILLING AS A SOCIAL STRATEGY

Infill serves both revenue and development imperatives, but it also may serve the social imperative. Even as many central cities have lost population relative to the larger metropolitan area, many downtowns have begun to experience residential growth. In three-quarters of the twenty-four cities studied by Rebecca Sohmer and Robert Lang, the downtown population increased during the 1990s.[23] Cities as diverse as Boston, Chicago, Denver, Los Angeles, and Memphis had repopulating downtowns. The downtown area growth is attributable to a number of factors, including demographics (e.g., the number of empty nesters and young professionals), distinctiveness (e.g., its history and style offer a sense of place), and geography (e.g., its central location).[24]

This increase in habitation has been fueled in most instances by infilling. The process of infilling, which is often supported through official city programs, involves converting vacant or underutilized land into housing.[25] The infill results in more efficient utilization of infrastructure and increased population density and thus is valued for its antisprawl effects. But infill programs also may have another effect: increases in the number of white residents in the area. Although the 1990–2000 pattern in most large U.S. cities was a loss of white population, in at least some cities the downtown area bucked the trend.[26] All told, the twenty-four downtowns in the Sohmer and Lang study increased their white population by 7.5 percent, compared with 1990. The numbers of Hispanics and blacks residing in the downtown area also increased, respectively by 4.8 and 6 percent. What makes the downtown pattern notable is that, overall, these same cities contained 10.5 percent fewer whites than they had in 1990 but 43 percent more Hispanics and 2.4 percent more blacks.

The relative position of the downtown area in Philadelphia, Phoenix, and Seattle varies dramatically. In Seattle from 1990 to 2000, the population in both the downtown and the city itself grew, although downtown's growth pace was much more robust (67 to 9 percent). In Philadelphia during the same period, population outflow occurred (-4.3 percent), but the downtown area actually grew (4.9 percent). Phoenix experienced the reverse situation: The city's population increased substantially (34.4 percent), but the downtown area suffered a loss (-9.1 percent). Thus in these three cities, downtown leads the larger growth trend (Seattle), it emerges as a growth node amid decline elsewhere in the city (Philadelphia), and it fails to hold its own even as the city grows (Phoenix).

Phoenix's Infill

In an effort to slow the downtown population exodus, Phoenix created an aggressive infill housing program in 1995. The goals of the program are straightforward:

- to encourage development of vacant or underutilized land located in the mature central portions of Phoenix;
- to encourage a wide variety of housing styles, types, and price ranges, appropriate to the surrounding neighborhoods; and
- to encourage and focus on owner-occupied housing to help fight blight and decay within the central city and promote neighborhood stability through home ownership.[27]

Developers of infill housing qualify for a series of incentives, including expedited review of plans, mitigation of "red tape," and granting of financial sweeteners such as fee waivers. But the infill program applies only to single-family residential projects, not to multifamily or commercial development. And only certain areas of the city are part of the infill area—although, over time, political exigencies have expanded the boundaries such that nearly every city council district contains some qualifying property.

Although its revenue and development components make the infill program attractive to the city, some of its aspects, such as the construction of affordable housing, also give it a social dimension. Some of the infill projects have been located in revitalization areas; although much of the housing is market rate, some is subsidized. Yet there are barriers to infill beyond simple economic factors such as higher development costs and greater market risk. In Phoenix in the mid-1990s, large portions of the infill area were plagued by high levels of anxiety about crime. The problem was particularly severe in the city's downtown. In addition to crime and the perception of crime, concerns over the quality of nearby schools and the presence of homeless people limited the appeal of infill.

One of the areas singled out for revitalization is a 3-square-mile section in South Phoenix known as Target Area B (TAB). With approximately 14,000 residents, the median household income in TAB is half of the citywide median, and its percentage of households living below the poverty level is three times the citywide figure.[28] Nearly 30 percent of TAB land is vacant, down from 37 percent in 1978. Much of the vacant land is in small parcels scattered throughout TAB, which, along with blighting conditions such as illegal dumping and junked automobiles, limits its development. By 1990, the city owned eighteen vacant parcels in TAB, most of them in areas zoned for commercial uses.

In 1993, the city advertised all eighteen properties for sale, but there was no interest in them, primarily due to the negative perception of the area and the availability of property in other, less troublesome areas. By 1996, Phoenix had channeled more than $25 million into the revitalization of TAB, and some of the available properties began to turn over. The intent, of course, is that the development of city-owned vacant land will stimulate additional investment. To achieve that objective, the city redoubled its blight elimination and code enforcement efforts in TAB.

Seattle's Densification

Seattle's housing concerns and infill strategies are qualitatively different from Phoenix's. Unlike Phoenix, Seattle has no (or very little) possibility of annexing additional land. From only 80,671 in 1900, Seattle's population surged to 315,312 by 1920 and, during that rapid-growth period, the city annexed ten major areas. The last series of annexations occurred in the early 1950s, when Seattle's population pushed over the half-million mark.[29] Population growth began to slow during the 1960s, as Seattle's borders were frozen and the economy softened. After the precipitous downturn in the aerospace industry in 1970–71, when Boeing laid off two-thirds of its 100,000-employee workforce and the population dipped under a half-million, the city began to regain its economic health in the late 1970s.

By 1997, the region was in the throes of a lengthy and sustained economic expansionary period. Population growth by 1997 had recouped the losses of the previous three decades, reaching 536,600, and the unemployment rate had fallen to about 3 percent. The total number of jobs in Seattle surged 21 percent in the 1980s, reaching 469,802 in 1990. The city expects to have more than 600,000 jobs by 2010, with high-technology industries as the fastest growth sector.[30] The city's population grew at a somewhat slower rate of 4.5 percent in the 1980s (from 493,000 in 1980 to 516,000 in 1990), indicating that much of the employment growth was taking place outside the city. The Puget Sound Regional Council (PSRC) projects that by 2010 Seattle's population will be just shy of 600,000.

Seattle's Department of Human Services estimated that the median family income required to make monthly payments for a housing mortgage fell short of the median housing price by more than $10,000 in 1990 (what the city calls the "financial gap"), compared with a positive gap of more than $3,000 in 1960.[31] The city's measure of housing needs showed that 30.2 percent of all city households were paying more than 30 percent of their income for housing. In the city's 1998 update to its comprehensive plan, it was reported that the value of the average house had increased by 850 percent since 1970, while household income had increased nearly 500 percent. The area's increased housing prices are partially attributable to Washington's Growth Management Act (GMA), a statute approved in 1990 and amended several times since then. Under GMA, an "urban growth boundary" was established around the urbanized area of King County, restricting the amount of developable land and protecting farmland and other unused land outside the boundary from further development.

GMA requires the adoption of local and countywide growth management policies, plans and regulations, the identification of urban growth areas, and concurrent planning for growth and infrastructure. The purposes of GMA include reducing sprawl, managing urban growth by reinforcing existing centers of activity, maintaining the current urban service structure, and encouraging efficient transportation systems.[32] King County adopted its plan in 1993, and together with the several counties surrounding it developed "VISION 2020" through the PSRC.

Counties and regions were required by GMA to create urban growth areas, or boundaries beyond which urban growth would be discouraged and "outside of which rural character will be maintained."[33] In King County, within which Seattle is located, the urban growth area in 1997 encompassed more than 461 square miles—the equivalent of only 21.6 percent of the county's landmass but more than 90 percent of its population.[34]

GMA mandated that a Countywide Planning Policy (CPP) set twenty-year growth targets for households and jobs. The CPP for King County created twelve "urban centers" (UCs), for which higher growth targets were established as a means of encouraging and concentrating growth.[35] Five UCs were designated in the city of Seattle. One, on the city's north side, called Northgate, centers on a large shopping mall, whereas the second, the University District, encompasses the area surrounding the University of Washington. The third UC is the First Hill–Capitol Hill area, which is adjacent to Seattle's central business district and houses a rapidly growing health services industry. The fourth UC is Seattle Center, which is next to and north of the central business district and prominently features the Space Needle at its core. Finally, Downtown Seattle is the fifth UC.

Downtown Seattle is by far the dominant UC in population and jobs. In 1998, the Downtown UC had 12,193 residents, with an expected increase of another 27,000 by 2020; the number of jobs was 163,000, and VISION 2020 projected another 62,000 jobs by 2020.[36] The First Hill–Capitol Hill UC, with 28,975 residents, is the second most populous UC, and plans call for an increase in its population to nearly 36,000 by 2020. The downtowns of nearby Redmond and Bellevue are also UCs, along with five others in King County, bringing the total in the four-county PSRC planning area to twenty-one.

The four-county region's UCs make up only 2 percent of the regional population but employ 29.7 percent of the urban growth area's workforce. The regional plan, VISION 2020, forecasts that by 2020, 8 percent of the population will reside in UCs that will contain 31.8 percent of the jobs. As a consequence of GMA and in-migration, the city's (and metropolitan area's) population has "densified" and will continue to do so. The PSRC forecasts increased population density in all twenty-one designated UCs in the Seattle metropolitan area by 2020.[37]

Increased densification is one of GMA's intended effects. The City of Seattle has also identified a subset of UCs, called urban villages, in which densification is also encouraged. Higher land prices in the UCs and urban villages has led to a housing affordability problem in Seattle and a premium on open space. Mayor Paul Shell's campaign strategy in

1997 focused in large part on the affordable housing issue. Blaming spiraling housing costs on limited supply, he advocated "mother-in-law apartments," expanding mixed-used structures such as multifamily apartments with retailing on the first floor, and smaller houses.[38] In a word, his was a clarion call for densification.

The Washington Center for Real Estate Research estimated that in 1997, 5.5 percent of Seattle's housing was priced at under $80,000.[39] Extreme housing pressures and a limited supply of vacant land has meant that land parcels once considered too steep to build on are being accommodated. One official referred to GMA's impact as "shoehorning people into the city!" Housing officials label low-income and low- to moderate-income housing as the "pressure point" in Seattle's political landscape. The result is that what might have remained vacant land in some cities has been turned into affordable housing in Seattle. For example, when the state failed to use all of the land it had purchased for a large interchange on Interstate 90, it deeded it to the city, and the city built affordable housing on the site.

These market pressures on land and housing benefit both developers and the city. Developers benefit because they can increase rents (average rents rose 9 percent between March 1997 and March 1998[40]); they also benefit because of Seattle's "density bonus" programs. Bonuses are offered to developers to provide not only low-income housing, but also two other items that get squeezed out in high-demand land markets: open space and historic structure preservation. Density bonuses come in the following forms. First, developers can increase the densification of multifamily dwellings if they are located in a mixed-use zoned area. The concession they make is that the first floor of these structures must be retail space. Second, developers can increase their floor-to-area ratio if, in exchange, they contribute to a low-income housing program, create open space, or contribute to historic preservation. Although not revenue generators, these density bonuses enhance the city's image of itself as a place that cares about its residents, its natural resources, and its history.

Developers are also granted the opportunity of using the transfer of development rights (TDR) between one site and another, thereby increasing density at a preferred location and preserving open space elsewhere.[41] TDR, which has been allowed since 1985, entails transferring unused buildable floor area to a "receiving area" to increase density at another site. The city's use of TDR during the high-growth period has preserved some low-income or affordable housing by allowing developers to build taller office structures in exchange for maintaining existing multifamily structures. The city estimated that TDR preserved 156 low-income housing units between 1985 and 1987 and another 181 units between 1991 and 1993.

Seattle does not have the redevelopment authority to condemn a part of the city, raze the structures, and redevelop the area. Rather, the primary development incentive is the market. Under a 1998 ordinance, the city can encourage more affordable housing by offering property tax abatement, but only for multifamily housing in nine target neighborhoods. The purpose, besides increasing the supply of multifamily housing for low- and moderate-income families, includes the "rehabilitation of existing vacant and underutilized buildings for multi-family housing."[42] The city's new tax abatement policy, then, is further recognition of the insufficient supply of affordable multifamily housing. The effect, then, is to increase residential density in those designated neighborhoods.

The city has considered relaxing its regulations on accessory dwelling units (ADUs), popularly known as mother-in-law apartments, to spur their use. Opponents of relaxing ADU rules argue that it would result in converting homes into duplexes and increasing absentee ownership, which would cause the quality of neighborhoods to deteriorate. Also, Seattle's rate of home ownership is at or near the top among large U.S. cities. Speculation would accelerate land and housing price increases at a faster rate, thereby reducing the affordability of housing for residents. Home ownership would consequently decline.

Thus in Seattle, a growing economy, a limited supply of vacant land, and GMA's strictures—along with the commitment of local officials—have combined to make densification the outcome for the foreseeable future.

Philadelphia's Density Question

The population exodus experienced by many older central cities has brought about a lower population density. Some cities are attempting to make the trend of "fewer people per square mile" work to their advantage. Low-density housing developments—such as Charlotte Gardens in New York City's South Bronx and Victoria Park in Detroit—run counter to infill strategies and have been criticized for "suburbanizing" the inner city.[43] Ignoring the critics, Philadelphia's housing officials have embarked upon a conscious de-densifying policy. In some neighborhoods targeted for redevelopment, ten dwelling units per acre have been built to replace the previous standard of twenty to thirty-five units per acre. According to planners, de-densification is a promising approach to Philadelphia's vacant land problems.

If the promotion of densification was an objective of GMA in Washington State, the postwar history of Philadelphia tells a different tale. In 1950, Philadelphia had more than 2 million people and almost 300,000 manufacturing jobs; less than half a century later, the population had slipped to under 1.5 million and manufacturing employment had decreased to 50,000. The deindustrialization of cities hit the old manufacturing centers hardest, but in Philadelphia the decline in employment was felt in all sectors. The city's Office of Housing and Community Development (OHCD) reported that between 1969 and 1994, total employment in Philadelphia plunged nearly a quarter-million jobs, from 950,000 to under 700,000.[44] With population and job loss came housing abandonment. By the mid-1990s, more than 27,000 houses were vacant and abandoned, and nearly two-thirds of those were in such dilapidated and dangerous condition that demolition was the only appropriate action.[45] But, according to OHCD, the city's budget could handle only 1,500 per year, thus leaving most of the structures "standing."

The city's approach to the effects of housing abandonment is essentially twofold: (1) Encourage rehabilitation of deteriorating housing stock; and (2) encourage demolition, community gardens, and side yards. The latter policy has resulted in increased vacant land and decreased density. In part, this strategy is influenced by two factors. First, the city no longer depends financially on property tax revenues. Consequently, the forgone property tax revenue is minuscule from land that no longer has a taxable structure on it (assuming the property was not tax delinquent in the first place). Moreover, the costs of protecting the health and safety of the neighbors often exceed the tax value of the structure.

The second factor is that the visual image of boarded-up and dilapidated structures, even if the housing is potentially valuable and reparable, is certainly less attractive than a community garden or a narrow side yard between two row houses on the street. The side yard garden depicted in figure 4.9 replaced what had become a litter-choked eyesore. The garden (secured by a fence) is credited with stabilizing this portion of the neighborhood. Razing abandoned structures for gardens and side yards, as one city planner noted, "will encourage reinvestment in the area . . . expansion, investor confidence, banker confidence." In other words, the charge is to de-densify the city, change the look and feel of the neighborhoods, and create vacant land to preserve the integrity of the neighborhoods and augment property values. In some parts of the city, entire neighborhoods are being refashioned into suburban-looking areas. Lawns, curved and tree-lined streets, and automobile-friendly designs have replaced high-density housing.[46] Increased sup-

FIGURE 4.9. A Side Yard in Philadelphia

plies of vacant land make de-densification a plausible strategy for Philadelphia that may contribute to a revival of the city.

VACANT LAND AS OPEN SPACE

Public space supports life. It provides the common ground where members of a community interact. In the words of Stephen Carr and his colleagues, it "is the stage upon which the drama of communal life unfolds."[47] Vacant land often becomes public space, informally as a result of usage,[48] or formally, as a result of designation. Vacant land, if accessible, may become a favorite gathering spot or a preferred shortcut through an area. Private landowners, wishing to restrict access to their property for a variety of reasons including liability, often fence off the vacant parcel. Most cities have policies that require owners to do so; failure to secure the parcel may result in governmental action, such as fencing the property and levying a fine against the owner.

In some cities, joint efforts by local government and developers have reclaimed moribund industrial waterfronts for public access. The festive marketplaces of Boston and Baltimore were among the first to undergo such a conversion. Abandoned structures were razed (although some of the historic buildings were adapted for reuse), and events were scheduled to attract people to the redeveloped area. Although the most successful redeveloped waterfronts end up with much retail activity, a major component in the formula is the presence of public space.

The rationale for creating public space is multifaceted, including economic development and environmental enhancement, but public welfare is a primary motivation. Public space should be meaningful to those who use it and responsive to their needs. For people living in cramped dwellings or for the homeless, public spaces become places for recreation and socialization.[49] Thus class-based patterns of use may emerge, and control issues may arise. Control issues in some cities have led to restrictions on public access, with the installation of high fences and lockable gates.

There is a de facto alternative to management of vacant land by governments, nonprofit organizations, and for-profit firms: community open space. Local residents may take over a vacant lot and develop it as a passive park or community garden, thus taking responsibility for the ongoing management or stewardship of the land. This can be an opportunity for grassroots democracy to flourish. "These community-controlled projects have become permanent parts of the open spaces of neighborhoods, forming an alternative park system designed, built, managed, and owned by those who use them."[50]

One of the central issues in community-controlled open space is ownership. Many abandoned properties sit idle because of complications related to ownership. The title may not be clear, and the city may be cautious about intervention. Into the ownership void slips a community group, often an informal neighborhood association. By sprucing up the lot, and perhaps transforming it into a passive park or garden, the organization gains a claim on the property. In the absence of market pressures, the organization may become the de facto owner of the lot, at least temporarily.

For years, New York City allowed interested neighborhood groups to maintain city-owned vacant lots as parks and gardens. But in 2000, when the city sought to reclaim those lots for development purposes, it encountered stiff resistance from the groups, which had come to consider the lots their own. Mayor Rudolph Giuliani and the City Council found themselves in a political imbroglio, which was resolved through a series of concessions to the affected neighborhoods. Vacant land as a community asset was never more obvious.

Open Space Protection in Bucks County, Pennsylvania

One suburban Philadelphia county has taken up the cause of open space protection through farmland preservation. In 1950, 66 percent of Bucks County's land was in farming; by 1990, the farmland figure had dropped below 20 percent. Many of the county's agricultural areas were being converted to subdivisions and strip malls. Local officials—alarmed not only by the pace of change but also by its direction—turned to Pennsylvania's Agricultural Land Preservation Program for relief. The state program allows a county to acquire agricultural conservation easements to protect viable agricultural lands from development. By 1999, Bucks County had preserved thirty-six farms totaling 3,213 acres of farmland. The goal is to reach 10,000 protected acres by 2007.

In a related move, Bucks County voters approved an open space preservation bond (ten years, $59 million) in 1997. The bond supports the preservation of farmland, the provision of park and recreation areas, and the protection of unique natural and environmental features in the county. The plan has several elements, but three of its central purposes are

- to recognize the value of significant open land and natural resources to the quality of life in Bucks County;
- to preserve farms in perpetuity by maximizing the county's use of the Pennsylvania Agricultural Land Preservation Program to purchase farmland easements; and
- to preserve a system of greenways, parks, trails, natural areas, scenic roads, and landscapes.[51]

The county works in partnership with fifty-four municipal governments in developing open space plans and in providing grants for land acquisition. Although the transformation of farmland to residential and commercial uses continues, the pace has slowed enough to give open space advocates cause for celebration.

Open Space Acquisition and Preservation in Phoenix

The city of Phoenix offers an interesting case, but not only because of its immense size (470 square miles as of 1998) and population growth rate (34.3 percent from 1990 [983,403] to 2000 [1,321,045]). Two other characteristics make the city worthy of note: its early commitment to open space and its use of Arizona state trust lands. Phoenix has a long tradition of open space acquisition and preservation. In 1925, the city purchased 13,000 acres of mountainous desert to create South Mountain Park. Now 16,500 acres, it is the nation's largest municipal park.[52] The acquisition of other large tracts of land has brought 27,000 acres of mountain preserves and desert parks under the city's control.

By 1998, the city had made plans to purchase relatively undisturbed desert land in the northern part of the city in an effort to preserve "our most unique asset, the Sonoran Desert."[53] There were many rationales supporting acquisition, including the expected increase in real property values near the open space, the positive impact on the tourism industry, and the provision of more recreational opportunities. However, one of the other items among the list of benefits was distinctive: the sociocultural aspect of the desert preserve. According to the city's plan:

> All citizens and visitors would benefit from a better historical awareness and appreciation of our own and past cultures of the Sonoran Desert. A desert preserve would provide opportunities for improved family cohesion through outdoor recreational activities and education programs. With carefully researched information comprehensively presented in programs and interpretive exhibits, the Sonoran Preserve has the potential for increasing pride in our local culture.[54]

The city's land acquisition goal is large, even by Phoenix standards: 21,000 acres. One factor that makes such a large acquisition conceivable is that 75 percent of the Sonoran Preserve Plan lands are Arizona State Trust Lands, owned by the Arizona State Land Department. By law, trust land can be sold only when the state's land commissioner designates it for sale, and it then must be sold or leased at market value, based on highest and best use. Under the Arizona Preserve Initiative, one of the designations for land disposition is conservation land. This facilitates the city's acquisition of the land. Figure 4.10 shows the distribution of state trust lands in the vicinity of the Sonoran Preserve. Immediately apparent is the vast expanse of land in metropolitan Phoenix still under the control of the State Land Department.

Three different concepts for the Sonoran Preserve were submitted for public review. One set out a concentrated concept that would cluster the preserve in a large contiguous parcel to create a regional park. Another offered a dispersed concept in which the preserve would be integrated into developed areas, thus providing greater access for users from their homes or workplaces. The semiconcentrated concept sought to blend the other two: Some areas would be set aside for conservation, while others would be accessible from adjacent developments. Regardless of the concept implemented, acquisition of land would be staged, and occur through fee-simple purchase and TDR. The city has a number of financing options available, including bonds, dedicated sales taxes, and desert preservation impact and infrastructure fees. In addi-

FIGURE 4.10. Arizona State Trust Lands near the Sonoran Preserve
Source: J. Burke and J. M. Ewan, *Sonoran Preserve Master Plan* (Tempe, Ariz.:
CAED Herberger Center for Design Excellence, 1998). Reprinted by permission of
J. Burke and J. M. Ewan.

tion, the city can pursue grants, fund raising, land exchanges, and do
nations as supplemental funding sources.

Although some of the land is designated for recreational use and environmental education, much of it is preserved as open space. Vast sections of the Sonoran Preserve leave the raw desert essentially undisturbed, with the vegetation and wildlife that it currently sustains.

Parkland as Open Space in Bellevue, Washington

Open space issues are highly salient in the city of Bellevue, Washington.
A negligible supply of vacant land, along with limited opportunities for
annexation and the pressures of the state's Growth Management Act,

makes the efficient use of land a central issue. The city has pursued the acquisition of parkland as one means of maintaining an adequate supply of open space. As a longtime official of the city's Parks and Community Services Department explained: "You can't rely on zoning to protect open space. It's only safe until the next election. Ownership is the answer."

Bellevue has embraced that philosophy wholeheartedly. By the late 1990s, approximately 10 percent of the city's parceled area was parkland. The approach is simple: Buy the open space; develop it in phases. Establishing trailheads and putting trails through the newly acquired land is an important step because it will bring people to the park. Additionally, connecting parks through a series of greenways, wildlife corridors, and trails is a long-term objective in the city's open space plan. As the plan states, "In the Pacific Northwest our cultural heritage is not embodied in cathedrals or museums, but in mountains, streams, lakes, forests, and views of these and other natural amenities."[55] Thus the city's open space plan refers to the need "to steward those open spaces and environmentally sensitive areas that characterize the unique natural system within our community."[56]

Figure 4.11 illustrates the natural beauty of Bellevue. The hillside park in the photograph is primarily vertical, with a pathway leading

FIGURE 4.11. The View from a Park in Bellevue, Washington

down to Lake Washington. The city has actively acquired land to assure public ownership of a sufficient natural resource base. And though some of the rationale for open space protection in Bellevue is driven by a land ethic akin to that of conservationist Aldo Leopold,[57] the rationale is not simply "parks for parks sake." A more instrumental "parks for people" intent exists as well.

Community Gardens on Vacant Land

In Philadelphia, an effort is under way to recast vacant land as a resource, as something with social benefit. Philadelphia, after all, is a city in which vacant parcels and abandoned buildings number in the tens of thousands. The Pennsylvania Horticultural Society (PHS) is one of the leaders in the "rethinking vacant land" movement:

> Instead of a blighting influence, vacant land can become an urban amenity. It can be converted into parks, community gardens, recreation areas, private yards, "commons" for new housing developments, managed fields, off-street parking, and other public open space. Vacant land can be incorporated into the fabric of neighborhoods, allowing city residents to enjoy the lower-density lifestyles sought by migrants to the suburbs.[58]

PHS operates several programs for vacant land renewal under its umbrella project, Philadelphia Green. Philadelphia Green has several facets, including a concentrated greening program known as Greene Countrie Townes. Its intent is more than simply converting vacant lots into community gardens. It is a multiyear effort that targets neighborhoods with greening projects in the hopes of awakening community spirit and commitment. Quite purposefully, greening has become a vehicle for community organizing. One of the transformational gardens in Philadelphia is shown in figure 4.12. As Jane Schukoske put it, "Community gardens build social capital not only by reclaiming or preserving urban space, but also by fostering collaboration among nearby residents across racial and generational lines."[59]

Philadelphia's program is similar to those in other cities. In the 1980s, Boston's Dudley Street neighborhood contained the highest concentration of vacant land in the city, 21 percent of all property. Since then, the area has undergone dramatic improvement, sparked by the creation of a community land trust to manage the vacant land. Gardening as a use for vacant land has become almost commonplace. Atlanta has its Community Gardening Initiative, Chicago has established Greencorps, and New York operates a Green Thumb program.

FIGURE 4.12. A Community Garden in Philadelphia

Estimates place the number of community gardening programs at more than 350 nationwide.[60]

The success of community gardens in stabilizing neighborhoods has, ironically, threatened their survival. As an area becomes more attractive for investment, community gardens located on unused public land become more vulnerable to development pressures. For example, in 2002, New York City announced plans to sell 131 gardens for development as affordable housing sites.[61] The resultant outcry from community activists and gardeners shelved the proposal—at least until city officials could devise a more acceptable alternative. In the meantime, a group intent on preserving the lots as gardens, the Trust for Public Land, raised sufficient funds to purchase several of them. The argument for their preservation was not simply the flowers and vegetables grown in the gardens but also the social connections created by their presence.

Perhaps the most interesting case of vacant land qua natural resource comes from New York City. An elevated railroad track that had been unused since the 1970s, known as the High Line, has undergone a natural transformation into weeds, grasses, bushes, and even a few small trees. Running for about 1.3 miles and about two stories high, this abandoned track offers a most unusual type of open space. Valued by some for its potential development as a midair park, perhaps as part of the national Rails to Trails system, it is valued by others in its natural state. As one of the High Line's devotees commented, "This is what spring in New York actually looks like when it's left up to Spring."[62]

CONCLUSION

Kevin Lynch's research on the images that residents hold of their city environments—their mental maps of the city—revealed an interesting twist.[63] Amid the recognizable districts, landmarks, and paths that people readily recalled were areas—sometimes large areas—that were simply unknown. Certain parts of Boston, for example, such as a region between the Back Bay and the South End, were a blank to Bostonians. In actuality, these areas were not vacant. But in the minds of those interviewed, they were unknown. In some instances, the absence of these areas from mental maps resulted from physical barriers, such as railroad tracks, that made knowing them difficult. In other cases, their disappearance was more perceptual. Regardless, some areas were, in a sense, virtual vacant land.

Real, tangible vacant land can serve a catalyst for achieving a vision, for building a city.[64] Usually, this involves the development process. But in many instances, there is a social component. A city may opt for a green wall: Create a park on vacant land separating a declining area of the city from a more prosperous section. Or the city may pursue a green magnet strategy: Purchase a small vacant lot in the downtown area to build a courtyard where people can interact. In both instances, the city is using vacant land to achieve a social objective. And though the social imperative may often take a back seat to the financial imperative when city officials make choices about vacant land, the illustrative data in this chapter suggest that the social imperative is at least operational, and in some instances dominant.

Vacant land often comes in small parcels, with shapes that weaken its development potential. In many downtown areas, these remnant parcels are scattered across different blocks, adjacent to retail stores, restaurants, and office buildings. In some cities, these leftover parcels have been joined with service alleys to create interconnected passageways and gallerias. The immediate effect is the transformation of a disorganized area into a series of coherent, pleasing spaces. Positive social benefits often result, such as an increased sense of personal safety and greater opportunities for interaction. Frequently, efforts to revitalize an area through new development are less than successful because they do not integrate the project with its environment. Detroit's Renaissance Center, isolated from its surroundings, was a powerful symbol of distance—and dissonance. Although it rose up from vacant land, it did not connect to adjacent areas. That does not have to be the case, however.

Vacant land can be the means of linking new development to the urban milieu, both physically and mentally. This is a subject to which we turn in chapter 5.

NOTES

1. Their preservation as natural resources is an indirect developmental asset.
2. Charles Tiebout, "A Pure Theory of Public Expenditures," *Journal of Political Economy* 64 (October 1956): 416–24. See, inter alia, Vincent Ostrom, Charles Tiebout, and Robert Warren, "The Organization of Government in Metropolitan Areas," *American Political Science Review* 55 (1961): 835–42; Wallace Oates and Robert Schwab, "Economic Competition among Jurisdictions," *Journal of Public Economics* 35 (April 1988): 333–54; Robert Stein, "Tiebout's Sorting Hypothesis," *Urban Affairs Quarterly* 23 (1987): 140–60; Kenneth Bickers and Robert Stein, "The Microfoundations of the Tiebout Model," *Urban Affairs Review* 34 (September 1998): 76–93; Christine Kelleher and David Lowery, "Tiebout Sorting and Selective Satisfaction with Urban Public Services: Testing the Variance Hypothesis," *Urban Affairs Review* 37 (January 2002): 420–31; Paul Peterson, *City Limits* (Chicago: University of Chicago Press, 1981); Mark Schneider, *The Competitive City* (Pittsburgh: University of Pittsburgh Press, 1989); Daphne Kenyon and John Kincaid, eds., *Competition among States and Local Governments* (Washington, D.C.: Urban Institute Press, 1991); Daphne Kenyon, "Theories of Interjurisdictional Competition," *New England Economic Review* (March–April 1997): 13–28; Thomas Dye, *American Federalism: Competition among Governments* (Lexington, Mass.: DC Heath, 1990); and Alan Altshuler, William Morrill, Harold Wolman, and Faith Mitchell, eds. *Governance and Opportunity in Metropolitan America* (Washington, D.C.: National Academy Press, 1999).
3. See, e.g., Susan Hansen, *The Politics of Taxation* (New York: Praeger, 1983); David Austen-Smith and Jeffrey Banks, "Electoral Accountability and Incumbency," in *Models of Strategic Choice in Politics,* ed. Peter Ordeshook (Ann Arbor: University of Michigan Press, 1989), 121–48; and Timothy Besley and Anne Case, "Incumbent Behavior: Vote-Seeking, Tax-Setting, and Yardstick Competition," *American Economic Review* 85 (March 1995): 25–45.
4. William A. Fischel, *The Homevoter Hypothesis: How Home Values Influence Local Government Taxation, School Finance, and Land-Use Policies* (Cambridge, Mass.: Harvard University Press, 2001).
5. The 30,000 figure was reported by city officials in response to the survey in 1998. Later data collected by the *Detroit Free Press* in 2000 pushed the estimate of vacant land closer to 40,000 parcels.
6. David Jacobson, *Place and Belonging in America* (Baltimore: Johns Hopkins University Press, 2002); Amos Rapoport, *The Meaning of the Built*

Environment: A Non-Verbal Communication Approach (Tucson: University of Arizona Press, 1990).

7. Jack L. Nasar, *The Evaluative Image of the City* (Thousand Oaks, Calif.: Sage Publications, 1998).

8. John A. Jakle and David Wilson, *Derelict Landscapes: The Wasting of America's Built Environment* (Savage, Md.: Rowman & Littlefield, 1992), 9; Alice Coleman, "Dead Space in the Dying Inner City," *International Journal of Environmental Studies* 19 (1982): 103–7.

9. James Q. Wilson and George L. Kelling, "Broken Windows: Police and Neighborhood Safety," *Atlantic Monthly*, March 1982, 29–38.

10. Arizona Prevention Resource Center, *Neighborhood Services Department: Make It Work!* (Phoenix: Arizona Prevention Resource Center, 1992), 2.

11. Kevin Lynch, *The Image of the City* (Cambridge, Mass.: MIT Press, 1960), 47.

12. Mark Alan Hughes and Anais Loizillon, "Over the Horizon: Jobs in the Suburbs of Major Metropolitan Areas," in *Urban Change in the United States and Western Europe*, 2nd edition, ed. Anita A. Summers, Paul C. Cheshire, and Lanfranco Senn (Washington, D.C.: Urban Institute Press, 1999), 35–58.

13. Hughes and Loizillon, "Over the Horizon."

14. David Lowery, "A Transaction Cost Model of Metropolitan Governance: Allocation Versus Redistribution in Urban America," *Journal of Public Administration Research and Theory* 10 (January 2000): 49–78.

15. Peter Dreier, John Mollenkopf, and Todd Swanstrom, *Place Matters: Metropolitics for the Twenty-First Century* (Lawrence: University Press of Kansas, 2001); William G. Gale and Janet Rothenberg Pack, eds., *Brookings-Wharton Papers on Urban Affairs 2001* (Washington, D.C.: Brookings Institution, 2001); Juliet F. Gainsborough, *Fenced Off: The Suburbanization of American Politics* (Washington, D.C.: Georgetown University Press, 2001); Lee Sigelman and Jeffrey R. Henig, "Crossing the Great Divide: Race and Preferences for Living in the City versus the Suburb," *Urban Affairs Review* 37 (September 2001): 3–18.

16. R. Schaffer and N. Smith, "The Gentrification of Harlem?" *Annals of the Association of American Geographers* 76, no. 3 (1986): 347–65.

17. William D. Solecki and Joan M. Welch, "Urban Parks: Green Spaces or Green Walls?" *Landscape and Urban Planning* 32 (1995): 93–106.

18. Paul H. Gobster, "Urban Parks as Green Walls or Green Magnets: Interracial Relations in Neighborhood Boundary Parks," *Landscape and Urban Planning* 41 (1998): 43–55.

19. The term "gated" is used generously in this instance.

20. Dolores Hayden, *The Power of Place: Urban Landscapes as Public History* (Cambridge, Mass.: MIT Press, 1995), 9.

21. Jennifer Dixon, "Detroit's Neglect Spawns Squatters," *Detroit Free Press*, July 7, 2000, 1.

22. Evictions can be pursued for health and safety reasons or in cases of criminal activity.

23. Rebecca R. Sohmer and Robert E. Lang, "Downtown Rebound," *Fannie Mae Foundation Census Note* (Washington, D.C.: Fannie Mae Foundation and Brookings Institution, 2001).

24. Sohmer and Lang, "Downtown Rebound."

25. Infill could involve nonresidential uses; however, it most commonly refers to the construction of housing in already-developed neighborhoods.

26. Brookings Institution Center on Urban and Metropolitan Policy, *Racial Change in the Nation's Largest Cities: Evidence from the 2000 Census*, April 2001; www.brookings.edu/es/urban/census/citygrowth.htm (June 1, 2003).

27. City of Phoenix, *Infill Housing Program* (Phoenix: City of Phoenix, Business Customer Service Center, 1998), 1.

28. City of Phoenix, *Target Area B Assessment* (Phoenix: City of Phoenix, Planning Department, 1998).

29. City of Seattle, *Seattle's Character* (Seattle: City of Seattle, Office for Long-Range Planning, 1991). The annexation map is on page 13.

30. Paul Summers and Daniel Carlson, with Michael Stanger, Saijun Xue, and Mike Miayasato, *Ten Steps to a High-Tech Future: The New Economy in Metropolitan Seattle*, Discussion Paper prepared for the Brookings Institution Center on Urban and Metropolitan Policy (Washington, D.C.: Brookings Institution, 2000).

31. Seattle's Comprehensive Plan, *Toward a Sustainable Seattle: A Plan for Managing Growth, 1994–2014 (as Amended November 25, 1997)* (Seattle: Seattle's Comprehensive Plan, 1997), appendices, A76.

32. For a discussion of GMA and Seattle, see Anne Vernez Moudon and LeRoy A. Heckman, "Seattle and the Central Puget Sound," in *Global City-Regions*, ed. Roger Simmonds and Gary Heck (London: Spon, 2000), chap. 11.

33. Puget Sound Regional Council, *1998 Regional Review: Monitoring Change in the Central Puget Sound* Region (Seattle: Puget Sound Regional Council, 1998), 29.

34. Puget Sound Regional Council, *1998 Regional Review*, 39.

35. See, e.g., King County, *1998 Annual Growth Report*, 1998; www.metrokc.gov/budget/agr/agr98 (June 1, 2003).

36. Data in this section are reported in Puget Sound Regional Council, *Urban Centers in the Central Puget Sound Region: A Baseline Summary and Comparison, Winter 1996–97* (Seattle: Puget Sound Regional Council, 1996), 2–21.

37. Puget Sound Regional Council, *Urban Centers in the Central Puget Sound Region*.

38. Susan Byrnes, "A Choice in How Seattle Grows," *Seattle Times*, November 2, 1997; www.seattletimes.com/extra/browse/html97/mayr_110297.html#background (May 2001).

39. Washington Center for Real Estate Research, *Washington State's Housing Market: A Supply/Demand Assessment, First Quarter 1999*, 1999; www.cbe.wsu.edu/~wcrer/HMUPDATE/MKTRPT9a.htm (May 2000).

40. City of Seattle, *Seattle Comprehensive Plan: Monitoring Our Progress, 1998* (Seattle: City of Seattle, Strategic Planning Office, 1998), 18.

41. City of Seattle, "Transferable Development Rights (TDR) Program" (City of Seattle, Department of Housing and Human Services, Seattle; unpublished, n.d.); Jane Voget, "Making Transfer of Development Rights Work for Downtown Preservation and Redevelopment" (City of Seattle, Department of Housing and Human Services, Seattle, draft, 1999).

42. City of Seattle, *Property Tax Exemption for Multifamily Housing* (Seattle: City of Seattle, Office of Housing, 1999).

43. Phyllis Myers, "The Varied Landscape of Park and Conservation Finance," *Nation's Cities Weekly,* June 2, 1997, 3.

44. City of Philadelphia, *Neighborhood Transformations: The Implementation of Philadelphia's Community Development Policy* (Philadelphia: City of Philadelphia, Office of Housing and Community Development, 1997).

45. City of Philadelphia, *Vacant Property Prescriptions: A Reinvestment Strategy* (Philadelphia: City of Philadelphia, Office of Housing and Community Development, 1996), 11.

46. An approach to neighborhood reinvestment based on his experience in Philadelphia's housing department can be found in: John Kromer, *Neighborhood Recovery: Reinvestment Policy for the New Hometown* (New Brunswick, N.J.: Rutgers University Press, 2000).

47. Stephen Carr, Mark Francis, Leanne G. Rivlin, and Andrew M. Stone, *Public Space* (New York: Cambridge University Press, 1992).

48. Richard Wilk and Michael B. Schiffer, "The Archaeology of Vacant Lots in Tucson, Arizona," *American Antiquity* 44 (July 1979): 530–36.

49. Carr et al., *Public Space*, 10, 167.

50. Carr et al., *Public Space*, 161.

51. Bucks County (Pa.), *Report of the Bucks County Open Space Task Force* (Doylestown, Pa.: Bucks County Open Space Task Force, 1996), 3.

52. J. Burke and J. M. Ewan, *Sonoran Preserve Master Plan* (Tempe, Ariz.: CAED Herberger Center for Design Excellence, 1998).

53. Burke and Ewan, *Sonoran Preserve Master Plan*, 3.

54. Burke and Ewan, *Sonoran Preserve Master Plan*, 9.

55. City of Bellevue (Wash.), *Bellevue Parks & Open Space System Plan* (Bellevue, Wash.: City of Bellevue, 1993), 6.

56. City of Bellevue, *Bellevue Parks & Open Space System Plan*, 1.

57. See Aldo Leopold, *The Sand County Almanac* (New York: Oxford University Press, 1949). In the foreword to his book (pp. xviii–xix), Leopold states, "We abuse land because we regard it as a commodity belonging to us. When we see land as a community to which we belong, we may begin to use it with love and respect."

58. Pennsylvania Horticultural Society, *Urban Vacant Land: Issues and Recommendations* (Philadelphia: Pennsylvania Horticultural Society, 1995), 19.

59. Jean E. Schukoske, "Community Development through Gardening: State and Local Policies Transforming Urban Open Space," *New York University Journal of Legislation and Public Policy* 3 (1999–2000): 357.

60. Pennsylvania Horticultural Society, *Urban Vacant Land*.

61. Vanita Gowda, "Whose Garden Is It?" *Governing*, March 2002, 40–41.

62. Adam Gopnik, "A Walk on the High Line," *New Yorker*, May 21, 2001, 45.

63. Lynch, *Image of the City*.

64. An interesting discussion of the catalytic role of architecture in designing U.S. cities is found in Wayne Attoe and Donn Logan, *American Urban Architecture: Catalysts in the Design of Cities* (Berkeley: University of California Press, 1989).

5

The Development Potential of Vacant Land

Amid the intergovernmental competition in a typical metropolitan area, local jurisdictions struggle to balance their revenue-generating capacity against service-delivery demands.[1] The vitality of the local economy is a key component in a jurisdiction's ability to achieve that balance. Thus, localities take actions designed to promote economic development. As we argued in an earlier study, *Cityscapes and Capital*, city officials use the resources available to them—for example, their regulatory authority, hortatory skills, investment choices—in an effort to spur economic vitality.[2] As we phrased it, they mobilize public capital on behalf of economic development. One of the primary resources a city controls is its territorial space, its land. At a minimum, a city has regulatory power over its land; in some instances, it may actually own land. In either case, city government is at the center of the development process, and land is an essential component in that process. In effect, then, governmental policies influence the development capacity and growth prospects of the city by affecting, among other things, the supply and quality of land.

The development imperative states that cities must pursue policies that promote economic vitality and enhance the image of the community. In accordance with this imperative, cities are induced to use or re-use vacant land in a productive manner. And although vacant land is seldom the leading issue in local elections, city officials contend that skillful management of land-related matters can pay political dividends.[3] Thus the development imperative is more than a simple matter of economic benefits and image enhancement; it has political value as well. This chapter focuses on the role vacant land plays in the development imperative.

ECONOMIC DEVELOPMENT IN METROPOLITAN AREAS

Metropolitan areas in the United States are highly fragmented, with a multiplicity of jurisdictions clamoring for pieces of the economic pie. As of 1997, the Census Bureau had tallied 87,453 local governments, up from 82,176 in 1987 and 79,862 in 1977. All these local governments have territorial boundaries that define their jurisdiction. To varying degrees, all these local governments raise revenue and provide services. This jurisdictional mix creates a market of governments that, according to Tiebout and others, "fosters the efficient allocation of public goods and widens the service choices available to citizens."[4]

Thus, in a given metropolitan area, localities compete with one another to attract people and firms. Competition occurs between jurisdictions with comparable powers (horizontal competition) and between local governments with different powers (vertical competition).[5] Although most analyses of competitive behavior have focused on tax levels and service quality, competition extends to land, and especially, land use.[6] Recall, for instance, the horizontal competition among Phoenix-area cities to annex revenue-producing territory (chapter 3). As an official in suburban Peoria commented, "If we didn't annex that area, another city [Phoenix] would have." Most metropolitan areas are marked by high degrees of horizontal competition, especially between a central city and its suburbs, as well as milder levels of vertical competition.[7]

The Mobilization of Public Capital

Localities adopt policies to augment or influence the economic growth potential of the underlying economy, namely, its investment, output, consumption, and income potential, as well as to influence fundamental changes in the structure of the local economy, including innovations in institutions, behavior, and technology. Land is a resource that both affects and is affected by economic development. Land's value is determined by its availability, condition, demand, use potential (zoning), government subsidy, access, plans and visions, prestige, symbolism, and social value.[8] As land is transformed into "place" through the workings of the private market and the actions of government, its value will change.

Throughout the country, cities have mobilized public capital in support of development projects.[9] Many cities find themselves playing the role of initiator and catalyst, providing whatever support might be necessary to get a project under way. In the era of the Urban Development Action Grant (UDAG) program, cities could apply for "gap financing" from the federal government, that is, funding designed to make a project feasible to a developer. In the post-UDAG era, cities often have to fill the gap themselves if they want to bring a project to fruition. Although there is much debate about the wisdom of development incentives, the fact remains that most cities mobilize public capital in some way in an effort to attract investment.[10] The effort, as a consequence, keeps the local economy healthy and lets the city maintain a competitive balance between taxes and services.[11]

Nearly all cities seek development, although certainly not the same type of development. In a national survey conducted in 1987, nearly 90 percent of mayors indicated that economic development was one of the top three priorities in their city, although their approaches and tools differed.[12] Some cities aggressively promote their development potential through incentives. That is, these cities give tax breaks, provide loans, and offer below-cost land, among other things, to attract investment. Other cities seeking development are more circumspect in their provision of incentives, often due to limitations in state law or city officials' reluctance to take risk. Still others opt for more of a maintenance role, choosing to manage growth and to tightly control the kind of investment entering the community.

Although economic development efforts seek a tangible return (e.g., new firms, expanded facilities, more jobs), there may be an additional intent: the enhancement of the city's image. Local officials may have aspirations for their city to compete with a different set of cities—those on a higher economic plane, in an urban hierarchical sense.[13] Attracting a professional sports franchise, even at tremendous cost to the city, signifies that the city has become "a major league city."[14] The new stadium (perhaps constructed with public funds) is a symbol that the city is flourishing, that it is ascendant. In some instances, symbolic value may be the sole return that a city receives from its investment.[15] The larger point is that image is not only an abstraction; it can serve as a guide for purposive action. Cities seek a positive image. As Gregory J. Ashworth and Henk Voogd contend, "The perception of cities, and the mental image held of them, become active components of economic success or failure."[16]

Land is a major component in the economic development process. More than two-thirds of cities with populations of 50,000 or more acquire land (68.6 percent) and sell land to developers (69.3 percent).[17]

tely 61 percent of the cities clear land in anticipation of redevelopment. The consolidation of land parcels occurs less frequently;
only about one-third of the cities do so. A similar figure is reported for
land write-downs, that is, the below-market sale of land to developers.
It is among the largest cities (populations greater than 200,000) that involvement in land-related development activities is highest. More than
75 percent of large cities acquire, clear, and sell land to developers, and
more than 50 percent consolidate lots and write-down land prices.

Vacant Land as an Economic Development Issue

With respect to vacant land, the most relevant development action
mentioned above is clearance. Sixty-one percent of city governments
have purposely made land vacant in their pursuit of development or,
more accurately, redevelopment. Most of these actions are fairly
modest, done on a parcel-by-parcel basis, rather than the old-style urban renewal whereby a city might raze block after block in the name
of slum clearance. The city's goals are simple:

- to clear the land of blighting structures;
- to prepare the land for subsequent redevelopment;
- if necessary, to take ownership of the land; and
- to return the land to productive use; that is, to successfully redevelop the parcel or to place it in protected (e.g., green space)
  status.

Cities are under tremendous competitive pressures, especially from
nearby jurisdictions, to exploit the development potential of their land.
City leaders make strategic decisions whether to target certain areas for
redevelopment, such as inner-city land or, instead, land at the fringe of
the city. Vacant land has different economic values depending on,
among other factors, its location. In general, metropolitan area land
prices tend to fall as the distance from the city's center increases.[18]
Local officials must also decide the level of subsidization of the redevelopment process and, ultimately, allowable land use.
    Vacant land created through abandonment threatens the value of
nearby property. A contagion effect occurs; that is, a vacant lot in the
middle of the block negatively affects the value of adjacent parcels. An
abandoned structure on a corner is similarly dampening, with the effect
extending to other blocks. In a study conducted in Philadelphia, each
vacant lot affected the value of as many as eight nearby properties.[19]
Figure 5.1 displays the "contagion" pattern for single and multiple va-

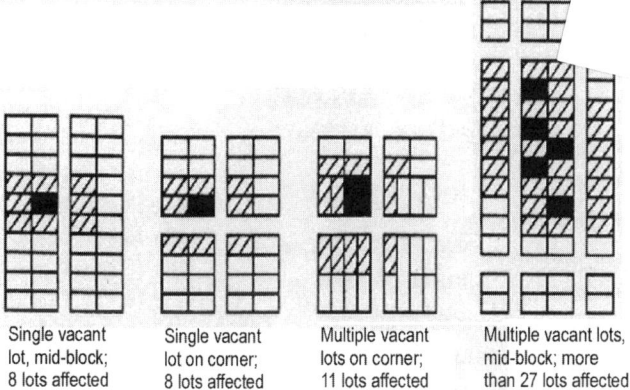

| Single vacant lot, mid-block; 8 lots affected | Single vacant lot on corner; 8 lots affected | Multiple vacant lots on corner; 11 lots affected | Multiple vacant lots, mid-block; more than 27 lots affected |

FIGURE 5.1. The Contagion Effect of Vacant Land: The Impact of Vacant Lots on Surrounding Properties
Source: Fairmount Ventures, Inc., "Vacant Land Management in Philadelphia Neighborhoods: Cost–Benefit Analysis," report prepared for the Pennsylvania Horticultural Society (PHS), April 1999. Reprinted by permission of PHS.

cant lots, visually demonstrating that vacant lots spread their undesirable effects beyond the borders of the lot.

Given the contagion effect and the prospect of triggering a downward spiral of neighboring properties, city strategies to reuse vacant land will certainly be—or should be—pursued vigorously. Even in a growing city like Peoria, portions of the older part of town are boarded up and vacant. Unless the city can encourage reuse of the vacant parcels and abandoned structures, it risks the reduction of property values in the neighborhood. But because the land is not held by the city but by private concerns, the city's options are limited.

City policies designed to encourage the development or reuse of a city's vacant land reflect important strategies. The decision, for example, to focus the city's development resources on its fringe or border reflects a particular need and set of circumstances and opportunities. These opportunities presumably have a higher potential payoff than those associated with mobilizing the city's development resources to reuse vacant land in its interior, that is, an "infill" strategy. We might expect, therefore, that a city's revenue-generating needs influence its pursuit of infill strategies. As we suggested in chapter 3, sales-tax-reliant cities seemingly have less incentive to pursue an infill strategy than do property-tax-reliant ones.

However, as is shown in table 5.1, the data from the vacant land survey do not bear this out. Indeed the percentage of sales tax cities with

TABLE 5.1.   City Infill Policy and Tax Reliance

Policy	Property Tax Cities	Sales Tax Cities	Income Tax Cities and both Income and Sales Tax Cities	All Cities
Infill policy	9	15	3	27
No infill policy	42	71	13	126
Percentage of cities with infill policy for city-owned land	17.6	17.4	18.8	17.6

Source: Data are from the authors' vacant land survey, 1997–98; see appendix A.

an infill policy is nearly identical to the percentage of property tax cities and to the percentage of income tax cities. Regardless of tax reliance, the infill policy figures do not exceed 19 percent. We should note, however, that our survey question only asked about infill policies for the re-use of city-owned vacant land, not about privately held vacant land. This caveat aside, it does not appear that cities have embraced infill policies systematically.

The development potential of vacant land is most obvious in so-called hot land markets. Boston, with the redevelopment of the land once occupied by the Boston State Hospital, offers an apt illustration.[20] The 175-acre site had sat idle since 1981. The state razed more than twenty buildings on the site and removed underground storage tanks, but it was unable to create a workable development plan. The pressure to "do something" with the largest publicly owned tract of undeveloped land in the city grew intense. Under legislation enacted by the Massachusetts legislature in 2000, the state retained ownership of the site but placed the City of Boston (i.e., the Boston Redevelopment Authority) in the role of lead developer. The new plan for the site included a multi-faceted business park, a large housing development, educational and health facilities, and a wildlife sanctuary. The development potential of the vacant land was high, given the robust local economy. As Boston mayor Thomas Menino exclaimed, "This site has languished too long. Give us the control of the development and we will rebuild one of the most valuable pieces of property in the city."[21]

Even though general-purpose local governments are responsible for regulating and managing land, they do not possess carte blanche authority, as the Boston example shows. A city's decision-making sphere is circumscribed by externally imposed rules, particularly those of state government and those of the marketplace, which affect land use policy.[22] These rules complicate a city's pursuit of the development imperative. Governmental vacant land policies, whether explicitly formulated in ordinances, state statutes, and interlocal agreements or implicitly followed via custom and tradition, can be classified as serving three purposes: capturing or stretching the political reach of the city;[23] recycling underused, abandoned, or contaminated land;[24] and constraining or regulating vacant land. These purposes are explored in the remainder of this chapter.

CAPTURING LAND

Annexation laws can encourage or discourage city expansion of its political reach. Between 1990 and 1996, cities added nearly 3.5 million acres of land in 45,000 annexations.[25] Cities in some states (e.g., Arizona) can stretch their political boundaries relatively easily. A majority of voters and a majority of landowners (based on assessed property values) in the area to be annexed must approve the action after a city puts the annexation question on the ballot. Because developers typically own most of the annexed land at the time of annexation, the likelihood of ballot rejection is low. Uncontroversial annexation may be effected in some states by, upon formal notification, a simple vote of the city council. However, in other states, annexation is more difficult or nonproductive.[26] The annexation question might require an extraordinary majority or a positive vote in both the extant city and the area to be annexed. It may be easy for residents of the annexed area to veto the action.

Felicitous state law is a necessary but not sufficient condition for annexation. A city's ability to annex also depends on the jurisdictional layout of the metropolitan area. A city surrounded by unincorporated territory may be able to expand its boundary, whereas a neighboring city ringed by incorporated places will not. In a state where municipal incorporation is fairly easy, it is more likely that a city will find incorporated suburbs at its borders. In fact, some jurisdictions incorporate defensively as an alternative to annexation by a neighboring city. The ease or difficulty of annexation is a major determinant of a city's land supply and thus influences the amount of vacant land in the city. The example of the Phoenix metropolitan area shows how the ability to annex influences a city's strategic behavior.

Peoria's Boundary Expansion

The map of north central Maricopa County, Arizona (figure 5.2), outlines the boundaries of incorporated places as of 1998.[27] The extent

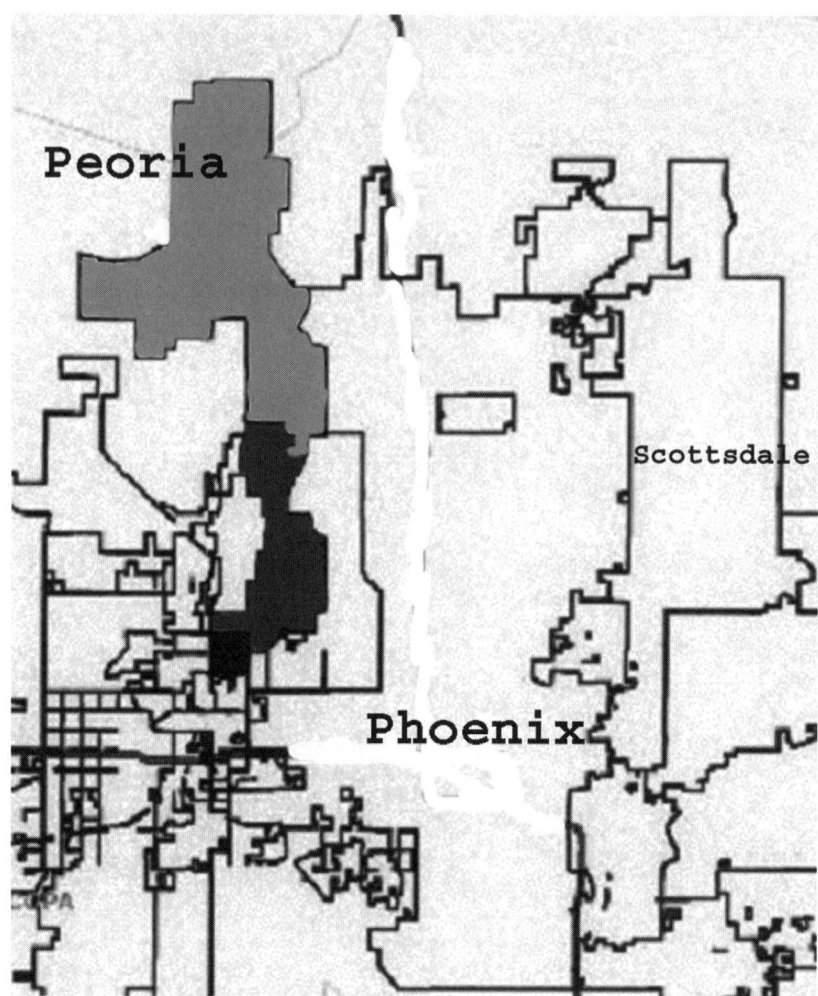

FIGURE 5.2. Incorporated Places in the North Central Portion of Maricopa County, Arizona

and rapidity of annexation by the City of Peoria is noteworthy. Peoria was incorporated in 1954 as a 1-square-mile city, an agricultural center west of Phoenix (the small area shaded black near the center of the map). Since then, the city has annexed land to the north, much of it in the mid-1990s when it annexed the dark gray area and then the last large parcel of land (the light gray color of the map), and now is more than 144 square miles in size. Annexation has been so aggressive to the north of the original city that the mayor was once jokingly referred to by the governor as "the mayor of South Utah"! Although annexation has probably come to a halt for the foreseeable future, the city's population has soared from just above 12,000 in 1980 to nearly 52,000 in 1990 and to 108,364 in 2000, a 114 percent increase in the past decade.

Although the state's annexation laws allow cities to expand aggressively, the reliance of Arizona's cities on sales tax revenue encourages or nearly requires aggressive annexation even before development. As Phoenix annexed land near the interstate highway on the north side of the city, its strategy was to capture prospective retail-center sites. Peoria's strategy was premised on two observations. First, Peoria's officials believed that Phoenix would soon annex to the west of Interstate 17 and thwart any northern expansion of the western Maricopa County cities, including Peoria. The reaction by Peoria, then, was a blocking strategy. Second, Peoria's officials, like all officials in Arizona cities, understand that residents contribute much less in property taxes from their residences than they receive in city government services. The property tax contribution to Peoria's general fund in its 1999–2000 operating budget was only 3 percent, whereas the sales tax contribution was 31 percent.[28]

Peoria, then, needed to promote retailing rather than allow neighboring cities to drain the sales tax payments of its residents to their coffers. And indeed retailing was encouraged along the city's border with Glendale (to the east of Peoria). In particular, the city granted a sales tax abatement to an automobile mall so that it would locate within the city's limits and less than a half-mile from two large communities (Glendale and the unincorporated community of Sun City). The revenue-generating capacity of car dealerships makes them especially desirable enterprises.[29] Figure 5.3 shows annexed land being readied for new commercial development. Throughout the Phoenix metropolitan area, the desert landscape is giving way to large-scale development.

Annexation has long been the vacant land policy of choice among Arizona municipalities. Phoenix, one of the nation's leaders in annexation, has good company in the Maricopa County metropolitan area. Chandler, Mesa, Scottsdale, Gilbert, and Peoria all have expanded their territorial limits substantially. Since 1990, annexation has been extensive, especially to the northwest (Peoria), north along the interstate (Phoenix), and to the southeast (Gilbert and Chandler). In just a few short years, these cities have increased their land supply to position themselves for future economic growth.

Annexation also has another developmental outcome: image enhancement. In Peoria, the sheer size of the annexation makes the city more of a player in the metropolitan area. It has shucked its status as an

FIGURE 5.3. Developing "Raw Dirt" Vacant Land in Peoria, Arizona

insignificant farming community west of Phoenix with the aim of becoming more like the full-service cities on Phoenix's east side. In Phoenix proper, the vast supply of developable land maintains the city's regional dominance; but more important, it enhances the city's image among its national and international competitors.

Aggressive Annexation in Phoenix

Peoria is one example of aggressive annexation; Phoenix is another. Annexation has been the means by which Phoenix has insured its continued dominance among metropolitan area communities. The map in figure 5.4 shows the territorial spread of Phoenix from 1950 (the square area in the center) to its 1990 form. The city expanded in all directions, adding large swaths of desert as well as smaller tracts of land. Annexation along major roadways has been a common practice, in anticipation of eventual commercial development. Annexations during the 1990s, not shown on the map, brought Phoenix to 470 square miles.

Why has the city pursed annexation as a conscious growth strategy? The public position is that Phoenix annexes because it, compared with other jurisdictions, will exert quality control over the newly added territory. More privately, Phoenix leaders acknowledge the city's continued need for sales tax revenue and its desire to prevent other cities from gaining that revenue. Thus the calculation is simple: annexation of land ripe for commercial development equals eventual sales tax revenue. Historically, Phoenix has received more than its share of metropolitan area retail sales taxes; but over time, the city's dominance in sales tax

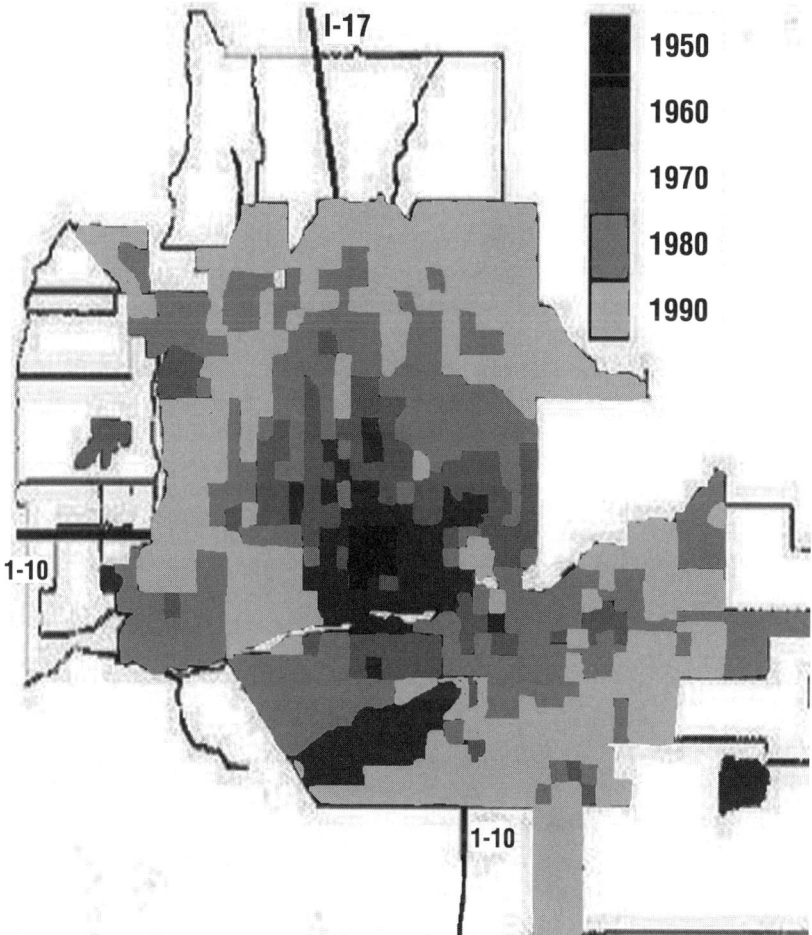

FIGURE 5.4. Phoenix's Annexations, 1950–90
Source: Ray Quay, Jim Mathien, and David Richert, "Phoenix's Strategic View of Growth," paper prepared for the American Planning Association annual meetings, San Diego, 1997. Reprinted by permission.

revenue has weakened as other jurisdictions have pursued similar strategies. As was noted above, to maintain its perceived "rightful" place in the metropolitan hierarchy and to compete nationally and globally, the city needs to continue its expansion.

Major cities annex for one of two reasons: (1) to control their own destiny or (2) to make sure the land does not become part of another city's destiny. Negotiated annexation is not uncommon. One example recounted by city officials involved a developer who, when readying an 8,000-acre parcel in the county for development, shopped his property to adjacent cities with the question: "What incentives can you give me in return for annexation?" Cities are keenly aware of other cities; the rivalry can be intense. The actions taken by one city may be in reaction to or in anticipation of actions by a rival jurisdiction.

Phoenix's large-scale annexation northward along Interstate 17 provides an illuminating case of strategic annexation. The Del Webb Corporation's Anthem residential development (an old Resolution Trust Corporation property) was under construction north of Carefree Highway in unincorporated Maricopa County. A large outlet mall is located adjacent to Anthem. The city annexed along I-17 and added the mall property to Phoenix, but Anthem remains outside it. The city and the developer weighed the benefits and costs of annexation (in terms of services, revenues, and regulations) and negotiated a deal in which Del Webb Corporation agreed to participate in infrastructure development along I-17 and the city agreed not to annex Anthem.[30]

The map in figure 5.5 displays the location of building permits granted by the City of Phoenix from July 1995 to June 1999. The greatest construction activity occurred in the northeastern section and along the southern edge on land that the city had annexed during the 1980s. Other census tracts with higher than average numbers of building permits were concentrated in the northern and western portions of the city, areas that also had been annexed fairly recently to the city. The distribution of building permits tends to confirm the Phoenix strategy of annexation in anticipation of development.

Tempe: Landlocked Redevelopment

Successful political strategies must adjust to changing conditions. The Peoria and Phoenix cases highlight the strategic behavior of cities capable of stretching their physical boundaries. But once that condition is restricted—that is, once a city becomes landlocked—the political strategy of boundary expansion changes and the imperative to compete with surrounding jurisdictions changes dramatically. The case of Tempe—a landlocked city that competes with four bordering cities (Mesa, Chandler, Phoenix, and Scottsdale)—is germane.

Landlocked cities have an incentive to cooperate with other jurisdictions in the retail inducement arena, but the cities that border them do not. Border cities have an incentive to establish retail centers at their edges, near the borders of others. The goal for both landlocked and border cities is to attract development that will maximize revenues. The directive is this: Saturate the market for your own residents and entice

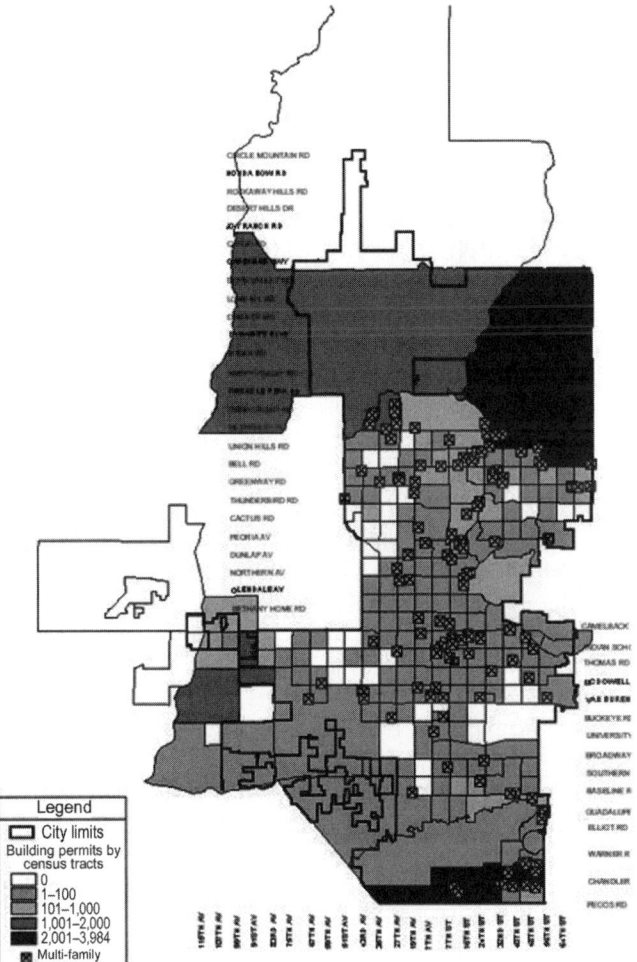

FIGURE 5.5. Construction Activity in Phoenix: Building Permits Issued from July 1995 to June 1999
Source: City of Phoenix, *Consolidated Plan for 2000–2005 and Annual Action Plan for 2000–2001.* Reprinted by permission of the City of Phoenix, Planning Department.

mobile residents of bordering cities to shop with you. Border cities with the ability to annex have more options than landlocked cities do, and thus the pressure to cooperate is less.

Tempe's development of its vacant land in the past two decades has been influenced by the actions of its border cities. Two major developments merit consideration. First, as was discussed above, Tempe's neighbor to the west, Phoenix, has pursued a policy of vigorous annexation. Phoenix annexed vacant land that separated the two cities and zoned much of it for residential construction. The City of Tempe responded by encouraging the conversion of its remaining large tract of vacant land into an extensive retail area, including an automobile mall. The intent? To lure residents just over the border in the newly annexed area of Phoenix to Tempe's new retail development.

The second illustration comes from the southeast corner of Tempe where, just across the border, its neighbor Chandler approved the construction of a shopping mall. The strategy of building commercial, revenue-generating facilities near the edge of the city should be expected, as it is with Tempe and indeed for any city dependent on a sales tax. In this instance, however, Tempe already had a large retail center on its border with Chandler called Arizona Mills. The dubious viability of two malls in close proximity soon pushed the two cities into discussion and negotiation. Having realized that residential density was not likely to increase, Chandler and Tempe concluded that only one mall could be sustained. Eventually, the two cities agreed to a mutually beneficial arrangement that maintained their revenue positions. Chandler agreed to discourage mall construction within a mile of its border with Tempe in exchange for Tempe's willingness to share some of the sales tax revenues from its mall located near Chandler's border.

The strategic interdependence between the two cities fostered cooperation between them rather than competition. Tempe will lose if Chandler builds a mall close to Tempe's existing mall. Tempe knows it and "bribes" Chandler by paying 20 percent of sales tax revenues in exchange for not building. The Tempe mall generates $7.5 million in sales tax revenues, and Chandler receives approximately $1.5 million annually. Both cities win sufficiently with the agreement and, most important, reduce the risk of losing. This arrangement has led to talk of additional sales tax sharing between the two cities.

Why would Chandler be willing to cooperate with Tempe and stop the mall wars? Indeed, why would any of the four bordering cities, all of which can still annex land and expand their territorial limits, want to cooperate with Tempe? Fast-growing Mesa and Phoenix, with their established and emerging commercial areas, have little reason to cooperate. Scottsdale can continue to expand, but it already has upscale shopping areas and developable vacant land close to the Tempe border and thus has no incentive to cooperate.

But why Chandler? The explanation may lie in the potential growth of Gilbert, Chandler's wealthier neighbor to the east-northeast. Gilbert has lost potential revenue to its neighbor to the north, Mesa, because Mesa has several malls along U.S. Route 60, a major east–west highway traversing the city. One-half mile south of Route 60 is Gilbert. As with the other jurisdictions in the metropolitan area, Gilbert's imperative is to build retail centers and annex developed land. If Gilbert's potential is frozen to the north (Mesa) and the population base has yet to develop to the south and east to support a mall, it leaves the west for development—along the border with Chandler. Chandler already has two large malls in its geographical center (and Tempe has one on Chandler's west side, and Mesa has one on its north side). Chandler's preferred outcome is the development of other malls to its east, which is where Gilbert is located. Chandler can encourage mall construction at a site near Gilbert's borders, thus serving both Chandler and Gilbert residents.

Of course, Gilbert has the same land development logic at work. Chandler's position is probably better because the city can count on revenues from Tempe's mall, rather than worry about Tempe building another mall near Chandler and draining potential revenues. A truce in offering retail incentives helps protect Chandler's northern and western neighbors and Tempe's southwestern neighbor. Yet Chandler's strategy of land development is expected to promote development of a retail center (a mall). Indeed, the most strategic location for the mall would be within 1.5 miles of Gilbert's borders to draw consumers from neighboring cities—exactly where a 400,000-square-foot mall was on the drawing boards. A truce, however, is an important strategy to the extent that the risk of financial loss in the development game is high. Predictably, the truce came to an end in 2003 when Chandler requested a modification to the "perpetual" 1996 memorandum of understanding with Tempe. The city's argument: "Since the time that the Memorandum of Understanding was implemented, there has been substantial commercial development within Chandler and the perpetual sharing agreement is no longer necessary."[31]

The location of developable vacant land is indicated by the cross-hatched patterns in figure 5.6. The city boundaries are marked with a solid line. Notice that the site that the City of Chandler readied for mall development (indicated by the dark square on the map) is within easy shopping distance for Gilbert consumers, close enough to the borders of Chandler to draw shoppers not only from Chandler but also from Gilbert. The site is far enough from Tempe, however (nearly 3 miles), to keep the truce between Tempe and Chandler from being an issue.

Moreover, Chandler is extending its corporate limits through annexation toward the south to block Gilbert's growth. Should the Gilbert threat be defeated (and Gilbert would have to annex more vacant and agricultural land to the south and east toward Queen Creek and establish retail centers farther from Chandler), Chandler and Gilbert would

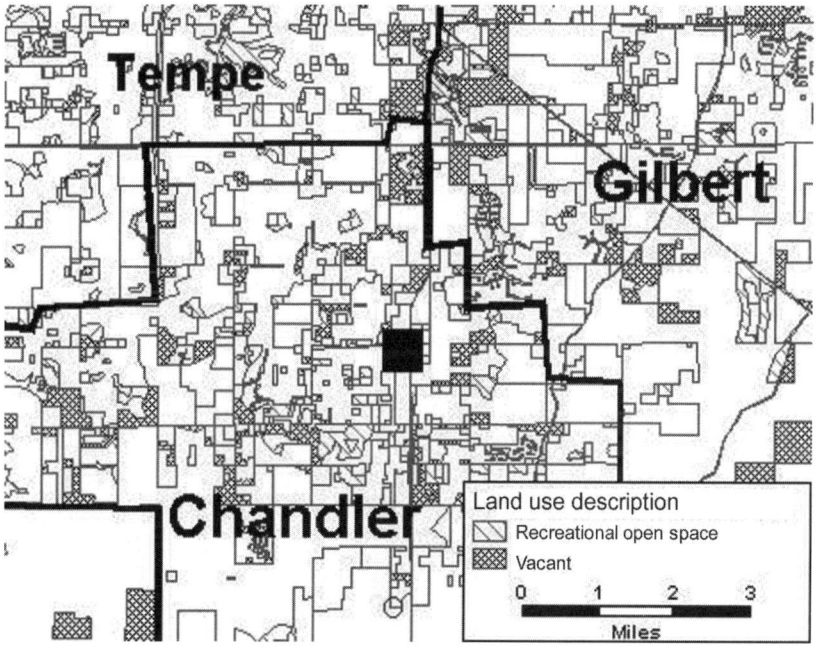

FIGURE 5.6. Land Use in Chandler, Arizona

be expected to race each other to annex the unincorporated land that is near them. If Chandler wins, Gilbert will become landlocked and its behavior will parallel Tempe's. Chandler's behavior, conversely, will mimic Peoria's. These actions should not be surprising, given the logic of the development imperative.

RECAPTURING AND RECYCLING VACANT LAND

The most persistent image of vacant land is the one that appears in the pages of newspapers and magazines, the one that strikes fear in the hearts of residents and passersby: a vacant lot that has become an informal waste dump or drug market. The challenge for communities is to recapture and recycle this kind of vacant land for its development potential. The problems associated with the ubiquitous vacant lots in Detroit, for example, are regularly reported in the local press.[32] In fact, the constant media pressure has kept the issue on the public agenda, forcing city officials to take action. Part of the problem for the city was an information deficit: Detroit simply did not know the location of abandoned property. There was no system in place to track when buildings became vacant.

Although the magnitude of the problem was especially severe in Detroit, in other cities as well, officials have sought accurate data on the location and condition of vacant parcels.[33] In 1984, the City of Cincinnati became one of the first in the nation to conduct a comprehensive, computerized inventory of its publicly and privately owned vacant industrial and commercial land. Cincinnati's effort was widely hailed, and other cities have followed suit, assembling zoning maps, tax records, aerial photographs, and data from the field into computerized land inventories.[34] The advent of geographic information system (GIS) technology has made the task much easier.

For Cincinnati, the impetus for its Site Finder inventory sprang from the city's ongoing economic development effort. Ready access to updated information—such as the location, size, physical features, ownership, zoning, and value of vacant parcels—gives the city a competitive advantage in firm recruitment and retention. Figure 5.7 displays the location of vacant parcels and formerly vacant but now developed parcels in Cincinnati. Cities as diverse and distant as Yakima, Washington, and Greenville, South Carolina, have borrowed from Cincinnati's Site Finder program to create their own inventories, specifically because of their interest in gauging each vacant parcel's development potential.[35]

Vacant Land and Economic Development Planning

Recycling vacant land as part of a larger economic development plan has become more standardized than it was in the past. In the early 1990s, New York City owned between 14,000 and 20,000 vacant lots.[36] (That the number was uncertain reflects the inadequacy of the data.) Even as the city continued to dispose of much of its vacant land at auction, officials began to work on a series of land disposition plans that focused on the transformation of vacant parcels into commercial centers, low-income housing, neighborhood parks, and community gardens. The first step was the creation of a vacant land database that contained relevant information about site location and condition. A comment by the director of the Department of City Planning typifies the new thinking: "This [city-owned vacant land] is an enormous resource . . . an enormous planning opportunity."[37]

Cleveland's Land Reutilization program stands out as a model for encouraging the reuse of vacant land and/or abandoned buildings.[38] The city aggressively seizes tax delinquent property and gives owners two weeks to reclaim it. If not reclaimed, the property is "land banked" by the city and sold for the amount owed in back taxes, or the market value, if greater. Boston has taken a hands-on, individualized

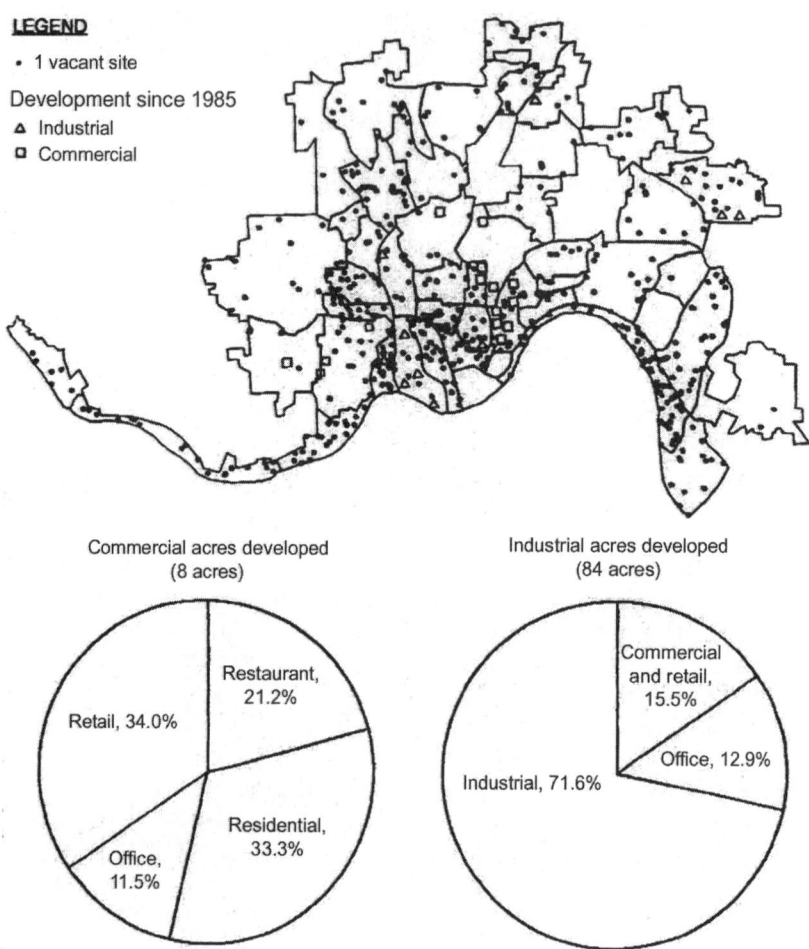

FIGURE 5.7. Cincinnati's "Site Finder" Locates Vacant Commercial and Industrial Land in Forty-Eight Communities
Source: Cincinnati City Planning Department, Planning and Management Support Office, *Information Report Issue 4*, December 1988. Reprinted by permission of the City of Cincinnati.

approach, using a request for proposals (RFP) process to dispose of city-owned vacant land. After determining the reuse preferences of nearby residents, the city's Public Facilities Department designs an appropriate RFP and circulates it to potential developers. The department enters into a direct contract with the organization or individual selected to redevelop the vacant parcel.

Maintaining, much less improving, city-owned vacant land can be costly. One means of sharing the burden is for city governments to turn to the private and nonprofit sectors for support. New York City began its City Spaces Plan to lease certain vacant properties to corporations in return for their cleanup and conversion to park or playground use.[39] The advantage to the corporation is the ability to use the space to advertise itself. There is a five-year minimum lease period, and the city retains title to the land parcels. Philadelphia has also sought to use financial support from the private sector in its vacant land redevelopment efforts. The Philadelphia Plan targets ten neighborhoods for the investment of more than $20 million in private funds during a ten-year period, much of it for open space development.[40]

The use of vacant land inventories as an economic development tool raises questions about the existence of an emergent "vacant land ethic" in some cities. That is, vacant land seems to be shedding its status as a residual category, as leftover space, and instead is becoming more intrinsic to a city's future vision. Cities that are pursuing master planning in the so-called new urbanist vein—Portland, Oregon, and San Jose are two prominent examples—see vacant land as one solution to growth pressures.[41] These initiatives are similar to but more comprehensive than previous, piecemeal efforts at infill development that seek to limit sprawl by shifting growth to the inner sections of a city. Available vacant parcels that have never been developed or have had structures razed but have not been reused are attractive alternatives to outer-edge development.[42]

To create a market for infill, cities use mechanisms such as density bonuses and low-interest loans, and they relax requirements for the minimum lot size. Infill, as a development tool, can be extended through the use of land banking, a somewhat complementary process. Vacant lots, owing to their "remnant" nature, are frequently small in size and irregular in shape. Land banking, which requires the assembly and often the improvement of contiguous parcels, may remedy size and shape problems, thus increasing the development potential of the assembled parcel. In high-demand land markets, land banking offers cities a way to manage and market a resource.

The Special Case of Brownfields

Used land comes in all shapes and sizes, each with its own history. One type of used land that poses special challenges for redevelopment is brownfields. As was noted in chapter 1, the U.S. Environmental Protection Agency (EPA) defines a brownfield as an abandoned, idled, or underused site where expansion or redevelopment is complicated by real or perceived contamination.[43] Given the contamination issue, brownfields often sit somewhat forlornly in a city's vacant land inventory. But the development potential of these polluted (or thought to be polluted) sites can be great. A comment in *Governing* offers an important point: "A simple truth is dawning on local governments: Industrial brownfields are the most obvious source of urban land ripe for redevelopment."[44]

The concept of brownfields grew out of the 1980 federal Superfund program.[45] Superfund contained liability provisions that penalized owners of polluted property with little regard to their actual contribution to the pollution. Even subsequent owners of the sites risked possible liability. The potential cost of cleanup and remediation of the property further limited the redevelopment of these properties.[46] At the same time, the availability of greenfields lessened the marketability of contaminated (or perceived to be contaminated) parcels. To an investor, the calculation was simple: Brownfields posed unacceptable risks and costs. As a consequence, these properties typically remained idle, even in cities experiencing intense development pressures.

Not all brownfields pose the same level of environmental threat; nor do they possess the same degree of marketability. Wright and Davlin classify brownfields into three tiers on the basis of their contamination levels and market potential.[47] Tier 1 sites pose some contamination issues but are economically viable development projects, whereas Tier 2 sites have either higher contamination or less marketability. Tier 3 sites include brownfields that are least likely to be redeveloped, posing high environmental risks and, even if remediated, possessing negligible economic potential. These tiers suggest a strategy for cities seeking to redevelop dormant properties. Because Tier 1 sites are likely to be redeveloped on their own, cities should target Tier 2 sites that, with sufficient incentives, could become Tier 1 parcels. Tier 3 sites, however, require massive public investment for an uncertain economic return; but the health risks they pose necessitate remediation. Redeveloping Tier 2 brownfields presents a challenge; Tier 3 parcels even more so.

Nationally, an estimated 600,000 brownfields mar the landscape.[48] Their land coverage is high; a study of 180 U.S. cities reported 19,000 brownfields covering nearly 180,000 acres.[49] Research on municipalities in New Jersey showed that one-third of the cities contained at least 1 brownfield site; 8 percent had 5 or more brownfields.[50] One city official commented on the difficulty of redeveloping these sites—and on their negative ripple effects. "Developers are only interested if we provide substantial tax breaks. The entire surrounding area is affected. We are frustrated by our inability to stop the decay."[51] The findings show that in the high-impact sites, the Tier 3 brownfields, redevelopment is complicated by a host of other negative factors. A brownfield site in Kansas City was described this way:

> For the next two years, a huge pile of bricks and a burnt-out concrete building marked the site. Located next to an abandoned rail yard littered with weeds and junk, it was worse than an eyesore—it was a "disastrous spectacle," in the words of one city official. Businesses in the area threatened to flee to the suburbs.[52]

Since the mid-1990s, EPA has funded a series of pilot programs and demonstration projects on the brownfields issue. The purpose of these projects—which have been subsumed into a comprehensive "Brownfields Initiative"—is to "prevent, assess, safely clean up, and sustainably reuse brownfields."[53] The agency provides grants to localities so that brownfields can be evaluated as to the extent of the pollution, the likely cleanup costs, and any attendant legal issues. By 2000, the program had led to the investigation of 30,000 sites (many of which turned out to be pollution free after all) and the cleanup of nearly 2,000 brownfields.[54] Since their inception, EPA's brownfield programs, in partnership with states and localities, have generated many redevelopment successes. In Buffalo, for instance, a steel fabrication site that had been abandoned for more than a decade was transformed into a $16 million, 22-acre hydroponic tomato farm and greenhouse facility providing nearly 200 new jobs.[55] In Birmingham, more than 1 million square feet of commercial and industrial space has been redeveloped in a brownfield area where, until recently, nearly half the parcels were vacant. For thirteen years, an abandoned can factory in New Orleans sat idle; in 2000, it was converted into an upscale residential complex, complete with retail stores.[56] These success stories demonstrate that brownfield redevelopment is not impossible.

In 1998, Phoenix initiated its Brownfields Land Recycling Program. The city targeted brownfields in a 20-square-mile section of central Phoenix for assessment, cleanup, and redevelopment. To qualify, a site must be zoned commercial or industrial, be vacant land or unoccupied or underused property, and have real or perceived contamination. The benefits to property owners and developers are many: tax incentives for cleanup costs, property marketing assistance, priority access to city departments, and liaison with regulatory agencies.[57] Even with the continued annexation of fringe land and the amassing of an ample supply of vacant land, demand for used land near the city's center remains. Targeted brownfield sites like the one pictured in figure 5.8 are expected to be redeveloped within a five-year window.

FIGURE 5.8. Brownfield Site in Phoenix

CONSTRAINING LAND USE

Growth management is an effort to regulate "the amount, timing, location, and character of development."[58] States that have enacted growth management statutes typically have done so in reaction to the rapid consumption of land and the destruction of ecologically vulnerable areas. Hawaii was the first state to adopt statewide land use controls in the 1960s, followed by Vermont (1970), Florida (1972), and Oregon (1973). Since those early actions, other states have followed suit, with urban sprawl as a powerful call to action.

The State of Washington passed its Growth Management Act (GMA) in 1990. The act effectively fixed city borders by restricting sprawl and by creating urban centers in which employment and population density are required to increase. The incentive for cities to expand their political boundaries is mitigated because the development potential for vacant (virgin) land is diminished by GMA. The urban growth boundary for the Seattle area is displayed in figure 5.9. The 1995 boundary is shaded light gray in the map; the modest extensions of the boundary in 1997 are shown as dark areas within the circles.

Seattle's Strategy

The political logic driving the reuse of vacant land puts Seattle in a fortuitous position. Both the revenue system of the city and the state's GMA have structured a political strategy toward vacant land and land policies more generally. Seattle is landlocked, with practically no possibility of annexation. It operates under GMA (as do all

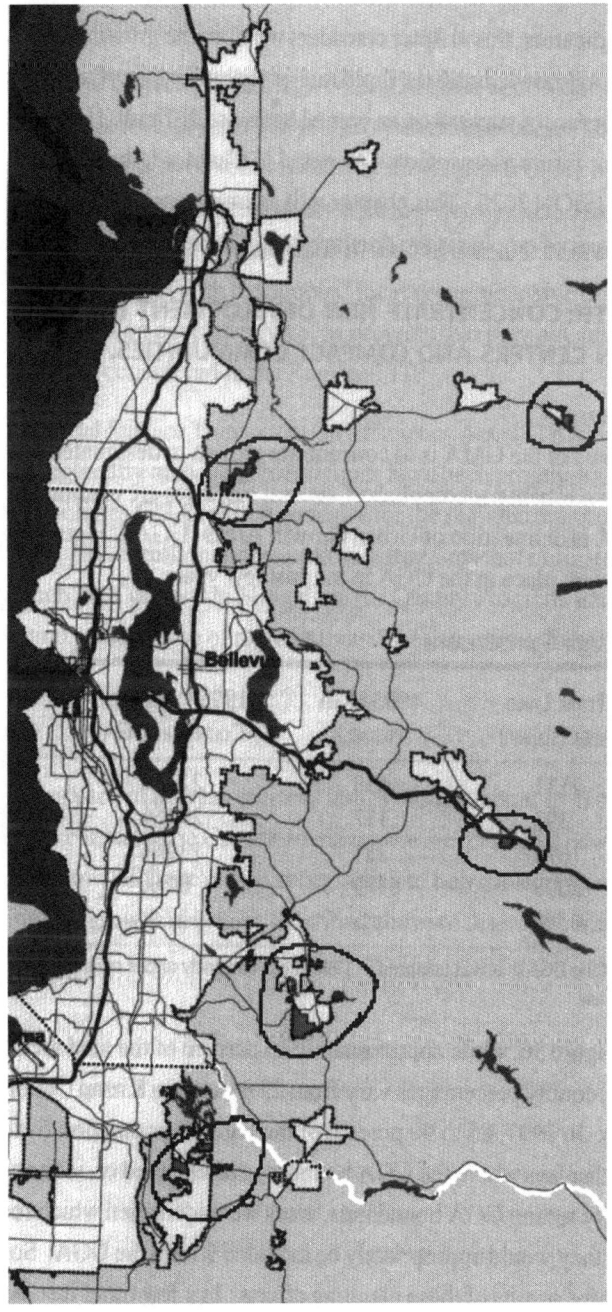

FIGURE 5.9. Urban Growth Boundary for the Seattle Metropolitan Area
Source: Puget Sound Regional Council, *1998 Regional Review*, December 1998,
40. Reprinted by permission of the Puget Sound Regional Council.

local governments in the state) and receives nearly two-thirds of its general tax revenues from nonproperty sources. As was discussed in chapter 3, the business and occupancy (B&O) tax and the sales tax are both broadly based taxes that include professional services. Less than 4 percent of the land is vacant, and most of that is in the form of temporary surface parking lots around commercial structures or on very steep slopes (and undevelopable without substantial costs) or, in residential areas, side lots that expand the backyards of residents who have no intention of developing the lot. Abandoned structures are, for the most part, in the process of being converted to productive use, and therefore are only "temporarily" abandoned.

GMA has nearly guaranteed that no new industrial sites will be created in the greater Seattle region, thereby protecting the vast industrial sites in south Seattle from being passed over for reutilization. GMA creates an insurance policy for Seattle's industrial base that economic forces will not jump to other cities. The vacancy rate for industrial property is virtually nonexistent. The Office of Economic Development estimated the 1998 vacancy rate at 1.7 percent. In fact, because of construction of the new stadiums and because of what several city and regional officials call a "loophole" in GMA that allows hotels, which are commercial enterprises, to be built near the stadium in an area zoned for industrial uses, the amount of industrial land is actually shrinking. One risk for Seattle, of course, is that the price of industrial-zoned land will rise to a level deemed unacceptable and industries will leave the city.

GMA also requires densification, meaning that Seattle's target population and employment levels will increase in areas zoned for such growth, especially urban growth centers and urban villages. This requirement has put enormous pressure on the land and housing markets, which appears to benefit both developers and the city. The program, amid a booming regional economy, has benefited developers because they can increase rents; they also benefit because of the density bonus programs of the city. If a developer locates in an area zoned for mixed uses, he can increase the densification of multifamily dwellings. (If he builds in an area zoned for multifamily housing, no increase in density is allowed.) The concession made by the developer is that the first floor of these structures must be retail space. The city benefits because the value of the building is greater than it would be in a multifamily-zoned area (and the property tax rate on multifamily structures is the same as on residential or any other property due to the state's uniform tax laws). The city also benefits because retailers must pay a B&O tax, while consumers pay a sales tax. Another density bonus program allows developers to increase the amount of square footage of a building if, in return, they contribute to a low-income housing program, build open spaces, or support historical preservation. As chapter 4 indicated, these density bonuses do not generate revenue but they do enhance the city's image of itself as a concerned and responsive place.

In the absence of state-mandated "urban growth centers," it is likely that the political strategy of cities to maximize revenues and/or minimize expenditures would have created these growth centers at precisely the same locations. The growth logic inherent in states whose cities are dependent on the sales tax results in developing growth poles near the political border of those cities. In the case of Seattle, we would expect major retail centers to be developed near the city's four corners. Indeed, before the establishment of urban growth centers and other urban growth boundary designations, the retail nodes of the city were the northeastern and northwestern corners, as well as the center of the city (the central business district, or CBD, and the medical and university area just to the east of the CBD). The southwestern and southeastern corners are urban villages. The urban growth centers, which are now required to have a higher population and employment density than other areas under GMA, we argue, have simply codified the development logic of Seattle because competition among cities and revenue-maximization strategies would have encouraged—and did indeed encourage—growth at those centers.

In light of the strong influx of migrants into the region, GMA's effect is to drive up the cost of land more than would be the case in its absence. Densification is encouraged, which benefits the city on two fronts. First, GMA restricts the amount of land available for residential, commercial, and industrial use, thereby increasing land values. As a consequence, property tax revenues are higher (the cap on property tax increases, known as the 106 percent rule, only affects buildings that have not been altered; higher-density reused buildings are not subject to the limit), and B&O taxes do not escape to neighboring jurisdictions because land availability is not much better elsewhere. The fortuitous position of cities, then, is that they can actually afford to reserve vacant land as open spaces and green space—because land demand is so high for the built spaces—without the risk of losing a revenue stream to vacant land.

Second, the city's revenue stream benefits financially from GMA because the assessed value of a mixed-use building with higher density in urban centers or urban villages is greater than it would be in a multi-family-zoned area. The property tax rate on buildings is at the same tax rate as on residential or any other property under the city's uniform tax laws. And the city's revenue stream doubly benefits the city's treasury because, as noted above, retailers must pay a B&O tax on the value of goods, whereas consumers pay a sales tax on goods.

The Role of Regional Organizations

Externally imposed rules such as state annexation laws and statewide growth management plans structure a city's strategic land behavior. Another external influence on city behavior is the presence of regional organizations. Regionally focused organizations, be they councils of governments, metropolitan planning organizations, or some other entity, constrain the choices available to a city. At the very least, they present another set of considerations for a city to weigh; and at most, they force a city to choose a less optimal (in its view) course of action.

Proximate communities are interdependent in many ways, but their governmental structures seldom reflect this condition. Economies tend to be regional, of course, irrespective of territorial limits and boundary lines.[59] Local governments often talk the language of regionalism, but historically they have been reluctant to embrace it. The creation of a regional organization happens in one of the three ways: The federal government makes it mandatory (or encourages it) through grant programs, state government passes a law requiring it, or local governments decide to do it. The key consideration is the amount of authority possessed by the regional organization. Are local jurisdictions willing to give up some of their power and authority to a regional entity in exchange for areawide solutions to common problems? The most common answer to the question has been "no." However, in a few areas such as Portland, Oregon, with its regional 2040 Plan and an elected metropolitan council, the answer has been "yes." And the willingness of local governments to think regionally appears to be increasing.[60]

Even before the passage of GMA, the Seattle metropolitan area had a regional orientation. For years, the Puget Sound Council of Governments (later to become the Puget Sound Regional Council) had sought to reconcile individual community interests with the larger regional interest. Growth pressures, especially in King County (which encompasses Seattle and its adjacent suburbs), provided sufficient impetus for regional action. In 1990, the regional council adopted a growth management, economic development, and transportation strategy for the region called VISION 2020. The implementation of GMA and VISION 2020 has created a powerful regional imperative. GMA is unequivocal; its Section RCW 36.70A.100 reads:[61]

> The comprehensive plan of each county or city that is adopted shall be coordinated with, and consistent with, the comprehensive plans adopted . . . [by] . . . other counties or cities with which the county or city has, in part, common borders or related regional issues.

Section RCW 36.70A.210 prescribes a meeting of counties and constituent cities:[62]

> Each county . . . shall convene a meeting with representatives of each city located within the county for the purpose of establishing a collaborative process that will provide a framework for the adoption of a county-wide planning policy.

Further, GMA established hearing boards to ensure that all municipalities and counties abide by the regionally based population, employment, and housing targets. (Subsequent amendments to GMA in the Buildable Lands Act further monitor the actions of localities.) Cities and counties do not have the choice to opt out of the regional framework established in GMA. The relevant hearing board for the Seattle area is the Central Puget Sound board, staffed by the Puget Sound Regional Council. If the board finds against the local government in question, sanctions can be imposed.

As a consequence of GMA and VISION 2020, cities are required to make land use decisions that mesh with regional strategies and targets. Within King County, cities operate under a set of countywide planning policies that set housing and employment targets. However, as several officials noted, even with the embrace of regionalism, it has been difficult to reconcile regional views and jurisdictional interests. And even as the cities work together, friction remains. Two Seattle-area cities provide an interesting example of strategic behavior within regional constraints.

Located east of Seattle are the cities of Bellevue and Redmond. The two cities, which are separated from Seattle by Lake Washington, share a common boundary. Bellevue is the larger of the two (with 109,000 residents in 2000 and 30 square miles); Redmond had a 2000 population of 45,000 and covers 15 square miles. Both cities are employment centers with more jobs than residents, and their downtown areas have been designated urban centers under GMA. Redmond's major employer, Microsoft Corporation, was once located in Bellevue. But when the City of Bellevue refused to change its zoning to accommodate Microsoft's campus development, the firm relocated to Redmond.[63] The section of Redmond in which Microsoft is located is surrounded by Bellevue on two sides. The area, known as Overlake, has become a significant commercial hub. Thus one of the sticking points for the two cities is the growing volume of "cut through" traffic from the south through Bellevue to Redmond. Bellevue, with concerns over meeting the transportation targets set via the GMA process, initiated a joint effort with Redmond to resolve the traffic problems.

For Redmond, the arrival and eventual expansion of Microsoft sparked a commercial boom that strained the city's capacity to handle growth. (Approximately one-quarter of the people employed in Redmond work for Microsoft.) By 1998, the city could not keep up with the demand for infrastructure, and the city council imposed a moratorium on new commercial development. And with the requirements of GMA and VISION 2020, the city has targets and goals that it is expected to achieve. Additional growth pressure on the city comes from the large planned developments outside Redmond in unincorporated King County. These developments, which were approved before GMA's implementation, have substantial urban effects and complicate Redmond's ability to reach its agreed-upon goals. And this has led to friction between Redmond and King County. One of the most contested King County planned developments is adjacent to the city of Redmond's 800-acre Watershed Preserve, land that the city has set aside as open space.

Bellevue has annexed small parcels within the urban growth area (as allowable under GMA), but generally the city is hemmed in by other cities and lakes. In a city without vast tracts of vacant land, the key land issue is the redevelopment of existing parcels to intensify use. Such actions enhance the city's revenue base and help the city reach its GMA targets. Thus in the downtown area of Bellevue, existing single-family dwellings are being redeveloped as mixed commercial-residential facilities. The basic question in Bellevue is how to use the land supply most efficiently. Figure 5.10 captures the downtown redevelopment scene: a single-family residence that is to be razed and replaced by a mixed-use condominium and retail development.

The city's comprehensive plan outlines its land use strategies:

- maintain commercial areas, do not expand them,
- do not create new commercial or industrial zones,
- do not change zoning boundaries,
- promote infill in existing commercial zones,
- focus growth into the downtown area, and
- intensify land use.

In the Seattle area, regionalism has taken root through the implementation of GMA and VISION 2020. Although regional organizations can trace their roots to the 1950s, it is evident that the passage of GMA has greatly strengthened them. From the perspective of local governments, regional organizations matter. As one Redmond official noted, in the past, a city's land use decisions were its own business. Now, under the scrutiny of regional organizations empowered by GMA, they are the region's business.

FIGURE 5.10.   Land Redevelopment in Bellevue, Washington

Zoning and Land Use

Since the nation's first zoning law was enacted by New York City in 1916, nearly all cities have adopted zoning as a mechanism to control their spatial development.[64] Missouri's statutes granting municipalities the right to zone property is typical: "For the purpose of promoting health, safety, morals or the general welfare of the community, the legislative body of all cities, towns, and villages is hereby empowered to regulate and restrict . . . the location and use of buildings, structures and land for trade, industry, residence or other purposes."[65] A city's zoning power directs the activities of a city in an orderly manner.

Land use maps graphically depict the spatial arrangement of these activities, usually by denoting residential, commercial, industrial, and open space use. Although property owners can appeal the zoning classification of their parcel, zoning and land use maps are fairly accurate portrayals of a city's personality. Increasingly, cities include a "vacant land" designation in their land use maps. In our survey, 65 percent of the responding municipalities indicated that vacant land was a category in their GIS data. Yet unlike the fairly stable categorizations of residential, commercial, industrial, and open space, vacant land is a transitional category, not a permanent or quasi-permanent use. Its metamorphosis into active use is not necessarily subject to an act of city council or zoning appeals board as long as the use to which it is put conforms to the land use designation.

The vacant land designations in land use maps do not provide sufficient information to a city in its effort to promote the use or reuse of its vacant land. For example, Seattle codes vacant land as "vacant," whether or not the vacant land is developable. Many of the parcels of land that are designated as vacant are adjacent lots to single-family homes that are used as side yards and, according to city officials, have always been used as side yards. They are vacant only because the city's land use map matches each parcel with a specific use marker; if the parcel has no structure on it, it is considered vacant. But these lots are, in most cases, not available for development or reuse. Philadelphia, likewise, describes the use of each parcel as commercial, residential, industrial, mixed use, or vacant. The row houses that have been razed because of their threat to the health and safety of the neighborhood are described as vacant land, even though their use is limited to residential purposes. Although the categories of land use are helpful in distinguishing the current use of a parcel, the designation "vacant" does not necessarily indicate a parcel's probable or likely future use.

Vacant land as a category of use, then, can have very different meanings. There may be a dilapidated structure on the land, old structures may have been razed, or perhaps there was never a structure on the land. In some cases, the land is available for use or reuse according to its zoning designation (e.g., vacant land zoned "residential" can be developed for residential purposes, but not for commercial use). But in other cases, the term "vacant land" means that the land is (and probably always was) vacant, and the possibility of use or reuse with a new building or structure is unlikely or undesired. Parcels adjacent to single-family homes that have always been used as a side yard or backyard illustrate this type of vacant land. It also might refer to undevelopable land or land that, due its steep slope or its odd shape, is unlikely to be anything other than vacant.

In each of these possible meanings of vacant land is an unstated assumption that warrants discussion. The assumption is that vacant land is unproductive or undevelopable or that it is not employed at its best and highest use. Although vacant land set aside as open space or green space does not fit this assumption—nor does vacant land that is a cliff or a slice of land between a highway and power plant—most other vacant land does. And in those cases, the implicit desire is that the vacant land is indeed just a transitional and short-term designation of a parcel of land. In other words, as a land use category, cities work to move the vacant land from its "unproductive" and "undesirable" status to a designated use category.

Vacant land tends to be a transitional category, not a permanent land use category. The length of time that a parcel remains attached to the "vacant" label becomes an important indicator of whether a city views its vacant land as a "good" or a "bad."[66] The vacant land survey asked cities to identify whether their supply of vacant land was expanding or shrinking and what causes contributed to that change. Although the majority of the responding cities noted that the supply of vacant land was expanding, most did not find this to be a cause for alarm. In fact, cities that are expanding their territorial mass, often through annexation, need more vacant land to accommodate growth. Vacant land, therefore, was considered "good," an opportunity for expansion and growth, a symbol of progress and advancement, a prized possession of dynamic cities. (Good vacant land is depicted in figure 5.11.)

Notwithstanding the expansion needs of growing cities, other cities pointed to vacant land as having been in a state of inactivity for "too long" (e.g., see figure 5.12). In these cases, vacant land has a temporal dimension that potentially harms the hoped-for prospects of using or reusing the land for productive purposes. Moreover, cities whose vacant land has languished in an unproductive state for some long, yet undefined, length of time fear that vacant land, like a virus, will spread

FIGURE 5.11.   "Good" Vacant Land

FIGURE 5.12. "Bad" Vacant Land: Vacant Too Long

through adjacent areas. The quicker the vacant land is put back into productive use, the less likely the decay will spread. The challenge confronting cities in which vacant land is considered "bad" is one of transforming the bad vacant land into good vacant land, whether it is part of a productive economic development activity or of open space, green space, art space, or side yards.

CONCLUSION

The physical evolution of a city takes place in a complex environment in which government plays a key role. Decisions about land development—which parcels to purchase, how to allocate various land uses, where to locate public facilities, how to sanction nonconforming uses, and the like—are decisions made by city government. We contend that the actions taken by city government reflect a political logic. That is, we argue that city governments behave strategically. They are motivated by three sometimes complementary, sometimes competing, imperatives: fiscal, social, and development. This chapter has focused on the development imperative: the maintenance of economic vitality and the enhancement of image.

Evidence from the Philadelphia and Phoenix metropolitan areas suggests that concerns of economic vitality are factored into land development decisions. As officials strive to maintain the economic health of the jurisdiction, they mobilize public capital. And vacant land is an important form of public capital. Many of a city's actions directly address economic development (e.g., the creation of a vacant land database that makes it easier to market property to potential investors, or the decision about where a new shopping mall should be located). Other actions seem aimed more at image enhancement, among other objectives (e.g., the demolition of dilapidated structures that clutter the cityscape). In effect, as cities pursue economic development, they try to maximize their supply of good vacant land while minimizing their stock of bad vacant land. If they are successful in doing so and economic vitality and enhanced image result, city officials are likely to engage in credit claiming. The political benefits of effective redevelopment of vacant land are potentially high.

External actors play a role in this process. In the cases cited in this chapter, the external actors have been state governments: Arizona and its annexation laws, Washington and its growth management statutes. States have always set the rules for their local governments, but what is increasingly being recognized is how those rules affect localities. In general, the recent trend has been to free local governments from some state constraints via the home rule mechanism.[67]

However, in the area of land use, a counter trend can be identified, at least in some states. Despite the traditional authority of general-purpose municipal governments to regulate and manage their land, the involvement of external actors has increased. In Washington, for example, simple city-level decisions to change the allowable density in a residential zone must meet a regional test. As concern over urban sprawl increases, more states are turning toward to growth management, or "smart growth," as a strategy.[68] This places states or newly empowered regional organizations in the midst of local land use decisions. And thus the strategic behavior of cities in pursuit of the development imperative changes.

NOTES

1. Helen Ladd and John Yinger, *America's Ailing Cities: Fiscal Health and the Design of Urban Policy* (Baltimore: Johns Hopkins University Press, 1989).
2. Michael A. Pagano and Ann O'M. Bowman, *Cityscapes and Capital: The Politics of Urban Development* (Baltimore: Johns Hopkins University Press, 1995), 21.
3. Philadelphia's 1999 mayoral campaign is an exception. Vacant land was a prominent issue in the campaign, and the eventual victor, John Street, commenced an ambitious effort to address his city's land problems.

4. Charles M. Tiebout, "A Pure Theory of Local Expenditures," *Journal of Political Economy* 64 (October 1964): 416–24; Vincent Ostrom, Charles M. Tiebout, and Robert Warren, "The Organization of Government in Metropolitan Areas: A Theory Inquiry," *American Political Science Review* 55 (October 1961): 831–42; Stephen L. Percy, Brett W. Hawkins, and Peter E. Maier, "Revisiting Tiebout: Moving Rationales and Interjurisdictional Relocation," *Publius: The Journal of Federalism* 25 (fall 1995): 1–17.

5. Daphne A. Kenyon and John Kincaid, eds., *Competition among States and Local Governments* (Washington, D.C.: Urban Institute Press, 1991).

6. In their study of the Milwaukee area, "Revisiting Tiebout," Percy, Hawkins, and Maier found that personal circumstances and employment considerations were important determinants of relocation. However, tax levels and service quality also played a part in cross-community moves, consistent with Tiebout's model.

7. Keeok Park, "Friends and Competitors: Policy Interactions between Local Governments in Metropolitan Areas," *Political Research Quarterly* 50 (December 1997): 723–50.

8. Alice Coleman, "Dead Space in the Dying Inner City," *International Journal of Environmental Studies* 19 (1987):103–7; C. Keuschnigg and S. B. Nielsen, "On the Phenomenon of Vacant Land," *Canadian Journal of Economics* (April 1996): S534–40; Neal Peirce, "Vacant Urban Land: Hidden Treasure?" *National Journal*, December 9, 1995, 3053.

9. Pagano and Bowman, *Cityscapes and Capital.*

10. See, e.g., Susan E. Clarke and Gary L. Gaile, *The Work of Cities* (Minneapolis: University of Minnesota Press, 1998); and Paul Brace, "The Changing Context of State Political Economy," *Journal of Politics* 53 (May 1991): 297–316.

11. Although a healthy local economy is important, there is not necessarily a consensus on the best way to create (or sustain) economic health.

12. Ann O'M. Bowman, *The Visible Hand: Major Issues in City Economic Policy* (Washington, D.C.: National League of Cities, 1987).

13. Brian J. L. Berry, *Growth Centers in the American Urban System*, vol. 1 (Cambridge, Mass.: Ballinger, 1973).

14. Charles C. Euchner, *Playing the Field: Why Sports Teams Move and Cities Fight to Keep Them* (Baltimore: Johns Hopkins University Press, 1993).

15. Pagano and Bowman, *Cityscapes and Capital*, 49.

16. Gregory J. Ashworth and Henk Voogd, *Selling the City: Marketing Approaches in Public Sector Urban Planning* (London: Belhaven Press, 1990), 3.

17. Bowman, *Visible Hand*, 14.

18. Peter F. Colwell and Henry J. Munneke, "Estimating a Price Surface for Vacant Land in an Urban Area," *Land Economics* 79 (February 2003): 15–28.

19. Fairmount Ventures, Inc., *Vacant Land Management in Philadelphia Neighborhoods: Cost–Benefit Analysis* (Philadelphia: Pennsylvania Horticultural Society, 1999).

20. Mitchell Zuckoff, "New Plan to Remake Mattapan Acreage," *Boston Globe*, July 16, 2000, A01.

21. Zuckoff, "New Plan," A01.
22. U.S. Advisory Commission on Intergovernmental Relations, *State Laws Governing Local Government Structure and Administration* (Washington, D.C.: U.S. Advisory Commission on Intergovernmental Relations, 1993).
23. For a discussion of annexation as political stretching, see Michael A. Pagano, "Metropolitan Limits: Intrametropolitan Disparities and Governance in U.S. Laboratories of Democracy," in *Governance and Opportunity in Metropolitan America*, ed. Alan Altshuler, William Morrill, Harold Wolman, and Faith Mitchell (Washington, D.C.: National Academy Press, 1999), 253–92.
24. Contaminated land is also referred to as "derelict" land.
25. Mary Edwards, "Annexation: A Winner-Take-All Process?" *State and Local Government Review* 31 (fall 1999): 221–31.
26. Jamie Palmer and Greg Lindsey, "Classifying State Approaches to Annexation," *State and Local Government Review* 33 (winter 2001): 60–73.
27. The data cited here were supplied by the Maricopa Association of Governments.
28. City of Peoria, "Annual Report," 1999; http://ci.peoria.az.us/AnnualReport /(June 1, 2003). The largest revenue element is state-shared revenue (from the state sales tax, income tax, and motor vehicle license tax), which amounts to 33 percent of total revenues.
29. Interviews with officials from the City of San Jose, California, indicate a similar strategy. These officials argued that the city was shifting its emphasis from its evolution during the past half-century as a residential city to a "mixed" city because of property tax limitations and because of the potential growth in sales tax revenues. The city's strategic plan, *2020 Plan*, put it best: "Generally, residential development on the fringe of the City costs more to serve than new growth in infill locations. Increased revenue from an industrial and commercial tax base is the most practical means of providing residents with reasonable levels of municipal services" (City of San Jose, Department of Planning, Building and Code Enforcement, *San Jose 2020 General Plan*, 1994, 16).
30. The Del Webb Corporation has secured an unusual arrangement for supplying water to its development. Anthem is supplied water leased from the Oaxan Indian community out of its Central Arizona Project water allocation.
31. City of Tempe, *Staff Summary Report*, prepared February 6, 2003; www.tempe.gov/clerk/history_02/20030206casg01.htm (June 1, 2003).
32. See the series of articles in the *Detroit Free Press* on Detroit's vacant land problems (e.g., Jennifer Dixon, "Detroit's Neglect Spawns Squatters: Makeshift Camps, Drugs and Prostitution Occupy Property," *Detroit Free Press*, July 7, 2000, 1; Cameron McWhirter, "Detroit Banks on Empty Lots: City Sees Cleveland as Model for Reviving Land for Development," *Detroit News*, February 15, 2001; www.detnews.com/2001/metro/0102/15/a01–188450.htm [June 1, 2003]).
33. For a review of the extant literature on inventories, see Ann O'M. Bowman and Michael A. Pagano, *Urban Vacant Land in the United States*, Working Paper (Cambridge, Mass.: Lincoln Institute of Land Policy, 1998).

34. Cynthia Carlson and Robert Duffy, "Cincinnati Takes Stock of Its Vacant Land," *Planning*, November 1985, 2–4.
35. David W. Jones, "Vacant Land Inventory and Development Assessment for the City of Greenville, S.C.," master's thesis, Clemson University, 1992.
36. David Gonzalez, "Vacant Lots, Except for Red Tape," *New York Times*, October 8, 1993, B1, B7.
37. Gonzalez, "Vacant Lots."
38. Pennsylvania Horticultural Society, *Urban Vacant Land: Issues and Recommendations* (Philadelphia: Pennsylvania Horticultural Society, 1995), 49.
39. "Greening New York's Waste Lands," *New York Times*, December 28, 1994, A12.
40. Pennsylvania Horticultural Society, *Urban Vacant Land*, 51.
41. Alan Ehrenhalt, "The Great Wall of Portland," *Governing*, May 1997, 20–24; Daniel Schneider, "To Halt Sprawl, San Jose Draws Green Line in Sand," *Christian Science Monitor,* April 17, 1996, 14.
42. Deborah Brett, "Assessing the Feasibility of Infill Development," *Urban Land*, April 1982, 3–9.
43. U.S. Environmental Protection Agency, *Brownfields Glossary of Terms*; www.epa.gov/swerosps/bf/glossary.htm#brow (June 1, 2003).
44. William Fulton and Paul Shigley, "The Greening of the Brown," *Governing*, December 2000, 31.
45. Sites that are part of the Superfund's National Priority List are not eligible for EPA's brownfield programs.
46. EPA has developed guidelines aimed at clarifying the liability of prospective purchasers, lenders, property owners, and others at brownfield sites. Although cleanup and remediation remain the primary goals, EPA can use its enforcement discretion to facilitate redevelopment.
47. Thomas K. Wright and Ann Davlin, "Overcoming Obstacles to Brownfield and Vacant Land Redevelopment," *Land Lines* 10 (September 1998): 1–3.
48. "Turning Brownfields to Green," *Governing*, December 2000, A16.
49. "Turning Brownfields to Green."
50. Michael Greenberg, Karen Lowrie, Laura Solitare, and Latoya Duncan, "Brownfields, TOADS, and the Struggle for Neighborhood Development: A Case Study of the State of New Jersey," *Urban Affairs Review* 35 (May 2000): 717–33.
51. Greenberg et al., "Brownfields," 724.
52. Fulton and Shigley, "Greening of the Brown," 31.
53. U.S. Environmental Protection Agency, *Brownfields Mission*; www.epa.gov/swerosps/bf/mission.htm (June 1, 2003).
54. "Turning Brownfields to Green."
55. U.S. Environmental Protection Agency, *Brownfield Success Stories*; www.epa.gov/swerosps/bf/success.htm (June 1, 2003).
56. Andrea Neighbours, "From Cans to Apartments in New Orleans," *New York Times,* March 26, 2000, 47.
57. The tax incentives include a tax deduction for expenses related to cleanup costs.

58. John M. Levy, *Contemporary Urban Planning*, 5th ed. (Upper Saddle River, N.J.: Prentice Hall, 2000), 215.

59. William R. Barnes and Larry C. Ledebur, *The New Regional Economies* (Thousand Oaks, Calif.: Sage, 1998).

60. Kathryn A. Foster, "Regional Impulses," *Journal of Urban Affairs* 19 (1997): 375–403.

61. Washington State Community, Trade, and Economic Development, *State of Washington's Growth Management Act and Related Laws 1998* (Olympia: Washington State Community, Trade and Economic Development, 1998), 11.

62. Washington State Community, Trade, and Economic Development, *State of Washington's Growth Management Act*, 15.

63. Microsoft still maintains offices in Bellevue. City officials are of mixed minds on the decision to deny Microsoft's request.

64. See, e.g., David Robertson and Dennis Judd, *The Development of American Public Policy* (Glenview, Ill.: Scott, Foresman, 1989).

65. Chapter 89, Section 89.020.1, of the Missouri statutes.

66. Abandoned structures, however, are almost always considered "not good," especially if they have been out of production for a period of time. Abandoned structures generate some city regulatory response, although the length of the abandonment (the longer, the more visual blight) and the disrepair of the facility (possibly threatening the health and safety of the citizens) precipitates more concern and action than vacant land.

67. Home rule increases the power of local governments to adopt policies and enact regulations on matters of local interest. See Dale Krane, Platon N. Rigos, and Melvin B. Hill Jr., *Home Rule in America: A Fifty-State Handbook* (Washington, D.C.: Congressional Quarterly Press, 2001).

68. Patricia E. Salkin, "Political Strategies for Modernizing State Land Use Statutes to Address Sprawl," paper presented at the Who Owns America? II conference, Madison, Wisc., June 4, 1998.

6

Strategic Uses of Vacant Land

That the use and reuse of vacant land are influenced by market forces is a well-known, accepted fact. That vacant land is affected by the decisions of local governments is not nearly so commonly acknowledged. And the notion that vacant land represents a resource for localities might strike some observers as nonsensical. But that is precisely what we have argued in the preceding pages. Just as decisions by private landowners to sell or hold a piece of property affect the supply of vacant land, so do choices by government to annex parcels, to tighten abandonment ordinances, to bulldoze dilapidated structures, to site a new public facility, to approve a rezoning request, or to subsidize a development project—to name but a few of the choices. Actions taken by private landowners and public officials also affect the quality of vacant land. Furthermore, vacant land is not an unequivocal "bad."[1] Certainly, some types of vacant land, such as contaminated brownfields and crumbling row houses turned drug havens, are difficult to count among a city's assets. But even they have potential value.

This chapter offers a spatial model of vacant land conversion, derived from the interaction of the three imperatives already discussed—fiscal, social, and developmental. Given these imperatives, how do city officials make strategic choices about vacant land? The model provides a guide as cities consider the tough question of how to transform vacant land into a resource. Several success stories are recounted, as are some cautionary tales.

A SPATIAL MODEL OF VACANT LAND

A return to the comment of Barry Wood, a student of European vacant land, is warranted: "The existence of vacant land offers Turin a unique opportunity to re-figure the city to meet the needs of the twenty-first century."[2] Upon reflection, the general sentiment that vacant land offers opportunities is accurate, but we disagree with the contention that Turin is somehow unique. Not so: City after city in the United States has an opportunity to re-figure itself for the future.

As we have argued throughout these pages, vacant land plays a vital role in city officials' strategic behavior. A parcel of vacant land is imbued not only with the "value" assigned to it by forces of supply and demand in the real estate market. Urban vacant land embodies characteristics derived from the three imperatives that we identified as essential to understanding city behavior. The city's fiscal structure makes the reuse status of vacant land more or less crucial in generating adequate revenues for the city's service-delivery responsibilities. Moreover, vacant land might also serve the purpose of creating buffers and fences, containing and restricting social groups and activities. And vacant land's potential as an element in a city's economic development arsenal can be vitally important to the city's economic growth prospects. These three imperatives individually or in tandem create the strategic space for city officials to probe the range of choices for vacant land.

Not all vacant land is equal. This point is depicted graphically in figure 6.1. The spatial location of a parcel of vacant land in the three-dimensional grid restricts or shapes its viability and potential to achieve the outcomes preferred by city officials. The cubes in figure 6.1 are not city specific, but rather land parcel specific. The condition of vacant land, as well as its purpose and characteristics, influence its placement on the large three-dimensional cube. Cities qua cities are not situated in the three-dimensional space because, as was noted above, parcels of vacant land vary not only across cities but also within a city. City officials take purposive actions structured by law, custom, and opportunity to convert a vacant land parcel. These actions are aimed at maximizing the individual or collective welfare of the community along any one or several of these three dimensions.

In figure 6.1, the imperatives are arrayed on the larger cube's surfaces in this manner: high development value on the front surface, and low development value on the back surface; high social value on the bottom surface, and low social value on the top surface; and high revenue value on the left side, and low revenue value on the right side. A vacant land parcel that has no revenue potential, that does not serve as a social buffer between groups and classes, and that cannot enhance the city's economic development profile will not capture the interest of city officials. The small checkerboard cube in the upper right corner of the larger cube depicts this type of land. The assessment of city officials who regard a parcel of vacant land as having the characteristics of the

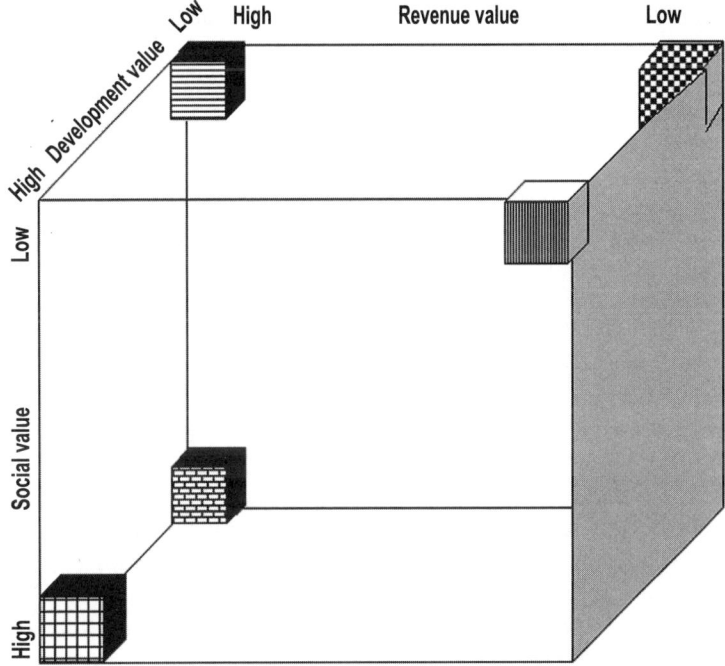

FIGURE 6.1. The Revenue, Social, and Development Values of Vacant Land in Three-Dimensional Space

checkerboard cube is that its use or reuse will have little or no effect on the collective well-being of the community and, consequently, their interest in the vacant parcel is expected to be lukewarm at best. At the opposite corner of the larger cube, however, is a vacant land parcel that has high revenue potential, that can serve a social purpose, and that does enhance the city's development potential. This small crosshatched cube depicts a vacant land parcel with high values on all three dimensions (or imperatives). City officials are more likely to actively and aggressively market this parcel. Their assessment, we suspect, would be that their preferred outcomes would be achieved by developing the parcel.

The three imperatives interact in different ways to produce a city's strategic actions toward vacant land. It is not uncommon for city officials to encourage the use or reuse of vacant land for development purposes, even if its revenue potential or the social value is uncertain. In this regard, as depicted by the vertically lined small cube in figure 6.1, city officials may believe that they are promoting the parcel's development potential when they grant tax abatements or create tax-increment-finance districts, even if revenue enhancement is risky. Moreover, encouraging the use or reuse of a parcel of vacant land might enhance the revenue-generating capacity of the city but simultaneously reduce property values. For example, what would an income-tax-dependent or sales-tax-dependent city lose by reusing a highly valued parcel of land as a public park, open space, or a parking lot? The parcel's value might not be in its revenue-producing value but rather in its attraction of high-income residents. The horizontally lined cube in figure 6.1 illustrates this possibility.

PUTTING VACANT LAND TO USE

The location of a parcel of vacant land in the cube shown in figure 6.1 depends on city officials' perceptions of the relative merits of the parcel vis-à-vis the three imperatives. In the hypothetical median city, we would expect to find a certain degree of dispersion of vacant land parcels, similar to the arrangement in figure 6.1. In other cities, vacant land might be concentrated at a few points. Cities with many "checkerboard cube" vacant properties face substantially different circumstances than cities where much vacant land is of the "cross-hatched cube" type. The real-world illustrations presented below reflect a variety of space within the three-dimensional cube. These examples do not exhaust the possibilities but rather highlight several dimensional combinations.

Chapter 4 explored the use of vacant land as a buffer or wall between land usages or income groups. One of the photographs from chapter 4 (shown again here as figure 6.2) illustrates how the three imperatives work together in a particular parcel. The revenue potential for the parcel depicted in the foreground on the right side of the photograph is fairly low. The land is zoned residential, yet property tax revenue generates very little of a city's cash needs. Its location on the boundary between a low-income neighborhood and a middle-income subdivision, means that the vacant land (and the wall, which shows that no home has access to the adjacent street or, therefore, to the low-income community) provides a buffer that is unlikely to be reduced in size. And its location in a residential neighborhood reduces its prospects of being converted into a commercial outlet, even if it could be successfully rezoned from residential to commercial use—especially given its proximity to a retail center two blocks away. Although market forces might encourage the vacant parcel's reuse for low-income housing, the likelihood of government intervention to encourage or otherwise facilitate its reuse is remote. Development options for higher-priced residential housing appear implausible because the land is surrounded by a low-income neighborhood, unless the entire neighborhood were "redevel-

FIGURE 6.2.   Walls and Income Classes in Peoria, Arizona

oped" as a subdivision. Otherwise, the social barrier of the vacant parcel in many ways parallels the purpose of the wall across the street. Its purpose is served, and it is unlikely to draw the attention of city officials any time soon.

Figure 6.3 depicts a vacant land parcel that was a prime candidate for recycling due to its high market value and its location near the heart of Philadelphia's central business district. Indeed, since this photograph was taken in 1999, the concert hall and recital theater have been constructed. All of this has occurred in a city where more than 31,000 parcels of land are vacant, most of them of low market or redevelopment value. The reuse of this city block in the heart of the city is expected to push neighboring property values upward and—because of the area's retail, lodging, and restaurant potential—to generate additional sales tax revenue. Its location is in a census tract that has already witnessed an increase in population of nearly 10 percent in the latest decennial census, even as the city declined by 4 percent.[3] The increase in the number of professionals and higher-income residents between 1990 and 2000 means that the parcel serves less a role as social buffer than as another element of the city's economic development program signaling a vibrant neighborhood. The city's decision to redevelop the land reflects city leaders' assessment of the parcel's very high revenue and development potential. Investment in the formerly vacant lot has the effect of increasing the value of other parcels in and near this section of the city.

Unlike the vacant parcels near the central core of Philadelphia, which have very high revenue-generating potential due to their commercial or entertainment attraction, most of the others have fairly low revenue-generating potential. Nor is the economic development potential great

FIGURE 6.3.   High-End Vacant Land on Philadelphia's Avenue of the Arts

for these scattered parcels. However, many of these vacant parcels possess social value, and they are turned into side yards or gardens, increasingly with the encouragement and tacit support of the city government. In other cases, vacant land is reused to provide low-income or subsidized housing. With little revenue-enhancing or development potential, Philadelphia has pursued a strategy of creating a low-density suburban feel with its housing programs. Figures 6.4 and 6.5 show new low-density, "suburb-within-the-city" housing in Philadelphia. Both of the new developments replace what originally were higher-density housing units that had been abandoned. This strategy is concentrated in particular in the area just north of the central city, as is denoted by the dark portions of the map in figure 6.6. These sections of Philadelphia contain the preponderance of publicly owned residential structures and vacant land parcels.

If transforming vacant land (and, in many instances, abandoned structures) into low-density housing stabilizes a neighborhood—even if it does not augment the city's treasury—the city's fiscal strategy of reducing outlays by making the neighborhood livable might be accomplished. Moreover, in the process, city expenses associated with managing and containing vacant land (the "bad" type) would decline. The Philadelphia City Planning Commission's exhortation to address the pernicious effects of vacant land and abandoned structures was based

FIGURE 6.4. Philadelphia's New Look: Lower-Density Row Houses

FIGURE 6.5. Philadelphia's New Look: Suburban-Style Housing

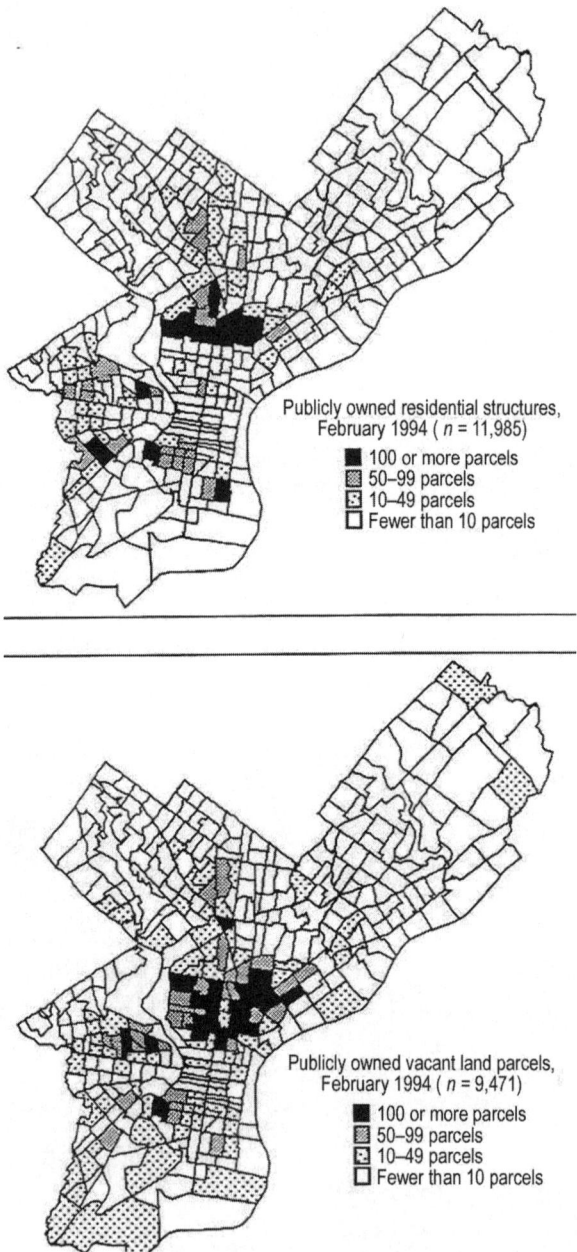

FIGURE 6.6.   Publicly Owned Residential Structures and Vacant Land Parcels, Philadelphia, 1994

Source: Philadelphia City Planning Commission, *Vacant Land in Philadelphia*, June 1995, 14. Reprinted by permission of the Philadelphia City Planning Commission.

on its assessment of the forgone revenues (tax effects) and of the city's demolition costs. But it also underscores the power of the social imperative. "The quality of life in these neighborhoods . . . [and] the perceived loss of social control and the cycle of neighborhood decline" are important considerations in reusing vacant land.[4]

When the golf course near downtown Redmond, Washington, ceased operation, the large tract of land remained vacant for a number of years. The city's population growth rate of 5 percent annually during the late 1980s and early 1990s intensified pressure for development. At the same time, a developer's plan to convert the green space into a commercial center met community resistance. The city's approach to the golf course's redevelopment was to require the developer to preserve the grove of trees shown in figure 6.7 in exchange for a height bonus: the construction of an additional floor in the project's hotel. This action allowed the city to reap the economic benefits of the new commercial center but at the same time reassure residents that city leaders were willing to impose some limitations on development.[5] The development potential of the old golf course property was sufficiently high that a portion of it could be successfully devoted to a social use: preservation of a slice of Redmond's past—and a buffer for the adjacent commercial development.

The vacant land along the Salt River in Tempe, Arizona, was a prime candidate for city-assisted development. Not only had the city exhausted

FIGURE 6.7. Preservation Efforts in Redmond, Washington: Vacant Land as Green Space

its annexable land; Tempe was also built out, with its last substantial area of developable real estate already having been brought to production in the southwest. Immediately to the north of Tempe's old downtown was land near and on the river basin of the frequently dry river. Its revenue potential, which as commercial real estate was assessed as quite high, and its development potential, as one of the precious few developable parcels left in the city, were both instrumental in city officials' care to ensure that the "right kind" of development took place. Residential development would be a drain on the city's revenue-generating capacity, whereas a commercial retailing venture would generate net revenue for the city.[6] Moreover, the location of the parcel is near the northern border of the city, just a short distance from Scottsdale. Developing the site for commercial retailing would attract residents of not just Tempe but also of other neighboring cities. The parcel's shopping shed, then, extends beyond the city's corporate boundaries and includes parts of Scottsdale as well as Phoenix. In addition to extending the proximate shopping shed for tax-revenue purposes, the city is marketing the site for broader tourist attraction. The vacant land that was converted into Town Lake (figure 6.8) was to become a training facility for the Olympic rowing team. An expansive hotel and restaurant complex for out-of-town conventioneers and other visitors has grown up nearby.

Many parcels of vacant land in Camden, New Jersey, possess the characteristics of the hypothetical "checkerboard cube" of figure 6.1: They are low on all three dimensions. For the vacant structures pictured in figure 6.9, the development potential is negligible, the social value is at best nonexistent, and the revenue potential has virtually evaporated.[7] This is due, in part, to the larger Camden context. Real estate values in the city have dropped or been flat; even new state investments such as the New Jersey State Aquarium have not generated the hoped-for spin-off development. Property taxes, the primary revenue source for New Jersey cities, contribute only approximately 20 percent of Camden's operating budget. Thus, both the development potential and the revenue value of vacant property such as that shown in figure 6.9 are low. The social considerations are just as prohibitive. Throughout Camden, dilapidated buildings have served as havens for squatters and drug dealers. In response, the city and local nonprofit organizations have instituted an effort to board up and secure abandoned structures to prevent them from becoming health and safety threats. The social effects of vacant parcels such as the one pictured are decidedly negative.

Admittedly, vacant land and abandoned structures in Camden represent an extreme case, given the preponderance of vacant parcels situated at or near the low end of all three dimensions. Still, Camden's

FIGURE 6.8.   Vacant Land in Tempe, Arizona: Salt River Project, Before and After Conversion into Town Lake

situation makes the larger point: When vacant land lacks revenue, social, and development value, its prospects for reuse are severely constrained.

APPROACHES TO REUSING VACANT LAND

Vacant land presents a variety of challenges to cities. An overabundance of vacant land depresses prices and reduces revenues; too little

FIGURE 6.9. "Checkerboard Cube" Abandoned Dwellings in Camden, New Jersey

vacant land limits development possibilities. Vast tracts of land may remain vacant for long periods, awaiting the "right" reuse project; small, scattered parcels complicate a comprehensive solution. The private ownership of vacant land may constrain a city's options, just as the perception of contamination makes reuse difficult. Vacant lots that are not secured may become dumping grounds and signal to passersby a neighborhood in decline.

The challenges may be especially daunting in cities with an abundance of "bad" vacant land. Even so, vacant land presents some compelling opportunities. Today's abandoned structures can be razed to create space for a park, and eventually perhaps a new structure. Contaminated soil can be removed and the land restored. Even a parcel that remains vacant for a long period may be converted into a temporary garden by enterprising neighbors. Land with unbuildable slopes and wetlands can be set aside for conservation as a natural habitat. And this is not to suggest that vacant land's sole value resides in its reuse. A vacant parcel lying fallow with natural vegetation may, from the perspective of city officials wishing to maximize the welfare of their community, be preferable to many kinds of reuse.

The transformation of vacant land requires the involvement of city government and, frequently, its active leadership. The city adopts ordinances regulating the management of vacant land, it reviews and approves a developer's reuse plans and may even design strategies for reuse, it underwrites some of the redevelopment costs, and it may even hold the title to the land itself. Thus, the role of city government is extensive. Our basic caution to city leaders grappling with the challenges presented by vacant land is this: A solution for one parcel is not a solution for all, just as a solution for one city is not a solution for all cities. City leaders must craft solutions that fit the situation, the context, the supply of available resources, and the opportunities.

The variability across cities and the need for approaches keyed to a given context was brought home in statistical analysis of our questionnaire data. In chapter 2, grouping the cities by region revealed apparent patterns: Southern cities had more vacant land as a percentage of their total land area than did Northeastern cities. When abandoned structures were the focus, Northeastern cities led the list and Western cities were at the bottom. Individually, changes in population and land area seemed potentially useful in explaining why some cities had proportionately more vacant land or abandoned structures. However, multivariate analysis found little statistical support for conventional explanations for why some cities had proportionately more vacant land than others.[8]

The statistical model presented in table 6.1 shows that region, population change, land area change, and economic growth do not yield statistically significant explanations. The most promising variable in the analysis is a composite measure developed by David Rusk that combines population density and land area change into a weighted "elasticity index."[9] Somewhat unsurprisingly, our analysis found that the more elastic the city, the more vacant land it has. After further probing, it became clear that expansion of city boundaries was into predevelopment areas where vacant land was awaiting conversion. In other words, there is more "good" than "bad" vacant land, and the former is associated with expanding or "elastic" cities. Beyond that finding, the statistical model of vacant land had negligible explanatory power.

Abandoned structures, however, were found to be a different proposition. The analysis supports the contention that the slower a city's population growth from 1980 to 1995, the higher its number of abandoned buildings. However, no other variable (e.g., region or economic growth) is statistically significant. The larger point is that the explanation for the proportionate amount of vacant land is not the same as the explanation for the number of abandoned buildings. Furthermore, in the analysis, when the focus shifts from vacant land to abandoned structures, sign changes occur in four of the six independent variables in the models. Vacant land and abandoned buildings may be related, but their causal linkages appear different. As a result, policies and programs should be appropriately tailored.

TABLE 6.1. Regression Analysis of Survey Data

Variable or Measure	Ratio of Vacant Land Area to Total Area (Unstandardized Coefficients)			Abandoned Structures per 1,000 Population (Unstandardized Coefficients)		
	B	Standard Error	Significance	B	Standard Error	Significance
Land area change, 1980–95	0.0010	0.0008	0.2196	-0.0034	0.0281	0.9032
Elasticity index [a]	*0.0389*	*0.0162*	*0.0196*	-0.6221	0.5325	0.2485
Fiscal position, 1996	-0.1171	0.1651	0.4809	-4.6383	3.2542	0.1605
Population change, 1980–95	0.0001	0.0006	0.8894	*-0.0355*	*0.0170*	*0.0423*
Region	-0.0344	0.0469	0.4656	0.0904	1.4205	0.9495
Economic growth, 1982–91	0.0159	0.0266	0.5535	0.6866	0.9562	0.4762
(Constant)	0.0503	0.0663	0.4509	6.5024	2.0904	0.0031
R^2	0.2399			0.2452		
Adjusted R^2	0.1599			0.1508		
Standard error of the estimate	0.1434			4.0790		
F-statistic	2.9988			2.5984		
Significance	*0.0129*			*0.0292*		
Degrees of freedom	63			54		

Note: Numbers in italics indicate variables that achieve conventional significance levels ($p < .05$).
[a] Elasticity index is from David Rusk, *Cities without Suburbs*, 2nd ed. (Baltimore: Johns Hopkins University Press, 1995).

A Universal Prescription: Information

Although no one approach can apply to all cities, one exhortation does apply to all: Know your vacant land. That is, know how much there is, where it is located, and what its characteristics are. This dictum operates as a first principle. Gerrit Knaap and Terry Moore refer to this as a vacant land inventory.[10] Without adequate knowledge of vacant land, a city cannot design policies and programs effectively. The survey results revealed that many cities lagged in the creation of information systems that contain even rudimentary data on their vacant land. As of 1998, 56 percent of the large cities relied on geographic information systems to track vacant land, but four in ten cities did not have vacant land in this systemic format.[11]

Without a reliable database containing information about derelict property throughout the city, a systematic response to vacant land will prove elusive, and policies will likely fall short of their intended effect. For decision makers, both public and private, to design successful intervention strategies, information about vacant land and abandoned structures needs to be accurate, timely, and computerized.

Monitoring abandoned or vacated structures seems even more problematic than tracking vacant land. Figure 6.10 reports the varied procedures cities use for learning about a structure's abandonment. By far, the notification method most frequently used was "calls from neighbors," selected as one of the top three methods by 73.6 percent of the cities. "Informal feedback" from city officials was relied upon more heavily than were regular inspections by city personnel, such as building inspectors, health and safety officials, or fire marshals. Figure 6.10 further suggests that tax delinquency and health inspections, two time-honored approaches to discovering abandonment, were relied on less frequently than calls from neighbors, informal feedback, and inspections, if they were employed at all.

Armed with up-to-date information, cities can go about managing and marketing vacant land. A geocoded database with parcel-level information on property value, tax status, infrastructure access, code violations, and zoning is an invaluable development tool. As the layers of information accumulate, a comprehensive picture of the city emerges. And city leaders then are in a much better position to evaluate how a specific property stacks up vis-à-vis the three imperatives.

Designing a Process for Recycling Vacant Land

As has been noted, cities differ with regard to the amount, type, and condition of their vacant land. But although the circumstances

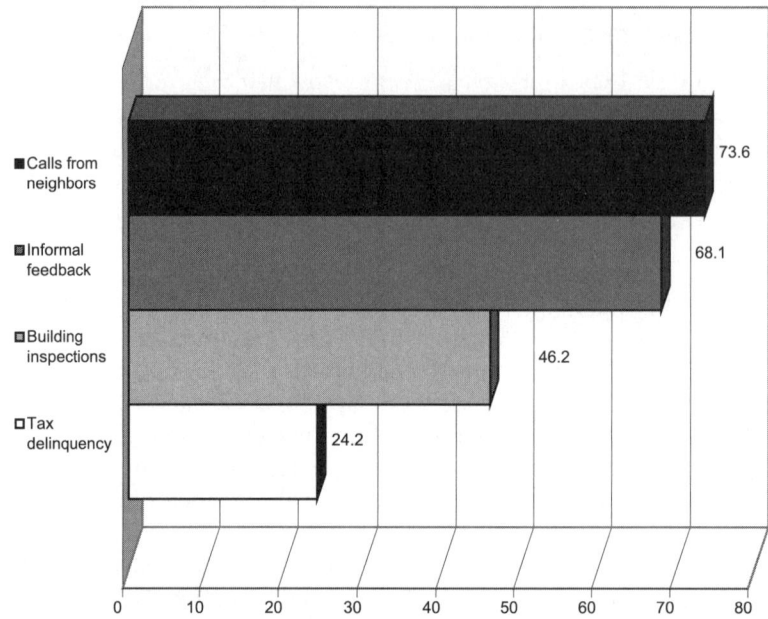

FIGURE 6.10. How Does Your City Know When a Structure Is Vacant? (percentage of responding cities that listed item among top three; $N = 91$)

combine differently in different places, some commonalities across cities allow for learning and, perhaps, emulation. We have noted already that cities need sufficient information to address vacant land, regardless of circumstance. Beyond that, cities may find a new set of policies, an alternative administrative structure, or different programs useful. In this section, a series of potential actions is presented. The intent here is not to prescribe but rather to highlight some notable tried-and-true approaches that may prove useful elsewhere.

ANTICIPATORY ACTIONS: VIGOROUS CODE ENFORCEMENT
In an effort to stem the negative consequences of vacant land and abandoned structures, the City of Phoenix enacted ordinances, created a new city department, and changed its procedures. A Neighborhood Preservation Ordinance was adopted in 1987, followed by a Property Maintenance Ordinance in 1991. As a result of the latter enactment, the Neighborhood Services Department (NSD) was created from pieces of eleven different city departments. The bureaucratic

consolidation was intended to reorient and intensify the focus on neighborhoods.

NSD's mission is neighborhood capacity building: preservation, revitalization, and development; one of the key responsibilities is code enforcement. Typically, the code enforcement process commences as the result of a complaint about a potential violation, such as lots overgrown with weeds or cluttered with refuse or structures that are unoccupied and unsafe or used by squatters. Vacant land complaints are handled through one process, and vacant structures are addressed in a different manner.

Phoenix is divided into twenty-three geographic areas called minidistricts, which are further subdivided into quarter-sections. When a complaint about a code violation on vacant land is received at NSD, it is assigned to an inspector in that minidistrict.[12] If an inspector finds a complaint to be valid, a thirty-day notice of violation (NOV) will be issued and sent to the property owner.[13] The goal of the NOV is to achieve voluntary compliance. On average, an estimated 50 to 60 percent of owners voluntarily comply (e.g., remove the litter, mow the weeds) upon receipt of the NOV. If the owner fails to take action, the city sets up an abatement team for the property.

At this point, the remediation process moves beyond the minidistrict; title and tax searches are conducted by the real estate division. A new thirty-day NOV containing abatement cost estimates is sent to all parties involved with the property. Realization of the financial liability for a city-contracted remedy stimulates a voluntary action by responsible parties in approximately 75 to 80 percent of the noncompliance cases. For the remainder, the team writes up the scope of the work necessary to abate the violation, obtains bids, and awards the job. The city pays the contractor and places an assessment against the property. Under Arizona law, tax liens have top priority for payback but enforcement costs are next to be reimbursed.

In the case of vacant structures, the city typically moves to board up unsecured buildings. If there is no rehabilitation plan for the property, then it becomes a demolition case. A title search will ensue, an NOV will be issued, and the city will petition the Rehabilitation Appeals Board to demolish the structure. The board, which is appointed by the mayor to hear requests for demolition and appeals of liens, has several options. Beyond simply upholding (or not) the city's NOV, it can give property owners a maximum of ninety days to rehabilitate or demolish the structure themselves. The board also has the power to forgive liens.[14] If the board supports the city's petition for demolition, then asbestos testing is done, an abatement plan is designed, a demolition contract is awarded to the successful bidder, and the building is razed. An assessment also is placed against the property. For structures located in historic preservation districts, a different set of procedures ensues, aimed less at demolition and more at restoration. [15]

In the five redevelopment areas in Phoenix, NSD is more proactive in identifying violations rather than simply waiting for complaints. In these areas, compliance is part of the larger goal of revitalizing neighborhoods, and additional resources can be leveraged. NSD takes a strategic approach in these areas and may opt not to cite each and every violation. As might be expected, over time, there has been some politicization of the process. It is not uncommon for a City Council member to get involved in a specific case in his or her district via the complaint process. Each council district receives funding for the neighborhood-empowering "Fight Back" program, and the boundaries of the city's infill program have been adjusted so that it reaches into nearly every council district.

The Code Enforcement section of NSD has become a problem-solving organization, providing resources for neighborhoods. The city's success in acquainting residents with the property maintenance program has led to more demands for code enforcement. In one illustrative year in the late 1990s, there were 31,000 complaints involving separate properties; on average, the cited properties had 2.5 violations. More broadly, Phoenix has sought to educate residents about the relationship between blight and crime. The antislumlord task force in Phoenix led to state legislation on the issue.

Because vacant land is often contested terrain, not everyone is supportive of the city's activist posture regarding property maintenance. Opposition has come from some property owners and from property rights advocates. Cost is a factor as well; during the 1990s, the city's annual demolition costs ran upward of $1 million. At the same time, however, voluntary compliance has increased. The increase in voluntary compliance is attributed not only to Phoenix's stepped-up NOV efforts but also to the Arizona statute that makes enforcement liens second in line for payoff. In addition to its administrative procedures, the city can use court-ordered abatement to gain access to vacant property, especially in cases of imminent hazard. In these instances, an enforcement officer and the city attorney determine the remedy.

In Phoenix, where City Council members are elected by districts, political campaigns are geared toward neighborhoods. The key to reelection is doing right by the neighborhoods in one's district, and as a result, neighborhood associations wield a lot of clout. Still, council members are cross-pressured because interest groups such as the Board of Realtors and landlord organizations are important in city politics.[16] Thus any new ordinance or procedure is likely to receive much scrutiny and debate with an eye on achieving a satisfactory balance of interests.

REDESIGNING THE ACQUISITION AND DISPOSITION PROCESSES

The magnitude of Philadelphia's problem of vacant land and abandoned structures is mind-boggling. Having been battered by the twin forces of suburbanization and deindustrialization, Philadelphia now is a much smaller city than it was in 1950. Some sections of the city have lost as many as half or even two-thirds of their 1950 population. In these areas, blocks of abandoned property are interrupted only occasionally by occupied structures. By 2000, more than 31,000 vacant lots and an estimated 54,000 abandoned structures contributed to widespread blight.[17] An estimated two-thirds of these properties are privately held; the remaining third is in public ownership, primarily in the city's hands. The city has acquired these parcels in various ways—for example, through the old urban renewal program and from sheriff sales of tax-delinquent properties.

Philadelphia's response to the vacant property situation has been criticized as "reactive," "fragmented," and woefully underpowered.[18] Particularly troublesome are the city's acquisition and disposition processes, which confound and exacerbate the problem. Even a simple action such as transferring a small side lot to an adjacent property owner is complicated.[19] After a series of studies of Philadelphia's vacant land situation, a working group on blight elimination came up with a set of short- and long-term recommendations.[20] At the top of the list was a reorientation to handling vacant land as "asset management."

Underlying Philadelphia's changed thinking was a realization that the logic of growth, which had driven the city for so long, was no longer appropriate. The key to Philadelphia's future is not growth but rather the creative management of decline and of its chief manifestation, blight. But this is not necessarily a negative enterprise. Ridding the city of blight will allow for new patterns of redevelopment with, in all likelihood, lower-density land use. The challenge to Philadelphia's leaders is to "understand vacant property as a generic resource."[21]

To get to the position of managing vacant land as an asset, the city has to implement several of the report's recommendations. At the most basic level was the compilation of a citywide database of abandoned structures and vacant lots. Related to that was the creation of an Office of Vacant Land Management within the administration. A fragmented administrative apparatus—in which as many as fifteen public agencies had some sort of responsibility for vacant land—has made it difficult to compile an inventory, much less to develop effective strategies.

Furthermore, the city's cumbersome procedures have frustrated the efforts of individuals and developers who have wanted to improve the land and/or purchase the property.[22] The lack of coordination across the various agencies has led to multiple directions and countermanded decisions.[23] As a result, vacant land sits idle year after year, joining other long-term vacancies. A new gateway office with the sole function of managing the city's vacant land would lead to a more coherent approach. A central goal of this approach, then, is to reduce the inventory of city-owned vacant land through the implementation of a vacant lot management system. The components of this system include a "clean and lien" program, whereby even more vacant land could fall into the city's hands, at least in the short term. The objective of the program is, once a parcel is acquired, to maintain it, perhaps consolidate it with other vacant properties nearby, and then transfer it to private ownership.

To facilitate the acquisition and disposition of vacant land and abandoned structures, the working group on blight elimination recommended several other actions. One is the identification of "hot spots" and target neighborhoods where immediate blight intervention is necessary. Another recommendation is the development of neighborhood investment plans to be monitored by Neighborhood Planning Councils. Community-based organizations are considered important complements to the city-sponsored activities. These groups can assist (or direct) the planning for neighborhood reuse and redevelopment as well as market vacant lots to residents and businesses. More diligent enforcement of the city code, coupled with increased penalties for violations and more media attention to the issue, are also recommended actions. Further, the working group suggested that state laws on foreclosure, condemnation, and property rights be reexamined in light of their impact on vacant land. In essence, the goal is a completely redesigned process and a new look for the city.

In 2001, Mayor John Street used many of the working group's recommendations for the Neighborhood Transformation Initiative (NTI), a five-year plan for reclaiming vacant land and converting it to a marketable asset. NTI's goals are grand; nearly $300 million is to be spent for blight removal, demolition, and land acquisition.[24] In its first year, NTI had led to the removal of 127,000 abandoned cars from the city's streets and the hauling off of 16,000 tons of debris from vacant lots. The number of code violation notices and warnings increased, as did the arrest of illegal dumpers. Still, it remains to be seen whether NTI can achieve the degree of transformation its supporters have promised.

Using Nongovernmental Actors

The primary focus of our research has been the role of city government in managing its vacant land. In some cities, including two of our fieldwork cities, nonprofit organizations play an especially important part. In Camden, community groups and faith-based organizations supplement the city's efforts. In Philadelphia, urban gardening groups have been instrumental in reusing vacant lots. In both cases, the coproduction of services by these groups grew out of deficiencies in the cities' efforts.

COMMUNITY GROUPS AND FAITH-BASED ORGANIZATIONS

As was noted above, abandoned structures are a ubiquitous presence in Camden. The city government, plagued by an array of problems, has been unable to mount a concerted effort to recycle and reuse the land.[25] City officials in this financially strapped community have struggled to try to keep track of city-owned vacant land and abandoned buildings on an ever-lengthening list. Nearly all these properties have come into the city's hands through foreclosures, most of them with tax liens and in substandard condition. In terms of the figure 6.1 diagram, Camden is awash in vacant property of the "checkerboard cube" variety: It does not help the city's revenue picture, it is of limited social value, and it possesses scant development potential.

Periodically, the city conducts an auction of vacant properties in an effort to attract buyers through an open bidding process. Because of the weak market for these properties, many of them remain in the city's hands for an extended period. This is the point at which nonprofit organizations intervene, focusing on redeveloping specific neighborhoods. Some of the groups are faith based; others are secular. In south Camden, Habitat for Humanity and Heart of Camden are active; in east Camden, it is the Saint Joseph's Carpenters Society. There are several groups involved in north Camden, including the North Camden Land Trust, which was spun out of a grassroots organization, Concerned Citizens of North Camden, and a group called Save Our Waterfront. Under the New Jersey Fair Share Housing Plan, city-owned property can be given to these nonprofits with stipulated uses, such as affordable housing. Nonprofit organizations attribute their expanded role to the city's lack of capacity; even as the city redeveloped its waterfront, neighborhood development was left to nonprofits and their expertise in housing.

It needs to be noted that reusing these properties is not easy. Even Camden's extremely low property values are not sufficient to lure investment. Many abandoned structures have large liens against them, and unless some mechanism exists for the elimination (or substantial reduction) of the debt, their reuse is unlikely. Assuming that a clear title can be provided, nonprofit organizations are frequently given a preference as residential redevelopers. With high hopes, Camden's nonprofits moved into the void created by the city's inaction and began to amass some redevelopment experience. But these organizations can be forces of opposition as well. Efforts to develop industrial parks on remediated brownfields encountered resistance from Heart of Camden, which feared that the development would isolate its neighborhood. Still, even as the city—with massive amounts of state aid—begins to pull itself out of its downward spiral, community groups and faith-based organizations continue to be a vital part of most neighborhoods.

URBAN GARDENERS

In Philadelphia, nonprofit organizations have been active in promoting the reuse of vacant land through community gardening. Foremost among the gardening organizations is the Pennsylvania Horticultural Society (PHS) and its Philadelphia Green program. PHS was founded in 1827 and promotes an array of horticultural experiences for local residents. As was mentioned in chapter 4, Philadelphia Green actively pursues the conversion of city-owned vacant land into community gardens. With a staff of forty, the program provides technical and educational assistance to community groups as they undertake this conversion. For example, they work with neighborhood-based community development corporations (CDCs) to incorporate the management of vacant land into CDC plans.[26] The larger intent underscores a social imperative: to improve the quality of life in these deteriorating neighborhoods. As one observer concluded, "Community gardens serve as a basic tool for teaching CDCs and neighborhood residents an effective way of dealing with [the] problem of vacant land."[27]

Community gardens are particularly compelling in cities whose population density is decreasing. Transforming vacant lots into gardens re-integrates the parcels "into the lower density fabric of the community."[28] Cities should design community gardening programs that are appropriate to the local context. The feasibility of community gardening hinges on a number of factors—such as the number, size, and location of vacant lots; the real estate market; the level of potential interest among gardeners; the local legal context; and the nonprofit and private-sector entities that exist or can be created to meet local needs.[29]

This last factor emphasizes the coproduction aspects of urban gardening. City governments are not the sole source of solutions for vacant land. Cities can support the creation of nonprofit land trusts to take title to and manage vacant lots; or if they prefer greater involvement, they can structure public–private partnerships. Schukoske derived a set of elements that characterize successful urban gardening programs. Among the list of twenty "best-practice" elements are these:

- creating an inventory of vacant lots (both public and private) in low-income neighborhoods, and making that information readily accessible to the public;
- authorizing contracts with private landowners for the lease of vacant lots (and providing favorable tax treatment to agreeable landowners);
- authorizing the use of municipal land for minimum terms long enough to elicit commitment by gardeners, such as five years; and providing for the possibility of permanent dedication to the parks department after five years' continuous use as a community garden;
- providing for interagency coordination of resources to facilitate creation and operation of community gardens;
- providing for the clearance of rubble and contamination where needed, and for regular trash collection; and
- preparing land for gardening by tilling and building raised beds, configuring some gardens for access by disabled gardeners.[30]

The role for city government is greater for certain program elements (e.g., contracts, land leases, and interagency coordination) than in other areas. Nonprofit organizations can take on some of the other responsibilities, thus supplementing a city's actions. In cities that are stretched to their limits by the magnitude of the vacant land situation, nonprofit organizations have the potential to play a leading role.

The Role of State Government

Local governments operate in a setting constrained by their state governments, as has been noted throughout the preceding chapters. The State of Washington's Growth Management Act influences the land use choices of Seattle, Bellevue, and Redmond. Arizona's annexation laws have set into motion the intercity scramble for territory (and tax revenue) in the Phoenix metropolitan area. Pennsylvania's Agricultural Land Preservation Program allows the purchase of farmland easements in Bucks County, just as the state's Spot Condemnation Act enables the City of Philadelphia to acquire vacant, tax-delinquent, and blighted properties. And in Camden, the State of New Jersey's involvement has moved beyond statutes and regulations into actually managing the city's finances.

In addressing the challenges and opportunities of vacant land, local jurisdictions need to work within state constraints. For localities, the optimum situation is for those constraints to be as favorable as possible. From the perspective of state governments, a different optimum exists, in which policies provide adequate uniformity statewide yet allow sufficient local customization. This is not an easy balance to achieve or maintain.

In seeking favorable constraints, localities might take some comfort from the recent tendency of state governments to rethink their dealings with local governments. Some observers have harkened the onset of a new era of state–local relations in which the two levels of government can function as governing partners.[31] Under this arrangement, often called "second-order devolution," the role for local government would expand beyond simple implementation of state directives to include the actual design of meaningful policies and programs.[32] Local problem solving would occur within a framework of active support from state government. As the state–local governance system is reshaped, "responsibility, authority, and discretion are devolved to lower levels of government."[33] By the same token, other observers are less optimistic, noting that increased responsibility also means increased costs for localities.[34]

LAND USE

Although land use traditionally has been an arena in which local governments have enjoyed much discretion, many states have begun to reinsert themselves into the mix.[35] One illustration is Maryland's 1997 Smart Growth Areas Act, which rewards local governments that target new growth to areas that already have infrastructure and denies state funding to infrastructure projects that encourage urban sprawl. Since the passage of this act, many other states have followed suit with their own smart growth provisions. Thus it is ironic that as states begin to loosen the reins on their local governments in many functional areas, they are tightening them with regard to land use.

Undoubtedly, these changes will affect vacant land—and the way in which cities manage and regulate it. So it is imperative that localities petition state governments to institute policies that are favorable and to repeal policies that have unfavorable consequences. The dilemma, of course, is that local governments' interests do not always coincide; central cities and their suburbs may, in fact, hold opposing views on a range of land use issues.

Each local jurisdiction described in this study has a unique relationship with its state government, one that has evolved over time. None of the cases offers an exportable, easy-to-emulate lesson for other localities seeking a favorable set of public policies. For example, Washington's Growth Management Act has a number of positive features, including its emphasis on regionalism, but its applicability to Arizona is limited.

The National Governors' Association, through its Center for Best Practices, has identified a smart growth approach called New Community Design (NCD) as one possible option for states seeking more effective land use. Its proponents contend that, if implemented, NCD will not only reduce sprawl but also improve a community's quality of life and bolster the local economy.[36] The primary elements of NCD include "extensive mixed land use, reduced land consumption, community centers, ample green space, transportation options, and building designs that reflect the local culture and harmonize with the natural environment."[37] Infill development, brownfield redevelopment, and preservation of open space are important strategies; thus the implications for vacant land are substantial.

States can support the adoption of NCD by providing localities with enabling legislation, financial support, and technical assistance. Examples of NCD actions include Delaware's statute on graduated impact fees, Utah's Quality Growth Awards, Rhode Island's model land use ordinances, Wisconsin's comprehensive planning requirements, and New Jersey's statewide building rehabilitation code. Were smart growth approaches like NCD to become the rule, many vacant land issues would change and, it is hoped, become more positive.

LOCAL-OPTION TAXES

Although all municipalities have access to the property tax (as was mentioned, most municipalities in Oklahoma do not exercise their authority to levy the tax), the authority to levy a sales or income tax is not universally shared. Diversifying a city's revenue portfolio holds many advantages, especially with regard to fiscal stability and tax equity. Indeed, the seminal work on city finances of Helen Ladd and John Yinger concludes with a call for revenue diversification (especially an income, or earnings, tax) as a means for expanding the tax base of central cities.[38] Nevertheless, the effects of a general tax structure on the spatial evolution of a city and on the selection process of development projects are less well known, although the inferences from this study suggest an important connection.

The authority to levy a local-option sales or income tax is, if not controlled, then certainly regulated by the state. For example, among states in the Western census region, Idaho, Montana, Nevada, and Oregon do not grant their cities a sales tax authority.[39] No New England state allows a local-option municipal sales tax.[40] Imbedded in any municipality's tax structure is a set of principles relating to individual and business tax burden, fairness, equity, revenue production, collectibility, and administration of the tax.[41]

Moreover, a state's control of its municipalities' general tax structure has implications for spatial development, sprawl, and abandonment, because any tax structure encourages a certain strategic behavior on the part of city officials whose interest is to maximize the community's well-being. In the absence of severe penalties or preconditions for territorial expansion of the municipal corporation, we should not be surprised to find cities with a sales tax reliance encouraging commercial development at the fringe of the corporate boundaries. Even if cheap land at the fringe of cities beckons developers and promotes sprawl, the revenue-generating logic of such enterprises does not escape the development calculus of city leaders. Their encouragement of fringe development, then, may be as much a function of the strategic logic underlying the city's general tax structure as it is a capitulation to real estate interests.[42] Officials in sales-tax-dependent cities affirmed the commercial development preferences of vacant land over residential development, and the development of vacant land along the city's fringe to capture a shopping shed that extends the city's fiscal reach.

Reliance on one source of general tax revenue, then, induces or at least influences a spatial development logic that might possibly be at odds with a state's concerns about sprawl and farmland preservation. Providing municipalities with access to all three general revenue sources should be considered by states in an effort to expand municipalities' revenue portfolio, but also with an eye toward the development logic that is being encouraged.

Sprawl and abandonment are not solely functions of the marketplace. Public policy intervention—in the form of designing or controlling the contours of the general tax structure—also plays a role, one that needs to be analyzed by states and municipalities.

STRATEGIC THINKING AND VACANT LAND

Kevin Lynch calls for a "visual plan" that is conscious of not just the physical shape of a city but also its impact on the image of the city— the mental map.[43] Vacant land is part of the mental map, but too often it is an unplanned, negative part. Dilapidation and disorder are the common images. But with some organization and initiative, the negative images can be transformed into more positive ones.

Vacant land can be a catalyst for achieving a vision, for building a city. It often provides a tabula rasa, a clean slate upon which new ideas can come to fruition. City leaders, their perspective perhaps teased by developers, gaze across a verdant meadow and envision a corporate office park, an upscale retail mall, a gated residential community. Their pulses quicken as they entertain thoughts of revenues flowing from the new development. Or those same city leaders might prefer a more public use of this space: multipurpose recreational facilities, a civic center or sports arena, a museum or performing arts venue, or perhaps a grand public plaza.

City leaders can easily engage in these sorts of visioning exercises when the vista is raw land. But when the vista is used land, the "seeing what might be" is a bit more challenging. Looking past the trash and weeds, the crumbling building, the possibly toxic soil requires more effort. And for good reason. The raw dirt carries far fewer negatives, both real and perceptual. Developing the raw dirt type of vacant land may mean higher infrastructure costs and raise concerns about urban sprawl, but reusing land generates a host of realities. Landownership may be disputed or uncertain. Parcels often lack sufficient size or appropriate shape, even with a clear title. Perfectly reusable land in a blighted area may signal a lack of market potential and be a harbinger of attendant social pathologies.[44]

The Brookings Institution, together with the organization CEOs for Cities, has identified a series of action steps for cities intent upon converting derelict land into valuable sites:

- Know your territory.
- Develop a citywide approach to redevelopment.
- Implement neighborhood plans in partnership with community stakeholders.
- Make government effective.
- Create a legal framework for sound redevelopment.
- Create marketable opportunities.
- Finance redevelopment.
- Build on natural and historic assets.
- Be sensitive to gentrification and relocation issues.
- Organize for success.[45]

These recommendations echo the argument of this book: First, think of vacant land as an asset; second, take actions that will make it so.

Thinking strategically about vacant land, especially in conditions of uncertainty, is a challenge for city officials. The three imperatives provide a guide. First, cities must pursue policies that enhance their fiscal condition; therefore, policymakers are motivated to consider vacant land options that either maximize revenues or minimize costs. Second, because cities must pursue policies that minimize social disruption and protect property values, policymakers are encouraged to assemble, zone, and dedicate vacant land for the purpose of simulating natural barriers and protecting property values. Third, cities must pursue policies that augment or, at a minimum, maintain the economic vitality and enhance the image of the community; thus, policymakers are induced to use or reuse vacant land to its highest and best use. Although real estate markets may vary and officials' preferences may differ, the imperatives help structure vacant land choices.

As this book has shed light on terra incognita, one of the lessons has been that vacant land is not an unalloyed "bad." Even the bleakest landscape of boarded-up buildings and trashed vacant lots can be renewed. The challenge for cities is to begin thinking about vacant land as a resource and to take actions that reflect this new thinking.

NOTES

1. See, e.g., the media portrayals of "bad" vacant land in Stephen Seplow, "Too Many Houses, Too Few Residents," *Philadelphia Inquirer*, May 10, 1999, A1; and Joseph Berger, "Tough Times and Tattered Image for Poughkeepsie," *New York Times*, October 5, 1998, 10.
2. Barry Wood, *Vacant Land in Europe*. Working Paper (Cambridge, Mass.: Lincoln Institute of Land Policy, 1998), 99.
3. Philadelphia City Planning Commission, "PCPC Map Gallery"; www .philaplanning.org/data/datamaps.html (June 1, 2003).
4. Philadelphia City Planning Commission, *Vacant Land in Philadelphia: A Report on Vacant Land Management and Neighborhood Restructuring* (Philadelphia: Philadelphia City Planning Commission, 1995), 15.
5. The concern over rapid growth intensified, the city's infrastructure became strained, and in 1998, Redmond imposed a six-month moratorium, which was subsequently renewed, on new commercial development.
6. The costs of providing services to residences are nearly double the property taxes received, according to estimates from Tempe's finance officers.
7. Camden's situation was so dire by the late 1990s that the State of New Jersey intervened and installed an oversight board for the city's finances. See Judith Havemann, "A City that Good Times Forgot; Blighted Camden, N.J., Reflects Inner Cities' Resistance to Renewal," *Washington Post*, April 1,

1999, A3. In December 2000, Milton Milan became the third Camden mayor in twenty years to be convicted of a felony.

8. See the discussion in Ann O'M. Bowman and Michael A. Pagano, "Transforming America's Cities: Policies and Conditions of Vacant Land," *Urban Affairs Review* 35 (March 2000): 559–81.

9. David Rusk, *Cities without Suburbs*, 2nd ed. (Baltimore: Johns Hopkins University Press, 1995).

10. Gerrit Knaap and Terry Moore, *Land Supply and Infrastructure Capacity: Monitoring for Smart Urban Growth*, working paper (Cambridge, Mass.: Lincoln Institute of Land Policy, 2000).

11. In the years that have elapsed since the survey was completed, anecdotal evidence suggests that more cities have improved their geographic information systems capability.

12. Common examples include overgrown vegetation, fire hazards, transients, litter, the parking of recreational vehicles, and, in one unusual case, the erection of a revival tent on a vacant lot.

13. Maricopa County provides the information on landownership to the city. With it, the city creates a Land Information System in the City Clerk's office.

14. The Rehabilitation Appeals Board, in the opinion of code enforcement officials, is quite responsive to property owners' appeals.

15. Previously, historic preservation district status meant that demolition could not occur; however, that provision has been relaxed.

16. In the late 1990s, city efforts to create a rental property registry stalled because of opposition from these groups.

17. City of Philadelphia, *A Blight Elimination Plan for Philadelphia's Neighborhoods* (Philadelphia: City of Philadelphia, Blight Elimination Subcommittee, 2000), 8.

18. City of Philadelphia, *Blight Elimination Plan*.

19. City of Philadelphia, *A Vacant Land Acquisition System for Philadelphia* (Philadelphia: City of Philadelphia, Acquisitions Subcommittee of the Select Committee on Vacant Land, 1999).

20. City of Philadelphia, *Vacant Land Acquisition System*.

21. Mark Alan Hughes, "Dirt into Dollars: Converting Vacant Land into Valuable Development," *Brookings Review* (summer 2000): 34–37.

22. An example of the cumbersome procedures is the requirement that the city council pass legislation so that city-owned vacant parcels can be sold or transferred.

23. John Kromer, *Vacant Property Prescriptions: A Reinvestment Strategy* (Philadelphia: City of Philadelphia Office of Housing and Community Development, 1996).

24. Rob Gurwitt, "Betting on the Bulldozer," *Governing*, July 2002: 28–34.

25. Dwight Orr and Angela Couloumbis, "Proposal for Camden Seeks Role for County," *Philadelphia Inquirer*, October 2, 2001, B1.

26. Parks & People Foundation, *Neighborhood Open Space Management: A Report on Greening Strategies in Baltimore and Six Other Cities* (Baltimore: Parks & People Foundation, 2000), 46.

27. Parks & People Foundation, *Neighborhood Open Space Management.*

28. Pennsylvania Horticultural Society, *Urban Vacant Land: Issues and Recommendations* (Philadelphia: Pennsylvania Horticultural Society, 1995), 90.

29. Jane E. Schukoske, "Community Development through Gardening: State and Local Policies Transforming Urban Open Space," *New York University Journal of Legislation and Public Policy* 3 (1999–2000): 390.

30. Schukoske, "Community Development through Gardening," 390–91.

31. Russell L. Hanson, ed., *Governing Partners: State–Local Relations in the United States* (Boulder, Colo.: Westview Press, 1998).

32. Beverly Cigler, "Emerging Trends in State–Local Relations," in *Governing Partners: State-Local Relations in the United States*, ed. Russell L. Hanson (Boulder, Colo.: Westview Press, 1998), 53–74.

33. Cigler, "Emerging Trends in State–Local Relations," 71.

34. Margaret Weir, "Central Cities' Loss of Power in State Politics," *Cityscape: A Journal of Policy Development and Research* 2 (May 1966): 23–40.

35. John M. Levy, *Contemporary Urban Planning*, 5th ed. (Upper Saddle River, N.J.: Prentice Hall, 2000).

36. Joel S. Hirschhorn and Paul Souza, *New Community Design to the Rescue: Fulfilling Another American Dream* (Washington, D.C.: National Governors' Association, 2001).

37. Hirschhorn and Paul Souza, *New Community Design to the Rescue*, 5.

38. Helen Ladd and John Yinger, *America's Ailing Cities: Fiscal Health and the Design of Urban Policy* (Baltimore: Johns Hopkins University Press, 1989).

39. This information is drawn from appendix A of *City Fiscal Conditions in 1999* (Washington, D.C.: National League of Cities, 1999), which in turn is drawn from a variety of sources, including *The State Tax Guide* published by Commerce Clearinghouse, Inc., and various cities and state municipal leagues, including the Alabama League of Municipalities, the Arkansas Municipal League, the Georgia Municipal Association, the City of Greensboro, the North Carolina Finance Department, the Association of Idaho Cities, the Indiana Association of Cities and Towns, the Iowa League of Cities, the City of Memphis Finance Department, the Michigan Municipal League, the League of Minnesota Cities, the New York State Conference of Mayors and Municipal Officials, the North Carolina League of Municipalities, the Tennessee Advisory Commission on Intergovernmental Relations, the Vermont League of Cities and Towns, and the League of Wisconsin Municipalities. Idaho permits a sales tax authority in resort cities with populations under 10,000; three have elected to levy the sales tax.

40. Vermont authorized a "transitional" sales tax from 1999 to 2002 that was authorized to mitigate local fiscal effects of state education financing reform.

41. John Mikesell, *Fiscal Administration*, 5th ed. (Fort Worth: Harcourt Brace College Publishers, 1999), chap. 6.

42. Kee Warner and Harvey Molotch, *Building Rules: How Local Controls Shape Community Environments and Economies* (Boulder, Colo.: Westview Press, 2000).

43. Kevin Lynch, *The Image of the City* (Cambridge, Mass.: MIT Press, 1960).

44. Jack L. Nasar, *The Evaluative Image of the City* (Thousand Oaks, Calif.: Sage Publications, 1998).

45. Paul C. Brophy and Jennifer S. Vey, *Seizing City Assets: Ten Stops to Urban Land Reform* (Washington, D.C.: Brookings Institution and CEOs for Cities, 2002).

APPENDIX A

Methodology

No comprehensive survey of the preponderance of vacant urban land and abandoned structures in the United States had been undertaken since the 1960s, and no assessment of city policy tools designed to use or reuse vacant urban land and abandoned structures had been attempted. Therefore, two major data collection efforts were undertaken for this project.

The first was designed to fill the gaps in our knowledge about vacant urban land. A survey was administered with the purposes of (1) estimating and assessing the amount of vacant land and abandoned structures in U.S. cities, (2) identifying and measuring the kinds of vacant land–related policies city governments have in place, and (3) analyzing the causal factors related to vacant land and city policies. Specifically, the following set of questions is addressed by the survey:

- How much vacant land exists in American cities?
- Is the amount of urban vacant land increasing or decreasing?
- What causes are associated with changes in vacant land supply?
- What are the ownership patterns for vacant land?
- What policies do cities use to regulate or manage their stock of vacant land and abandoned buildings?
- Are certain characteristics such as region, population change, or fiscal stress associated with the amount of vacant land or with city policies?

To find answers for these questions, a survey was mailed to city officials (typically, but not always, a planning director) in U.S. cities with populations of 50,000 or more in late 1997 and early 1998 (figure A.1). To minimize the likelihood of definitional disparities, a definition of vacant land was printed on the questionnaire. It read: *"Vacant land in-*

cludes not only publicly-owned and privately-owned unused or aban-doned land or land that once had structures on it, but also the land that supports structures that have been abandoned, derelict, boarded up, partially destroyed, or razed."

The survey research proceeded in two stages. In the first stage, a four-page questionnaire (reproduced as figure A.1) requested informa-tion from city officials about (1) the causes of vacant land and aban-doned structures in their cities, (2) policies designed to regulate pri-vately held vacant land and abandoned structures, and (3) policies governing city-owned vacant land and abandoned structures. Although the questions were structured, respondents were provided ample op-portunity to explain their answers, as well as to offer caveats and clari-fications. For cities indicating that they had a geographic information system that included information on vacant land, a second survey was sent. This short (one-page) instrument focused on detailed, descriptive data as to the amount and type of vacant land, its ownership character-istics, its location, and its assessed value.

Efforts were made to attain an acceptable response rate. A single mailing of the first questionnaire, bolstered by reminder postcards and follow-up telephone contacts, produced 186 responses, for an overall response rate of 35 percent. The response rate for smaller cities (50,000–100,000 population) depressed the overall rate; the nation's largest cities (the 197 cities with populations greater than 100,000) re-sponded at a 50.25 percent rate ($N = 99$). An examination of the re-sponses revealed no discernible over- or underrepresentation of partic-ular regions or government structures.

A total of eighty-one cities received the second survey, and thirty-two (39.5 percent) responded. The purpose of the second survey was to disaggregate the total amount of vacant land which was indicated on the first survey. The survey requested cities to divide vacant land ac-cording to public and private ownership. Further, private ownership was divided into its zoned use, and public vacant land was divided by the level of government that owned it. Finally, cities were asked to disaggregate privately owned and publicly owned land by location, namely, land on the "fringe" of the city or near the core of the built city. The assessed value of taxable vacant land and abandoned structures was also requested. Many of the questionnaires were returned only par-tially completed, frequently with a notation that the level of specificity requested was impossible for the city official to provide.

As data-rich as the surveys proved to be, they were not designed to address a key follow-up issue: the impact of city policies on the use or reuse of vacant land. In other words, how successful have city policies been in reducing the supply, the location, or the kind of vacant land?

VACANT LAND/ABANDONED STRUCTURES SURVEY

The Lincoln Institute of Land Policy is sponsoring a project to gauge the magnitude of urban vacant land in the United States and to identify city government policies that are directed at the use and re-use of urban vacant and fringe land and of abandoned structures. This is the only nationwide, comprehensive assessment of urban vacant land policy that we are aware of. We expect the database from the survey to provide the foundation for in-depth analyses of the effectiveness of cities' vacant land policies. The deadline for submitting the survey is *15 December 1997.*

Thank you in advance for participating in this project. A summary of the report will be sent to the name who appears below unless we hear otherwise.

City Name: _____ Population: _____

Name of Contact Person : _____ Title: _____

Address: _____

City: _____ State: _____ Zip Code: _____

Telephone Number: (   )_____ e-mail address: _____

Fax Number: (   ) _____

I. **VACANT LAND**. Vacant land includes not only publicly-owned and privately-owned unused or abandoned land or land that once had structures on it, but also the land that supports structures that have been abandoned, derelict, boarded up, partially destroyed or razed.

   A. Does your city have a **GIS map of the city**? Yes   No
       If yes, does it contain data on **vacant land and/or abandoned buildings**? Yes   No
       If yes, does it also contain data on public and private **ownership of vacant land**? Yes   No

   B. **Causes of Vacant Land/Abandoned Structures**
       Answer either or both part 1 and part 2 below, as appropriate to your city's situation.

       1. If the amount of vacant land or the number of abandoned structures in your city has **increased** during the past decade, what are the causes? (Check all that apply.)
           _____ Deindustrialization   _____ City land-use policies
           _____ Suburbanization   _____ Annexation
           _____ Population migration out of the region

FIGURE A.1.   The Survey Instrument Administered December 1997–May 1998

_____ Transportation problems _____ Disinvestment
_____ Access to capital _____ City real estate tax policies
_____ Land assembly problems _____ Contamination of
                                                land/structures
_____ Other:_____

2. If the amount of vacant land or the number of abandoned structures in your city has **decreased** during the past decade, what are the causes? (Check all that apply.)
_____ Population in-migration _____ A growing local economy
_____ City policy to encourage land reuse (e.g., infill)
_____ Micro-enterprises _____ Private development initiatives
_____ City land-use policies _____ City real estate tax policies
_____ Other: _____

C. Which of the following current **conditions** accurately describe the physical characteristics of vacant land and structures in your city. (Check all that apply.)
Vacant land tends to be:
_____ In oversupply _____ In the wrong location
_____ In undersupply _____ Odd-shaped parcels
_____ Vacant too long _____ Not assembled in sufficiently large
                                        parcels
_____ Other (please explain) _____

D. How does your **city know officially** when a structure is vacant? Rank from 1 (most frequent) to 7 (least frequent).
____ a building inspection system (e.g., annual or monthly inspections)
____ calls from neighbors ____ tax delinquency
____ city officials/departments informal feedback
____ a period of time must have passed since last occupied
____ health inspection
____ other (please specify)
_____

E. **Vacant Land/Abandoned Structures Census**. Please indicate the amount of vacant land within the legal boundary of your city as of 1 July 1997. Vacant land includes not only unused or abandoned land or land that once had structures on it, but also the land that supports structures that have been abandoned, derelict, boarded up, partially destroyed or razed. **If precise figures are unavailable, please estimate or provide approximations.**

FIGURE A.1. _Continued_

1. ***Total*** Land Area within City Limits:_____ acres or square miles (circle one) Year of estimate: 19___

2. Estimate or approximate the amount of usable vacant land within your city's limits (***excluding unusable land***, such as streets, rights of way, underwater land, wetlands, flood plains, etc.) _____

3. Estimate or approximate the number of abandoned structures within your city's limits: _____

II. City government policies that regulate or affect the use or reuse of vacant land/abandoned structures.

A. Does your city have ordinances or other policies that ***regulate the use of privately-owned vacant land and/or abandoned structures***? **Yes   No**
   If yes, please answer the following questions:

   1. ***Health and Safety***: Does your city have an unoccupied structures policy that is premised on the city's need to protect the citizens' "health and safety" for:
      (a) commercial/industrial structures? **Yes   No**
      (b) residential structures? **Yes   No**
      Comments: _____
      _____

   2. ***Foreclosures:*** Does your **city** or the **county** (circle one) have the authority to foreclose on property whose owners are in tax arrears?
      If you circled **"city,"** does your city foreclose after the property tax has been in arrears for a certain period of time: (a) for commercial/industrial property? **Yes   No** If yes, how long? _____ days/months/years
      (b) for residential property? **Yes   No**
      If yes, how long? _____ days/months/years

   3. ***Fines***: Does your city have the authority to fine owners of unoccupied:
      (a) commercial/industrial structures? **Yes   No**
      If yes, what is the fine schedule? _____
      If yes, under what conditions (e.g., health hazard)? _____
      (b) residential structures? **Yes   No**
      If yes, what is the fine schedule? _____
      If yes, under what conditions (e.g., health hazard)? _____

4. *"Abandonment Tax":* Does your city have the authority to tax unoccupied:

(a) commercial/industrial structures? **Yes No** If yes, how much more is the "abandonment tax" compared to the standard property tax? _____

(b) residential structures? **Yes No** If yes, how much more is the "abandonment" tax compared to the standard property tax? _____

5. *Registration Fee:* Does your city require owners of unoccupied *commercial/industrial* structures to register with the city? **Yes No** If yes, what is the registration fee?

_____

6. *Razing Fee:* Does your city require owners of unoccupied structures to compensate the city for the *city's cost* of demolition or razing? **Yes No** If yes, how much (full amount or partial) _____

7. *Special Programs:* Does your city have special programs that specifically address vacant land or abandoned structure issues, such as a policy dealing with illegal dumping on vacant lots, or controlling vandalism of abandoned structures? **Yes No** If yes, please identify _____

_____

B. Does your city have ordinances, programs, or other policies that regulate the use or disposition of *city-owned* vacant land or abandoned structures? **Yes No**

If yes, please answer the following questions:

1. Does the city have a policy to dispose of city-owned land/structures at *fair market value or below* (Circle one)? If **"below,"** how much below? _____

2. When the city sells vacant/abandoned land, *does the city offer other inducements* or subsidies as an incentive to purchase? **Yes No** If yes, please describe _____

3. How much of the city-owned vacant land was acquired *through tax foreclosures?*_____

4. Approximately *how many vacant lots* are owned by the city? _____ *abandoned buildings?* _____

FIGURE A.1. *Continued*

5. What is the approximate *assessed value of city-owned vacant land/buildings*? _____
   What is the approximate assessed value of city-owned vacant land/buildings that were acquired through *tax foreclosures?*
   _____

6. Does the city have a policy for the reuse of city-owned vacant land and buildings *near the core* of the city (an "infill" policy) that is different from the city's policy governing the use or reuse of city-owned vacant land *at the fringe* of the city? **Yes No** If yes, please explain: _____
   _____

7. Does the city have a policy for the reuse of *abandoned structures* that is different from the city's policy governing the reuse of *vacant land?* **Yes   No** If yes, please explain: _____
   _____

8. Does the city have any *special programs* that encourage neighborhood or citizen or community participation or involvement, such as neighborhood weed-maintenance or trans clean-up programs, or a voluntary building repair and maintenance program, or a program to care for city-owned lots? **Yes No** If yes, please explain: _____
   _____
   _____

III. Miscellaneous.

A. Is there something else about *your city's vacant land policy* that you would like to tell us? If so, add your comments here:
   _____

B. The second phase of this study will focus on policy solutions and their effectiveness in addressing vacant land problems. If called on, would you be willing to be a participant as one of a handful of case study cities? If so, whom should we contact and at what address? _____

C. If you have materials on your city's vacant land policy that we should be aware of, *please send them* along with this survey.

What works in a given context? Are policies transferable? Do cities that have implemented the same policies experience the same results? Do city policies matter? What is the impact of the policy (or its absence) on the supply of city-owned vacant land? Do the outcomes vary, given different policy packages from one city to another?

The second data collection effort, therefore, was designed to examine these clusters of cities in detail, collecting information and data on their vacant and fringe land experiments. In-depth interviews with key city officials and other governmentally linked elites were supplemented with archival research on extant land policy and actions.

Fieldwork was necessary for three reasons. First, it provided multiple points of access so that we could gain a full picture of the vacant land issue in the city. Our primary interest was in government actions, and we scheduled interviews with relevant elected and appointed city officials. However, our survey indicated that in many communities much of the vacant land restoration activity is undertaken by government-supported groups, rather than being directed by a particular office at city hall. It was through fieldwork that these connections were pursued.

Second, fieldwork was necessary because the survey asked respondents if they would be willing to participate in the case study portion of the project and because a key contact person was identified in each survey. Thus, through fieldwork we were able to gain access to the key policy officials and archival data as well as to nongovernmental groups and individuals.

Third, fieldwork enabled us to separate direct and indirect effects, as well as intended and unintended consequences. As we found from our survey results, a city's supply of vacant land might have changed, but could the change be attributed to city policies? Cause and effect were particularly difficult threads to untangle, but the "up-close" perspective offered by structured and focused fieldwork facilitated the assessment of policy effectiveness.

Three metropolitan regions were selected for in-depth, detailed study. Sites were chosen to reflect a rich diversity of the vacant land condition, based on responses to the national survey on vacant land. *Phoenix* was chosen because of the abundance of vacant land at the fringe of the city of Phoenix and at the fringe of neighboring cities, the state's liberal annexation laws, and the existence of a landlocked city surrounded by cities with nearly limitless boundaries. In *Seattle*, the vacant land situation is different: There is comparatively little vacant land; furthermore, local jurisdictions must abide by the state's Growth Management Act. *Philadelphia* is different still: Vacant land and abandoned structures define the core of the metropolitan area. In each of the three metropolitan areas, officials in three localities (the major city and two nearby cities) were interviewed, as were leaders of the areawide planning organization or council of governments. The site visits were undertaken between January and May 1999, and the principal investigators collected primary and interview data at each site for a total of one week each or six person-weeks of activity.

The following questions and data requests, which we submitted to several city officials before the actual site visits, directed the site visits.

Interview Questions:

   I. Policy creation. What precipitated the creation of a policy on infill, brownfields, reuse, financial penalty, greenbelt, etc. What image/vision did policymakers have?
  II. Policy actors. Who are the "policy entrepreneurs"?
 III. Policy goal. What was the intended impact/output of the policy? What constitutes an acceptable outcome? How do policymakers know when the goal has been reached? What is a satisfactory outcome?
  IV. Policy implementation. Who has responsibility for implementing and monitoring the policies? Are all policies implemented by the same city agency or do multiple agencies implement urban vacant land (UVL) policies? Level and extent of interorganizational coordination and competition.
   V. Experimental effects. Do other (non-UVL) policies interfere with successful implementation of UVL policies?
  VI. Intergovernmental effects. Do other cities' and local governments' policies interfere with successful implementation of UVL policies? If so, what's the city's response? Is there intergovernmental coordination of UVL policies?

Data Requests:

   I. Census data on land area and change, population, racial composition, density, income, voting behavior, occupations, home ownership, business formation, etc.
  II. Government characteristics, election districts/wards, business or downtown districts (autonomous or semiautonomous development boards).
 III. Commuting patterns, city finances, state restrictions.
  IV. Evidence of cooperation or conflict among municipal/local governments, such as regional councils, metropolitan planning organizations.

V. Geographic information system footprints of the areas, if they include vacant land and abandoned structures; public (city and others) vs. private ownership.

VI. Zoning and land use maps, and city plan (comprehensive).

VII. Press coverage of land use and redevelopment.

Because county assessors' offices keep records on the assessed value
and property tax liabilities of all parcels of land and structures, it is a
straightforward process of identifying the spatial distribution of property tax revenue generation in a city. The same cannot be said of
sales tax collection. Sales taxes are collected at the point of transaction but are not recorded in any easily retrievable electronic file. Consequently, data on the spatial location of sales tax collections were
estimated for only two cities, Tempe and Seattle (Phoenix, Peoria,
and Philadelphia could not provide estimates). Tempe was able to aggregate sales tax collections by a few sites that were identified by the
authors. Those estimates were provided for four regional sites for the
period 1992 through 1999. The spatial assignment of sales tax collections in Seattle was based on a set of assumptions that were developed in consultation with an official in the city's finance department.
The principal assumption was that the city's total retail sales tax collections were apportioned to the city's planning zones (called Fore-
cast Analysis Zones, or FAZs) according to the FAZ's proportion of
the city's total population, as estimated by the Puget Sound Regional
Council. This estimating technique provides a very crude estimate of
the retail sales tax dollars apportioned to each FAZ. The Puget Sound
Regional Council defines an FAZ as a geographic area made up of one
or more census tracts.

Data on vacant land were collected in each of the site visit cities from
cities' planning departments. Philadelphia provided addresses and assessed valuations of each vacant parcel, as did Tempe. Seattle,
Redmond, Bellevue, Bucks County, Peoria, and Phoenix provided data
on the location and geographic size of the vacant parcels. Data for Camden were unavailable.

The following individuals, most of whom are city officials, were interviewed and/or provided data for the site visits, which were conducted by the authors for one full week in January 1999 (Phoenix),
March 1999 (Seattle), and May 1999 (Philadephia).

Phoenix: Jim Brooks, Jim Burke, John Burke, Elizabeth Burns, Arlen
Colton, Russ Conway, Michelle Dodds, Michael Dollin, Leslie Dornfeld,
Ray Garewal, Phil Gordon, Mitch Hayden, Sandy Holland, Brian Kear-
ney, Don Kouth, Kate Krietor, Jo Marie, Charlene McDonald, John
McIntosh, Rick Naimark, Donna Neill, John Nelson, Fred Osgood, John

Parks, Joe Parma, Ray Quay, Rosanne Sanchez, Tracy Sato, Paul Seivert, Isabel Templeton, Sandy Treese, Neil Urban, Bob Wotjan, and Rich Zacher.

Tempe: Gary Brown, Neil Calfee, Ash Campbell, Don Cassano, Len Copple, Dave Farkler, Pat Flynn Neil Giuliano, Harvey Hubbs, Randy Hurlburt, Atis Krigers, Joseph Lewis, and Harry Mitchell.

Peoria: Jenifer Corey, Chad Daines, Terrence Ellis, Ken Forgia, Scott Friend, Phil Gardner, John Keegan, and Debra Stark.

Seattle: Norman Abbott, Elizabeth Butler, Richard Conlin, Elsie Crossman, Tom Hauger, Tom Kirn, Bob Laird, Glen Lee, Matthew Moeller, Anne Vernez Moudon, Rocky Piro, Janeen Smith, Jane Voget, and Ben Wolters.

Redmond: Richard Cole, John Couch, Lenda Crawford, Sharon Dorning, Rosemarie Ives, Tom Paine, the Redmond Code Enforcement Team, and Tim Trihimovich.

Bellevue: Gary Ameling, Randy Bannecker, Adam Hoard, Tom Lindquist, Lee Springgate, Dan Stroh, and Stephanie Warden.

Philadelphia: Richard Bickel, Julia Chapman, John Houk, Mark Hughes, Gary Jastrzab, Nancy Kammerdeiner, Barbara Kaplan, Don Kligerman, John Kromer, Joe Leonardo, Deborah McColloch, Jeremy Nowak, Michael Nutter, Sandy Salzman, and Barry Seymour.

Camden: Barbara Brennan, Richard Cinaglia, Sean Closky, Brian Finnie, Orion Joyner, and Thomas Roberts.

Bucks County: Robert Cormack, Richard Harvey, Michael Kane, and Vitor Vicente.

Data from San Jose were also collected and the following city officials were interviewed in person in March 2000: Del Borgsdorf, Darrel Dearborn, Kent Edens, Craig Parada, Timothy Steele, and Dhez Woodworth. Telephone interviews with officials from several other cities were conducted in January and February 2002, including Columbia (Fred Delk, Jim Gambrell, and Leona Plaugh), Columbus (Ellen Barncy, Ken Ferell, Gary Guglielmi, and Donna Hunter) and Oklahoma City (Mark Carleton, Jim Couch, John Dugan, David Jones, Russell Lewis, Wiley Rice, and J. Clare Woodside). Their help and support are acknowledged.

The authors are grateful for the candor and support from all the above individuals during the site visits.

APPENDIX B

Demographic, Economic, and Political Data for the Three Site-Visit Metropolitan Areas

TABLE B.1.   Data for Phoenix, Tempe, and Peoria, Arizona

Characteristic	Phoenix	Tempe	Peoria
Population			
1960	439,170	24,897	2,593
1970	581,562	62,907	4,792
1980	789,704	106,919	12,171
1990	988,983	142,056	51,154
2000	1,321,045	158,625	108,364
Percentage population change			
1960–70	32.4	152.7	84.8
1970–80	35.8	70.0	153.8
1980–90	25.2	32.9	320.3
1990–2000	33.6	11.7	111.8
Area (square miles)			
1960	187	22	2
1970	248	25	3
1980	375	39	27
1990	420	40	62
2000	475	40	138
Government structure			
1960–2000	CM	CM	CM
Top economic sectors			

1960	Manufacturing
	Wholesale/retail
	  trade
	FIRE
		Manufacturing
		Educational
		  services
		Wholesale/retail
		  trade
			n.a.

1970	Manufacturing
	Wholesale/retail
	  trade
	
	Construction
		Manufacturing
		Elementary and
		  secondary schools
		  and colleges
		Wholesale/retail
		  trade
			n.a.

1980	Wholesale/retail
	  trade
	Manufacturing
	FIRE
		Wholesale/retail
		  trade
		Manufacturing
		Elementary and
		  secondary schools
		  and colleges
			Wholesale/retail
			  trade
			Manufacturing
			Construction

1990	Wholesale/retail
	  trade
	Manufacturing
	FIRE
		Wholesale/retail
		  trade
		Manufacturing
		Elementary and
		  secondary schools
		  and colleges
			Wholesale/retail
			  trade
			Manufacturing
			
			FIRE

Note: CM = council-manager; FIRE = finance, insurance, and real estate; n.a. = not available.

TABLE B.2. Data for Seattle, Bellevue, and Redmond, Washington

Characteristic	Seattle	Bellevue	Redmond
Population			
1960	557,087	12,809	1,426
1970	530,831	61,102	11,031
1980	493,846	73,903	23,318
1990	516,259	98,628	36,090
2000	563,374	109,569	45,256
Percentage population change			
1960–70	1.7	377.0	673.6
1970–80	–7.0	20.8	111.6
1980–90	4.6	33.5	54.8
1990–2000	9.1	11.1	25.4
Area (square miles)			
1960	89	6	n.a.
1970	84	24	10
1980	84	25	13
1990	84	26	14
2000	84	31	16
Government structure			
1960–2000	MC	CM	MC
Top economic sectors			
1960	Manufacturing Wholesale/retail trade FIRE	Manufacturing Wholesale/retail trade FIRE	n.a.
1970	Manufacturing Wholesale/retail trade Elementary and secondary schools and colleges	Manufacturing Wholesale/retail trade Elementary and secondary schools and colleges	Manufacturing Wholesale/retail trade FIRE
1980	Wholesale/retail trade Manufacturing Elementary and secondary schools and colleges	Wholesale/retail trade Manufacturing FIRE	Wholesale/retail trade Manufacturing FIRE
1990	Wholesale/retail trade Manufacturing FIRE	Wholesale/retail trade Manufacturing FIRE	Wholesale/retail trade Manufacturing FIRE

Note: CM = council-manager; MC = mayor-council; FIRE = finance, insurance, and real estate; n.a. = not available.

TABLE B.3.   Data for Philadelphia, Bucks County, Pennsylvania, and Camden, New Jersey

Characteristic	Philadelphia	Bucks County	Camden
Population			
1960	2,002,512	308,567	117,159
1970	1,948,609	415,056	102,551
1980	1,688,210	479,180	84,910
1990	1,585,577	541,174	87,460
2000	1,517,550	597,635	79,904
Percentage population change			
1960–70	−2.7	34.5	−12.5
1970–80	−13.4	15.4	−17.2
1980–90	−6.1	12.9	3.0
1990–2000	−4.3	10.4	−8.6
Area (square miles)			
1960	127	617	9
1970	129	614	9
1980	136	610	9
1990	135	608	9
2000	135	607	9
Government structure			
1960–2000	MC	CO to CM	CO to MC
Top economic sectors			
1960	Manufacturing	Manufacturing	Manufacturing
	Wholesale/retail trade	Wholesale/retail trade	Wholesale/retail trade
	Public administration	Public administration	Public administration
1970	Manufacturing	Manufacturing	Manufacturing
	Wholesale/retail trade	Wholesale/retail trade	Wholesale/retail trade
	Elementary and secondary schools and collegs	Elementary and secondary schools and colleges	Public administration
1980	Manufacturing	Manufacturing	Manufacturing
	Wholesale/retail trade	Wholesale/retail trade	Wholesale/retail trade
	Elementary and secondary schools and colleges	Elementary and secondary schools and colleges	Elementary and secondary schools and colleges
1990	Wholesale/retail trade	Wholesale/retail trade	Manufacturing
	Manufacturing	Manufacturing	Wholesale/retail trade
	Elementary and secondary schools and colleges	Elementary and secondary schools and colleges	Elementary and secondary schools and colleges

Note: CM = council-manager; CO = commission; MC = mayor-council; FIRE = finance, insurance, and real estate; n.a. = not available.

APPENDIX C

Data on Vacant Land and Abandoned Structures

from the Survey and Data on Population and Area from the Census (for cities with population greater than 100,000)

Data on Vacant Land and Abandoned Structures

City	State	Population, 1995	Percentage Change in Population, 1980–95	City Area (acres)	Percentage Change in City Land Area, 1980–95	Vacant Land (acres)	Ratio of Vacant Land to Total Land Area (percent)	No. of Abandoned Structures	No. of Abandoned Structures per 1,000 Inhabitants
Mobile	AL	206,685	3.11	101,018	-4.07			2,009	9.7201
Little Rock	AR	181,295	14.74	76,800			26.0	600	3.3095
Mesa	AZ	364,876	139.41	78,733	60.65	27,328	34.7		
Phoenix	AZ	1,220,000	54.49	300,160	29.60	128,000	42.6		
Tempe	AZ	158,315	48.07	25,600	4.22	1,950	7.6		
Anaheim	CA	295,452	34.61	31,911	6.24	4,517	14.2	50	0.1692
Concord	CA	115,000	10.83	19,200	0.68	9,600	50.0	100	0.8696
Fontana	CA	104,201	183.12	23,040	45.31	13,824	60.0		
Fullerton	CA	122,804	20.11	14,238	0.00	532	3.7	24	0.1954
Garden Grove	CA	153,824	24.75	11,200	2.29	168	1.5		
Glendale	CA	195,623	40.68	6,303	0.00	1,540	24.4	146	0.7463
Hayward	CA	124,000	32.50	27,520	11.54	1,000	3.6	75	0.6048
Huntington Beach	CA	200,000	9.29	17,600	3.33	528	3.0		
Inglewood	CA	117,300	24.57	5,664	3.37	40	0.7	5	0.0426
Irvine	CA	127,000	104.40	27,520	0.95	11,008	40.0	0	0.0000
Moreno Valley	CA	133,000		32,000		12,800	40.0	250	1.8797
Orange	CA	122,000	33.41	15,040	9.91	300	2.0	1	0.0082
Pasadena	CA	138,925	17.66	14,720	-0.43	450	3.1		
Salinas	CA	123,329	53.24	11,970	23.18	927	7.7	0	0.0000
San Diego	CA	1,197,000	36.64	211,200	1.25	30,080	14.2	200	0.1671
San Jose	CA	873,286	38.75	113,024	8.42	8,785	7.8	0	0.0000
Santa Clara	CA	100,030	14.06	12,350	-4.19	254	2.1	5	0.0500

City	State								
Santa Clarita	CA	142,000		28,800		10,800	37.5	19	0.1338
Santa Rosa	CA	132,000	59.69	25,216	26.69	3,500	13.9	19	0.1439
Stockton	CA	236,000	59.16	35,648	31.50	11,407	32.0	175	0.7415
Sunnyvale	CA	129,250	21.23	14,016	-4.78	11,520		9	0.0696
Vallejo	CA	100,000	24.53	32,960	25.31	17,920	54.4	500	5.0000
Bridgeport	CT	142,000	-0.38	10,880	8.84			150	1.0563
New Haven	CT	123,000	-2.45	12,800	0.00	700	5.5	524	4.2602
Stamford	CT	110,000	7.35	24,320	-1.05	3,648	15.0		
Washington[a]	DC	572,059	-5.74	43,712	11.24	1,485	3.4	3,970	0.6939
Jacksonville	FL	711,933	31.62	485,488	0.00	16,726	3.4	2,800	0.0039
Orlando	FL	173,122	34.94	62,733	70.38	18,000	28.7	400	2.3105
Pembroke Pines	FL	116,000	224.24	21,760	99.38	2,560	11.8	1	0.0086
Tallahassee	FL	140,643	72.47	49,542	126.07	19,756	39.9		
Atlanta	GA	425,000	-0.01	84,480	0.61	5,895	7.0		
Boise	ID	167,000	63.33	34,900	17.30	5,000	14.3		
Aurora	IL	120,000	47.61	23,680	31.37	5,920	25.0	20	0.1667
Chicago[a]	IL	2896016	4.03	146,176	0.53	10,000	6.84	4,000	0.1381
Naperville	IL	120,000	181.68	23,040	36.10	3,000	13.0	3	0.0250
Fort Wayne	IN	195,680	13.51	49,056	19.20	4,480	9.1		
South Bend	IN	105,511	-3.84	24,960	0.28	1,500	6.0	500	4.7388
Louisville	KY	386,300	29.23	40,960	3.50	1,750	4.3	2,200	5.6995
Baton Rouge	LA	220,000	81.49	48,000	19.97	4,480	9.3		
Boston[a]	MA	589,141	2.59	30,208	-2.48	180	0.6	5	0.00848
Worcester	MA	171,226	5.83	24,620	0.53	2,361	9.6	50	0.29200
Baltimore	MD	675,000	-14.20	53,760	0.62	1,000	1.9	15,000	22.2222
Detroit	MI	1,027,000	-14.66	88,768	2.29			10,000	9.7371
Livonia	MI	108,850	3.85	23,040	2.59	5,884		4	0.0367
St Paul[a]	MN	287151	5.48	33,792	0.00			317	0.1292

City	State	Population, 1995	Percentage Change in Population, 1980–95	City Area (acres)	Percentage Change in City Land Area, 1980–95	Vacant Land (acres)	Ratio of Vacant Land to Total Land Area (percent)	No. of Abandoned Structures	No. of Abandoned Structures per 1,000 Inhabitants
Kansas City	MO	442,300	-1.28	203,520	-1.52	12,800	6.3	5,000	11.3045
Springfield	MO	150,604	13.14	46,144	4.78	7,842	17.0	1,121	7.4434
Charlotte	NC	460,000	45.81	111,552	24.77	32,000	21.4	1,000	2.1739
Durham	NC	167,000	65.10	57,600	70.69	8,640	15.0	50	0.2994
Albuquerque	NM	419,681	26.06	103,680	38.72	25,600	24.7	20	0.0477
Reno	NV	160,000	58.80	39,104	85.48	600	1.5	20	0.1250
New York	NY	7,400,000	4.64	205,952	2.45	20,000	9.7		
Syracuse	NY	160,000	-5.94	16,064	5.46			500	3.1250
Akron	OH	223,000	-5.98	39,808	8.17			300	1.3453
Cincinnati	OH	362,040	-5.96	49,280	0.00	493	1.0	1,000	2.7621
Columbus	OH	660,000	16.81	135,488	5.53	16,867	12.4	1,000	1.5152
Dayton	OH	182,005	-5.96	32,640	13.64	5,773	17.7		
Salem	OR	120,800	35.59	29,018	12.77	1,925	6.6		
Erie	PA	108,718	-8.73	51,200	1.38	1,536	3.0	225	2.0696
Philadelphia	PA	1,478,002	-12.45	86,144	-0.66			54,000	36.5400
Providence	RI	160,728	2.50	11,840	-2.12	1,776	15.0	800	4.9774
Columbia	SC	104,000	2.74	22,818	9.34	3,052	13.4	100	0.9615
Knoxville	TN	167,535	-4.29	62,637	0.13			92	0.5491
Nashville	TN	536,360	17.71	336,000	-1.29	81,948	24.4		
Amarillo	TX	158,000	5.88	56,730	9.74	25,528	45.0	200	1.2658
Beaumont	TX	114,323	-3.20	54,669	9.88			500	4.3736
Fort Worth	TX	484,500	25.79	192,403	17.03	83,064	43.2		
Grand Prairie	TX	111,811	56.46	50,025	12.85	14,673	29.3		

City	State								
Lubbock	TX	196,679	12.80	67,424	14.90	12,113	18.0	3	0.0261
Mesquite	TX	115,000	71.51	26,747	24.06	7,000	26.2	150	1.5000
Midland	TX	100,000	41.79	38,400	92.40	16,000	41.7	10	0.0488
Plano	TX	205,000	183.42	45,210	41.45	2,600	5.8	3,000	2.6891
San Antonio	TX	1,115,600	41.94	248,320	26.76	51,402	20.7	25	0.2083
Ogden	UT	120,000	86.32	17,280	.00	3,000	17.4	8	0.0748
Provo	UT	107,000	44.38	27,456	10.29	11,455	41.7	500	3.0599
Salt Lake City	UT	163,405	0.23	77,718	44.95			0	0.0000
Alexandria	VA	117,000	13.35	10,048	2.00	60	0.6	180	0.9826
Newport News	VA	183,185	26.42	44,288	4.59	4,000	9.0	3,000	1.5416
Richmond[a]	VA	197,790	-2.59	40,000	3.99	4,800	12.0	650	1.5476
Virginia Beach	VA	425,000	60.18	196,480	-2.97	48,000	24.4		
Seattle	WA	536,000	8.54	53,800	.00	2,000	3.7		
Spokane	WA	189,000	10.33	36,672	8.12	4,713	12.9		
Madison	WI	201,786	18.27	42,918	7.24	380	0.9	1	0.0050
Milwaukee[a]	WI	596,974	-4.95	61,312	-0.31	3,198	5.22		

[a]Data on these cities were collected in 2002; as a consequence, changes in population and land area refer to 1980–2000.

Source: Except as noted above, the vacant land and abandoned structures data are taken from the survey administered in 1997 and 1998. The cities listed in this appendix are the large cities that provided information about the amount of vacant land and/or the number of abandoned structures. Other large cities answered many questions on the survey but did not provide numerical data on vacant land and abandoned structures; these cities were Ann Arbor, MI; Birmingham, AL; Grand Rapids, MI; Green Bay, WI; Henderson, NV; Lafayette, LA: Laredo, TX; McAllen, TX; Omaha; Pittsburgh; Portland, OR; Raleigh; Riverside, CA; Rochester; Thousand Oaks, CA; and Wichita.

Bibliography

Accordino, John, and Gary T. Johnson. "Addressing the Vacant and Abandoned Property Problem." *Journal of Urban Affairs* 22 (2000): 301–15.

Altshuler, Alan, William Morrill, Harold Wolman, and Faith Mitchell, eds. *Governance and Opportunity in Metropolitan America*. Washington, D.C.: National Academy Press, 1999.

Arizona Prevention Resource Center. *Neighborhood Services Department: Make It Work!* Phoenix: Arizona Prevention Resource Center, 1992.

Ashworth, Gregory J., and Henk Voogd. *Selling the City: Marketing Approaches in Public Sector Urban Planning*. London: Belhaven Press, 1990.

Attoe, Wayne, and Donn Logan. *American Urban Architecture: Catalysts in the Design of Cities*. Berkeley: University of California Press, 1989.

Austen-Smith, David, and Jeffrey Banks. "Electoral Accountability and Incumbency." In *Models of Strategic Choice in Politics*, ed. Peter Ordeshook. Ann Arbor: University of Michigan Press, 1989.

Barnes, William R., and Larry C. Ledebur. *The New Regional Economies*. Thousand Oaks, Calif.: Sage Publications, 1998.

Berger, Joseph. "Tough Times and Tattered Image for Poughkeepsie." *New York Times*, October 5, 1998, 10.

Bernard, Richard M. "Oklahoma City: Booming Sooner." In *Sunbelt Cities: Politics and Growth Since World War II*, ed. Richard M. Bernard and Bradley R. Rice. Austin: University of Texas Press, 1983.

Berry, Brian J. L. *Growth Centers in the American Urban System, Vol. I* . Cambridge, Mass.: Ballinger, 1973.

Besley, Timothy, and Anne Case. "Incumbent Behavior: Vote-Seeking, Tax-Setting, and Yardstick Competition." *American Economic Review* 85 (March 1995): 25–45.

Bickers, Kenneth, and Robert Stein. "The Microfoundations of the Tiebout Model." *Urban Affairs Review* 34 (September 1998): 76–93.

Bowman, Ann O'M. *The Visible Hand: Major Issues in City Economic Policy*. Washington, D.C.: National League of Cities, 1987.

Bowman, Ann O'M., and Michael A. Pagano. "Transforming America's Cities: Policies and Conditions of Vacant Land." *Urban Affairs Review* 35 (March 2000): 559–81.

———. *Urban Vacant Land in the United States*. Working Paper. Cambridge, Mass.: Lincoln Institute of Land Policy, 1998.

Brace, Paul. "The Changing Context of State Political Economy." *Journal of Politics* 53 (May 1991): 297–316.

Brett, Deborah. "Assessing the Feasibility of Infill Development." *Urban Land*, April 1982, 3–9.

Brookings Institution Center on Urban and Metropolitan Policy. *Racial Change in the Nation's Largest Cities: Evidence from the 2000 Census.* April 2001. www.brookings.edu/es/urban/census/citygrowth.htm (June 1, 2003).

Brophy, Paul, and Jennifer Vey. *Seizing City Assets: Ten Steps to Urban Land Reform.* Survey Series. Washington, D.C.: Brookings Institution and CEOs for Cities, 2002.

Bucks County (Pa.). *Report of the Bucks County Open Space Task Force.* Doylestown: Bucks County Open Space Task Force 1996.

Burke, J., and J. M. Ewan, *Sonoran Preserve Master Plan.* Tempe, Ariz.: CAED Herberger Center for Design Excellence, 1998.

Byrnes, Susan. "A Choice in How Seattle Grows." *Seattle Times*, November 2, 1997. www.seattletimes.com/extra/browse/html97/mayr_110297.html# background (May 2001).

Carlson, Cynthia, and Robert Duffy. Cincinnati Takes Stock of Its Vacant Land. *Planning* (November 1985): 2–4.

Carr, Stephen, Mark Francis, Leanne G. Rivlin, and Andrew M. Stone. *Public Space.* New York: Cambridge University Press, 1992.

Cigler, Beverly. "Emerging Trends in State–Local Relations." In *Governing Partners: State-Local Relations in the United States*, ed. Russell L. Hanson. Boulder, Colo.: Westview Press, 1998.

Cisneros, Henry G. "Urban Land and the Urban Prospect." *Cityscape: A Journal of Policy Development and Research* 3 (December 1996): 115–26.

City of Bellevue (Wash.). *Bellevue Parks & Open Space System Plan.* Bellevue, Wash.: City of Bellevue, 1993.

City of Camden (N.J.). *Multi-Year Recovery Plan, Fiscal Years 2001–2003.* 2001. www.state.nj.us/dca/camdensummary.pdf (June 1, 2003).

―――. *Overall Economic Development Program 1998–2004.* Camden, N.J.: City of Camden, Department of Development and Planning, 1998.

City of Columbia (S.C.). Planning and Development Services. *Columbia, SC Demographics, Development and Growth.* 2001. www.columbiasc.net/city /adobeforms/grfinl01.pdf (May 2002).

City of Columbus (Ohio). *City of Columbus 2002 Budget.* 2002 http://mayor. ci.columbus.oh.us/2002Budget/PDF/Financialoverview.pdf (June 1, 2003).

City of Oklahoma City. Department of Finance. *FY2001–2002 Budget Revenue Summary.* 2002. www.okc-cityhall.org/ (May 2002).

City of Peoria (Ariz.). *Annual Report, 1999.* http://ci.peoria.az.us /AnnualReport/(June 1, 2003).

City of Philadelphia. *A Blight Elimination Plan for Philadelphia's Neighborhoods.* Philadelphia: City of Philadelphia, Blight Elimination Subcommittee, 2000.

―――. *Comprehensive Annual Financial Report, 1999.* 2000. www.phila.gov /atservice/reports/annual99/ (June 1, 2000).

―――. *Neighborhood Transformations: The Implementation of Philadelphia's Community Development Policy.* Philadelphia: City of Philadelphia, Office of Housing and Community Development, 1997.

―――. *Quality of Life.* 2000. www.phila.gov/transition/QualityOfLife.htm (June 1, 2000).

―――. *A Vacant Land Acquisition System for Philadelphia.* Philadelphia: City of Philadelphia, Acquisitions Subcommittee of the Select Committee on Vacant Land, 1999.

———. *Vacant Property Prescriptions: A Reinvestment Strategy*. Philadelphia: City of Philadelphia, Office of Housing and Community Development, 1996.

City of Phoenix. *Infill Housing Program*. Phoenix: City of Phoenix, Business Customer Service Center, 1998.

———. *Target Area B Assessment*. Phoenix: City of Phoenix, Planning Department, 1998.

City of San Jose. Department of Planning, Building and Code Enforcement. *San Jose 2020 General Plan*. San Jose: City of San Jose, Department of Planning, Building and Code Enforcement, 1994.

City of Seattle. *Comprehensive Annual Financial Report, 1997*. Seattle: City of Seattle, 1997.

———. *1999–2000 Proposed Budget* 2000. www.ci.seattle.wa.us/budget/ 99_00bud/REVENUE.htm (March 2001).

———. *Property Tax Exemption for Multifamily Housing*. Seattle: City of Seattle, Office of Housing, 1999.

———. *Seattle's Character*. Seattle: City of Seattle, Office for Long-Range Planning, 1991.

———. *Seattle Comprehensive Plan: Monitoring Our Progress, 1998*. Seattle: City of Seattle, Strategic Planning Office, 1998.

———. "Transferable Development Rights (TDR) Program." City of Seattle, Department of Housing and Human Services, Seattle. Unpublished, n.d.

City of Tempe (Ariz.). *Staff Summary Report*, February 6, 2003. www.tempe. gov/clerk/history_02/20030206casg01.htm (June 1, 2003).

Civic Trust. *Urban Wasteland Now*. London: Civic Trust, 1988.

Clarke, Susan E., and Gary L. Gaile. *The Work of Cities*. Minneapolis: University of Minnesota Press, 1998.

Coleman, Alice. "Dead Space in the Dying Inner City." *International Journal of Environmental Studies* 19 (1982): 103–7.

Colwell, Peter F., and Henry J. Munneke. "Estimating a Price Surface for Vacant Land in an Urban Area." *Land Economics* 79 (February 2003): 15–28.

Dixit, Avinash K., and Barry J. Nalebuss. *Thinking Strategically*. New York: W. W. Norton, 1991.

Dixon, Jennifer. "Detroit's Neglect Spawns Squatters: Makeshift Camps, Drugs and Prostitution Occupy Property." *Detroit Free Press*, July 7, 2000, 1.

Downs, Anthony. *An Economic Theory of Democracy*. New York: Harper & Row, 1957.

Dreier, Peter, John Mollenkopf, and Todd Swanstrom. *Place Matters: Metropolitics for the Twenty-First Century*. Lawrence: University Press of Kansas, 2001.

Dye, Thomas. *American Federalism: Competition among Governments*. Lexington, Mass.: DC Heath, 1990.

Edwards, Mary. "Annexation: A Winner-Take-All Process?" *State and Local Government Review* 31 (fall 1999): 221–31.

Ehrenhalt, Alan. "The Great Wall of Portland." *Governing*, May 1997, 20–24.

Euchner, Charles C. *Playing the Field: Why Sports Teams Move and Cities Fight to Keep Them*. Baltimore: Johns Hopkins University Press, 1993.

Fairmount Ventures, Inc. *Vacant Land Management in Philadelphia Neighborhoods: Cost–Benefit Analysis*. Philadelphia: Pennsylvania Horticultural Society, 1999.

Fischel, William A. *The Homevoter Hypothesis: How Home Values Influence Local Government Taxation, School Finance, and Land-Use Policies*. Cambridge, Mass.: Harvard University Press, 2001.

Flanagan, Barbara. "Good Design Creates Another Palm Beach Success Story." *New York Times*, June 12, 1997, B1, B8.

Forgette, Richard, and Michael Pagano. "Fiscal Structures and Metropolitan Tax Base Sharing." Paper presented at the annual meeting of the American Political Science Association, San Francisco, September 1, 2001.

Foster, Kathryn A. "Regional Impulses." *Journal of Urban Affairs* 19, no. 4 (1997): 375–403.

Fulton, William. *The Reluctant Metropolis: The Politics of Urban Growth in Los Angeles.* Baltimore: Johns Hopkins University Press, 1997.

Fulton, William, and Paul Shigley. "The Greening of the Brown." *Governing*, December 2000, 31.

Gainsborough, Juliet F. *Fenced Off: The Suburbanization of American Politics.* Washington, D.C.: Georgetown University Press, 2001.

Gale, William G., and Janet Rothenberg Pack, eds. *Brookings-Wharton Papers on Urban Affairs 2001.* Washington, D.C.: Brookings Institution Press, 2001.

Gobster, Paul H. "Urban Parks as Green Walls or Green Magnets: Interracial Relations in Neighborhood Boundary Parks." *Landscape and Urban Planning* 41 (1998): 43–55.

Gonzalez, David. "Vacant Lots, Except for Red Tape." *New York Times*, October 8, 1993, B1, B7.

Gopnik, Adam. "A Walk on the High Line." *New Yorker*, May 21, 2001, 45.

Gowda, Vanita. "Whose Garden Is It?" *Governing*, March 2002, 40–41.

Greenberg, Michael, Karen Lowrie, Laura Solitare, and Latoya Duncan. "Brownfields, TOADS, and the Struggle for Neighborhood Development: A Case Study of the State of New Jersey." *Urban Affairs Review* 35 (May 2000): 717–33.

Greenberg, Michael R., Frank J. Popper, and Bernadette M. West. "The TOADS: A New American Urban Epidemic." *Urban Affairs Quarterly* 25 (March 1990): 435–54.

"Greening New York's Waste Lands." *New York Times*, December 28, 1994, A12.

Gurwitt, Rob. "Betting on the Bulldozer." *Governing*, July 2002, 28–34.

Hampton, Kumasi R. "Land Use Controls and Temporarily Obsolete, Abandoned, and Derelict Sites (T.O.A.D.S.) in Cincinnati's Basin Area." Master's thesis, University of Cincinnati, 1995.

Hanson, Russell L., ed. *Governing Partners: State–Local Relations in the United States.* Boulder, Colo.: Westview Press, 1998.

Hanson, Susan. *The Politics of Taxation.* New York: Praeger, 1983.

Harden, Blaine. "Neighbors Give Central Park a Wealthy Glow." *New York Times*, November 22, 1999, A1, A29.

Havemann, Judith. "A City That Good Times Forgot: Blighted Camden, N.J., Reflects Inner Cities' Resistance to Renewal." *Washington Post*, April 1, 1999, A3.

Hayden, Dolores. *The Power of Place: Urban Landscapes as Public History.* Cambridge, Mass.: MIT Press, 1995.

Hirschhorn, Joel S., and Paul Souza. *New Community Design to the Rescue: Fulfilling Another American Dream.* Washington, D.C.: National Governors' Association, 2001.

Hough, Michael. "Design with City Nature: An Overview of Some Issues." In *The Ecological City*, ed. Rutherford H. Platt, Rowan Rountree, and Pamela Muick. Amherst: University of Massachusetts Press, 1994.

Hughes, Mark Alan. Dirt into Dollars: Converting Vacant Land into Valuable Development. *Brookings Review* (summer 2000): 34–37.

Hughes, Mark Alan, and Anais Loizillon. "Over the Horizon: Jobs in the Suburbs of Major Metropolitan Areas." In *Urban Change in the United States and Western Europe*, 2nd edition, ed. Anita A. Summers, Paul C. Cheshire, and Lanfranco Senn. Washington, D.C.: Urban Institute Press, 1999.

Jacobson, David. *Place and Belonging in America.* Baltimore: Johns Hopkins University Press, 2002.

Jakle, John A., and David Wilson. *Derelict Landscapes: The Wasting of America's Built Environment.* Savage, Md.: Rowman & Littlefield, 1992.

Jones, David W. "Vacant Land Inventory and Development Assessment for the City of Greenville, S.C." Master's thesis, Clemson University, 1992.

Kelleher, Christine, and David Lowery. "Tiebout Sorting and Selective Satisfaction with Urban Public Services: Testing the Variance Hypothesis." *Urban Affairs Review* 37 (January 2002): 420–31.

Kemmis, Daniel. *Community and the Politics of Place.* Norman: University of Oklahoma Press, 1990.

Kenyon, Daphne. "Theories of Interjurisdictional Competition." *New England Economic Review* (March–April 1997): 13–28.

Kenyon, Daphne A., and John Kincaid, eds. *Competition among States and Local Governments.* Washington, D.C.: Urban Institute Press, 1991.

Keuschnigg, C., and S. B. Nielsen. "On the Phenomenon of Vacant Land." *Canadian Journal of Economics* (April 1996): S534–40.

King County (Wash.). *1998 Annual Growth Report.* 1998. www.metrokc.gov /budget/agr/agr98 (June 1, 2003).

Kittower, Diane. "Turning an Airport into an Urban Village." *Governing*, May 2000, 90.

Kivell, Philip. *Land and the City: Patterns and Processes of Urban Change.* London: Routledge, 1993.

Knaap, Gerrit, and Terry Moore. *Land Supply and Infrastructure Capacity: Monitoring for Smart Urban Growth.* Working Paper. Cambridge, Mass.: Lincoln Institute of Land Policy, 2000.

Krane, Dale, Platon N. Rigos, and Melvin B. Hill Jr. *Home Rule in America: A Fifty-State Handbook.* Washington, D.C.: Congressional Quarterly Press, 2001.

Kromer, John. *Neighborhood Recovery: Reinvestment Policy for the New Hometown.* New Brunswick, N.J.: Rutgers University Press, 2000.

———. *Vacant Property Prescriptions: A Reinvestment Strategy.* Philadelphia: City of Philadelphia Office of Housing and Community Development, 1996.

Ladd, Helen, and John Yinger. *America's Ailing Cities: Fiscal Health and the Design of Urban Policy.* Baltimore: Johns Hopkins University Press, 1989.

Lake, David A., and Robert Powell, eds. *Strategic Choice and International Relations.* Princeton, N.J.: Princeton University Press, 1999.

Leopold, Aldo. *The Sand County Almanac.* New York: Oxford University Press, 1949.

Levy, John M. *Contemporary Urban Planning*, 5th ed. Upper Saddle River, N.J.: Prentice Hall, 2000.

Lewis, Paul G. "Retail Politics: Local Sales Taxes and the Fiscalization of Land Use." *Economic Development Quarterly* 15 (February 2001): 21–35.

Lowery, David. "A Transaction Cost Model of Metropolitan Governance: Allocation Versus Redistribution in Urban America." *Journal of Public Administration Research and Theory* 10 (January 2000): 49–78.

Lynch, Kevin. *The Image of the City*. Cambridge, Mass.: MIT Press, 1960.

Manvel, A. D. "Land Use in 106 Large Cities." In *Three Land Research Studies*. Research Report 12. Washington, D.C.: Prepared for the consideration of the National Commission on Urban Problems, 1968.

McDonough, Gary. "The Geography of Emptiness." In *The Cultural Meaning of Urban Space*, ed. Robert Rotenberg and Gary McDonough. Westport, Conn.: Bergin & Garvey, 1993.

McWhirter, Cameron. "Detroit Banks on Empty Lots: City Sees Cleveland as Model for Reviving Land for Development." *Detroit News*, February 15, 2001. www.detnews.com/2001/metro/0102/15/a01-188450.htm (June 1, 2003).

Meyers, Roy. *Strategic Budgeting*. Ann Arbor: University of Michigan Press, 1994.

Mikesell, John. *Fiscal Administration*, 5th ed. Fort Worth: Harcourt Brace College Publishers, 1999.

Moudon, Anne Vernez, and LeRoy A. Heckman. "Seattle and the Central Puget Sound." In *Global City-Regions*, ed. Roger Simmonds and Gary Hack. London: Spon, 2000.

Myers, Phyllis. "The Varied Landscape of Park and Conservation Finance." *Nation's Cities Weekly*, June 2, 1997, 3.

Nasar, Jack L. *The Evaluative Image of the City*. Thousand Oaks, Calif.: Sage Publications, 1998.

National Association of State Budget Officers. *Fiscal Survey of the States, December 2000*. Washington, D.C.: National Association of State Budget Officers, 2000.

Neighbours, Andrea. "From Cans to Apartments in New Orleans." *New York Times*, March 26, 2000, 47.

New York City Independent Budget Office. *Big City, Big Bucks: NYC's Changing Income Distribution*. New York: New York City Independent Budget Office, 2000.

Niedercorn, John H., and Edward F. R. Hearle. *Recent Land-Use Trends in Forty-Eight Large American Cities*. Memorandum RM-3664-1-FF. Santa Monica, Calif.: RAND Corporation, 1963.

Northam, Ray. "Vacant Urban Land in the American City." *Land Economics* 47 (1971): 345–55.

Noto, Nonna. Local Income Taxes on Nonresidents in the Nation's 25 Largest Cities. Congressional Research Service memorandum, March 4, 2002 (draft), Congressional Research Service, Washington, D.C.

Oates, Wallace, and Robert Schwab. "Economic Competition among Jurisdictions." *Journal of Public Economics* 35 (April 1988): 333–54.

Orr, Dwight. and Angela Couloumbis. "Proposal for Camden Seeks Role for County." *Philadelphia Inquirer*, October 2, 2001, B1.

Ostrom, Vincent, Charles M. Tiebout, and Robert Warren. "The Organization of Government in Metropolitan Areas: A Theory Inquiry." *American Political Science Review* 55 (October 1961): 831–42.

Pagano, Michael A. *City Fiscal Conditions in 1999*. Washington, D.C.: National League of Cities, 1999.

———. *City Fiscal Structures and Land Development*. Discussion paper prepared for Brookings Institution Center on Urban and Metropolitan Policy and for CEOs for Cities. April 2003. www.brookings.edu/es/urban/publications/paganovacant.htm (June 1, 2003).

———. "Metropolitan Limits: Intrametropolitan Disparities and Governance in US Laboratories of Democracy." In *Governance and Opportunity in Metropolitan America*, ed. Alan Altshuler, William Morrill, Harold Wolman, and Faith Mitchell. Washington, D.C.: National Academy Press, 1999.

Pagano, Michael A., and Ann O'M. Bowman. *Cityscapes and Capital: The Politics of Urban Development*. Baltimore: Johns Hopkins University Press, 1995.

Pagano, Michael A., and Richard G. Forgette. "Regionalism and Municipal Tax Structures: Assessing Tax-Base Sharing in Ohio Metropolitan Areas." Paper presented at the annual meeting of the Association for Budgeting and Financial Management, Kansas City, October 10, 2002.

Palmer, Jamie, and Greg Lindsey. "Classifying State Approaches to Annexation." *State and Local Government Review* 33 (winter 2001): 60–73.

Park, Keeok. "Friends and Competitors: Policy Interactions between Local Governments in Metropolitan Areas." *Political Research Quarterly* 50 (December 1997): 723–50.

Parks & People Foundation. *Neighborhood Open Space Management: A Report on Greening Strategies in Baltimore and Six Other Cities*. Baltimore: Parks & People Foundation, 2000.

Peirce, Neal. "Vacant Urban Land: Hidden Treasure?" *National Journal*, December 9, 1995, 3053.

Pennsylvania Horticultural Society. *Urban Vacant Land: Issues and Recommendations*. Philadelphia: Pennsylvania Horticultural Society, 1995.

Percy, Stephen L., Brett W. Hawkins, and Peter E. Maier. Revisiting Tiebout: Moving Rationales and Interjurisdictional Relocation. *Publius: Journal of Federalism* 25 (fall 1995): 1–17.

Peterson, Paul. *City Limits*. Chicago: University of Chicago Press, 1981.

Philadelphia City Planning Commission. "PCPC Map Gallery." www.philaplanning.org/data/datamaps.html (June 1, 2003).

———. *Vacant Land in Philadelphia: A Report on Vacant Land Management and Neighborhood Restructuring*. Philadelphia: Philadelphia City Planning Commission, 1995.

Poracsky, Joseph, and Michael C. Houck. "The Metropolitan Portland Urban Natural Resource Program." In *The Ecological City*, ed. Rutherford H. Platt, Rowan Rountree, and Pamela Muick. Amherst: University of Massachusetts Press, 1994.

Puget Sound Regional Council. *1998 Regional Review: Monitoring Change in the Central Puget Sound Region*. Seattle: Puget Sound Regional Council, 1998.

———. *Urban Centers in the Central Puget Sound Region: A Baseline Summary and Comparison, Winter 1996–97*. Seattle: Puget Sound Regional Council, 1996.

Rapoport, Amos. *The Meaning of the Built Environment: A Non-Verbal Communication Approach*. Tucson: University of Arizona Press, 1990.

Robertson, David, and Dennis Judd. *The Development of American Public Policy*. Glenview, Ill.: Scott, Foresman and Co., 1989.

Rusk, David. *Cities without Suburbs*, 2d ed. Baltimore: Johns Hopkins University Press, 1995.

Salkin, Patricia E. "Political Strategies for Modernizing State Land Use Statutes to Address Sprawl." Paper presented at the Who Owns America? II conference, Madison, Wisc., June 4, 1998.

Schaffer, R., and N. Smith. "The Gentrification of Harlem?" *Annals of the Association of American Geographers* 76 (1986): 347–65.

Schneider, Daniel. "To Halt Sprawl, San Jose Draws Green Line in Sand." *Christian Science Monitor,* April 17, 1996, 14.

Schneider, Mark. *The Competitive City.* Pittsburgh: University of Pittsburgh Press, 1989.

Schukoske, Jane E. "Community Development through Gardening: State and Local Policies Transforming Urban Open Space." *New York University Journal of Legislation and Public Policy* 3 (1999–2000): 351–92.

Seattle's Comprehensive Plan. *Toward a Sustainable Seattle: A Plan for Managing Growth, 1994–2014 (as Amended November 25, 1997).* Seattle: Seattle's Comprehensive Plan, 1997.

Seplow, Stephen. "Too Many Houses, Too Few Residents." *Philadelphia Inquirer,* May 10, 1999, 1.

Shepsle, Kenneth A., and Mark S. Bonchek. *Analyzing Politics: Rationality, Behavior, and Institutions.* New York: W. W. Norton, 1997.

Sigelman, Lee, and Jeffrey R. Henig. "Crossing the Great Divide: Race and Preferences for Living in the City Versus the Suburb." *Urban Affairs Review* 37 (September 2001): 3–18.

Smith, Neil, Paul Caris, and Elvin Wyly. "The 'Camden Syndrome' and the Menace of Suburban Decline: Residential Disinvestment and Its Discontents in Camden County, New Jersey." *Urban Affairs Review* 36 (March 2001): 497–531.

Sohmer, Rebecca R., and Robert E. Lang. "Downtown Rebound." *Fannie Mae Foundation Census Note.* Washington, D.C.: Fannie Mae Foundation and the Brookings Institution, 2001.

Solecki, William D., and Joan M. Welch. "Urban Parks: Green Spaces or Green Walls?" *Landscape and Urban Planning* 32 (1995): 93–106.

Spinner, Jackie. "Decaying Buildings Targeted: D.C. to Acquire, Repair or Demolish 2,000 Properties." *Washington Post,* April 8, 2000, E1.

Spirn, Ann Whiston. *The Granite Garden.* New York: Basic Books, 1984.

Stein, Robert. "Tiebout's Sorting Hypothesis." *Urban Affairs Quarterly* 23, no. 1 (1987): 140–60.

Summers, Paul, and Daniel Carlson, with Michael Stanger, Saijun Xue, and Mike Miayasato. *Ten Steps to a High-Tech Future: The New Economy in Metropolitan Seattle.* Discussion paper prepared for Brookings Institution Center on Urban and Metropolitan Policy. Washington, D.C.: Brookings Institution, 2000.

Tiebout, Charles M. "A Pure Theory of Local Expenditures." *Journal of Political Economy* 64 (October 1964): 416–24.

Turner, Frederick Jackson. *The Frontier in American History.* New York: H. Holt & Co., 1920.

"Turning Brownfields to Green." *Governing,* December 2000, A16.

U.S. Advisory Commission on Intergovernmental Relations. *State Laws Governing Local Government Structure and Administration.* Washington, D.C.: U.S. Advisory Commission on Intergovernmental Relations, 1993.

U. S. Environmental Protection Agency. *Brownfields Glossary of Terms.* www.epa.gov/swerosps/bf/glossary.htm#brow (June 1, 2003).

———. *Brownfields Mission.* www.epa.gov/swerosps/bf/mission.htm (June 1, 2003).

———. *Brownfield Success Stories.* www.epa.gov/swerosps/bf/success.htm (June 1, 2003).

U.S. General Accounting Office. *Superfund: Proposals to Remove Barriers to Brownfield Redevelopment.* GAO/T-RCED-97–87. Washington, D.C.: U.S. General Accounting Office, 1997.

Voget, Jane. "Making Transfer of Development Rights Work for Downtown Preservation and Redevelopment." City of Seattle, Department of Housing and Human Services, Seattle (draft), 1999.

Warner, Kee, and Harvey Molotch. *Building Rules: How Local Controls Shape Community Environments and Economies.* Boulder, Colo.: Westview, 2000.

Washington Center for Real Estate Research. *Washington State's Housing Market: A Supply/Demand Assessment, First Quarter 1999.* 1999 www.cbe.wsu .edu/~wcrer/HMUPDATE/MKTRPT9a.htm (May 2000).

Washington State Community, Trade, and Economic Development. *State of Washington's Growth Management Act and Related Laws 1998.* Olympia: Washington State Community, Trade, and Economic Development, 1998.

Wassmer, Robert W. *Influences of the "Fiscalization of Land Use" and Urban-Growth Boundaries* (revised). Sacramento: California Senate Office of Research, 2001.

Weimer, David, and Aidan R. Vining. *Policy Analysis,* 3d ed. Upper Saddle River, N.J.: Prentice Hall, 1999.

Weir, Margaret. "Central Cities' Loss of Power in State Politics." *Cityscape: A Journal of Policy Development and Research* 2 (May 1996): 23–40.

Wilk, Richard, and Michael B. Schiffer. "The Archaeology of Vacant Lots in Tucson, Arizona." *American Antiquity* 44 (July 1979): 530–36.

Wilson, James Q., and George L. Kelling. "Broken Windows: Police and Neighborhood Safety." *Atlantic Monthly,* March 1982, 29–38.

Wood, Barry. *Vacant Land in Europe.* Working Paper. Cambridge, Mass.: Lincoln Institute of Land Policy, 1998.

Wright, Thomas K., and Ann Davlin. "Overcoming Obstacles to Brownfield and Vacant Land Redevelopment." *Land Lines* 10 (September 1998): 1–3.

Zuckoff, Mitchell. "New Plan to Remake Mattapan Acreage," *Boston Globe,* July 16, 2000, A01.

Zukin, Sharon. *Landscapes of Power.* Berkeley: University of California Press, 1991.

Index